Lecture Notes of the Institute for Computer Sciences, Social Informatics and Telecommunications Engineering   191

More information about this series at http://www.springer.com/series/8197

Ramón Agüero · Yasir Zaki
Bernd-Ludwig Wenning · Anna Förster
Andreas Timm-Giel (Eds.)

Mobile Networks
and Management

8th International Conference, MONAMI 2016
Abu Dhabi, United Arab Emirates, October 23–24, 2016
Proceedings

 Springer

Editors
Ramón Agüero
University of Cantabria
Santander
Spain

Yasir Zaki
New York University
Abu Dhabi
United Arab Emirates

Bernd-Ludwig Wenning
Cork Institute of Technology
Cork
Ireland

Anna Förster
University of Bremen
Bremen
Germany

Andreas Timm-Giel
Hamburg University of Technology
Hamburg
Germany

ISSN 1867-8211   ISSN 1867-822X (electronic)
Lecture Notes of the Institute for Computer Sciences, Social Informatics
and Telecommunications Engineering
ISBN 978-3-319-52711-6   ISBN 978-3-319-52712-3 (eBook)
DOI 10.1007/978-3-319-52712-3

Library of Congress Control Number: 2016963651

Printed on acid-free paper

This Springer imprint is published by Springer Nature
The registered company is Springer International Publishing AG
The registered company address is: Gewerbestrasse 11, 6330 Cham, Switzerland

Preface

This volume is the result of the 8th EAI International Conference on Mobile Networks and Management (MONAMI), which was held in Abu Dhabi, United Arab Emirates, during October 23–24, 2016, hosted by New York University Abu Dhabi.

The MONAMI conference series aims at bringing together top researchers, academics, and practitioners specializing in the area of mobile network management, service management, virtualization and object management. Multi-access and resource management, mobility management, and network management have emerged as core topics in the design, deployment, and operation of current and future networks. Yet, they are treated as separate, isolated domains with very little interaction between the experts in these fields and lack cross-pollination. Recently, new avant-garde techniques and solutions have emerged; as notable examples, network function virtualization, software-defined networking, network virtualization, and the cloud paradigm have taken root. All in all, these techniques bring about new requirements and scientific challenges, and migration strategies are required to provide a smooth transition from today's legacy systems to future systems. At the same time, new wireless broadband access technologies, in what has been referred to as 5G, are posing new challenges and requirements that need to be taken into account; energy efficiency, densification, off-loading are examples of the new issues the scientific community is currently addressing.

Dr. Polly Huang from National Taiwan University officially opened the conference with her vision on "User-Centric Multimedia Networking for the Mobile Era — How to Strike a Balance between User Demand and Scarce Resources." In addition, the conference featured a half-day tutorial: "Programming and Networking for the Internet of Things Using RIOT, the Friendly OS for the IoT," presented by Peter Kietzmann (HAW Hamburg/RIOT Community).

After a thorough peer-review process, 16 papers were selected for inclusion in the main track of the technical program. Most papers were reviewed by three competent researchers, including at least one Technical Program Committee (TPC) member. This volume includes the revised versions of all papers that were presented at MONAMI 2016 in a single-track format. All MONAMI 2016 newcomers acknowledged the collegial atmosphere that characterizes the conference, making it an excellent venue, not only for presenting novel research work, but also for fostering stimulating discussions between the attendees.

This volume is organized thematically in four parts, starting with "Cloud Computing and Software Defined Networking" in Part I. "Internet-of-Things and Vehicular Networks" are discussed in Part II. Part III presents novel "Techniques and Algorithms for Cellular Networks," while Part IV deals with "Security and Self-Organizing Networks."

We close this short preface to the volume by acknowledging the vital role that the TPC members and additional referees played during the review process. Their efforts ensured that all submitted papers received a proper evaluation. We thank EAI and ICST for assisting with organization matters, and New York University for hosting

MONAMI 2016. The team that put together this year's event is large and required the sincere commitment of many folks. Although too many to recognize here by name, their effort should be highlighted. We particularly thank Barbara Fertalova, Ivana Allen, and Sinziana Vieriu for their administrative support on behalf of EAI, and Prof. Imrich Chlamtac of CREATE-NET for his continuous support of the conference. Finally, we thank all delegates for attending MONAMI 2016 and making it such a vibrant conference!

November 2016   Yasir Zaki
                                                    Ramón Agüero
                                                     Anna Förster
                                              Bernd-Ludwig Wenning

Organization

General Chairs

Yasir Zaki   New York University Abu Dhabi,
                          United Arab Emirates
Ramón Agüero   University of Cantabria, Spain

TPC Chairs

Bernd-Ludwig Wenning   Cork Institute of Technology, Ireland
Anna Förster   University of Bremen, Germany

Publications Chair

Andreas Timm-Giel   Hamburg University of Technology, Germany

Web Chair

Thomas Pötsch   New York University Abu Dhabi,
                          United Arab Emirates

Publicity and Social Media Chair

Thomas Zinner   University of Würzbürg, Germany

Keynote and Tutorials Chair

Koojana Kuladinithi   University of Bremen, Germany

Conference Manager

Barbara Fertalova   EAI - European Alliance for Innovation

Contents

Cloud Computing and Software Defined Networking

Simulation Framework for Distributed SDN-Controller Architectures in OMNeT++

Nicholas Gray[✉], Thomas Zinner, Steffen Gebert, and Phuoc Tran-Gia

Institute of Computer Science, University of Würzburg,
Am Hubland, 97074 Würzburg, Germany
{nicholas.gray,zinner,steffen.gebert,trangia}@informatik.uni-wuerzburg.de

Abstract. SDN introduces the separation of network control and network data plane. The control plane is removed from distributed network entities and logically centralized as the SDN controller. To provide resilience and performance such a logically centralized controller may again be physically distributed. Scenarios featuring distributed controller architectures include data center deployments, where controller instances synchronize states on small distances and delays, or continental WAN deployments with long distances and delays between controllers. The contribution of this paper is an OMNeT++ based simulation framework for assessing the performance of distributed SDN controller architectures. Relevant protocols and controller applications are modelled with a high level of detail. Further, an exemplary implementation of two different controller architectures, namely Hyperflow and Kandoo, is included. Initial results based on the provided implementations are presented.

1 Introduction

Software Defined Networking (SDN) [11] promotes the separation of the control and data plane in communication networks. While the data plane is kept distributed, the control plane is logically centralized in a controller and serves as interface for configuration purposes. Devices in the data plane are controlled via the southbound API using communication protocols like OpenFlow [15]. Thus, SDN provides a higher configuration flexibility and enables the network operator to dynamically react to changing network parameters. This results in a more efficient resource utilization as well as in a reduction of the management efforts. Hence, SDN is enjoying an increasing popularity and is already deployed in live production environments, i.e. Google's B4 backbone [9].

Despite the advantages of a centralized control plane, it also imposes new challenges in terms of resiliency and scalability limitations. Today's data centres, for example, are required to handle 150 million flows per second, while current OpenFlow controllers only have the ability to process a fraction of this demand [22]. One possible approach to address the scalability issues is to distribute the load among several controller instances while keeping the management logically centralized. In this context a variety of distributed controller architectures have been proposed, e.g., Hyperflow or Kandoo. The impact of different

© ICST Institute for Computer Sciences, Social Informatics and Telecommunications Engineering 2017
R. Agüero et al. (Eds.): MONAMI 2016, LNICST 191, pp. 3–18, 2017.
DOI: 10.1007/978-3-319-52712-3_1

controller architectures on relevant performance metrics like latencies or the resulting architectural overhead have not been in the focus of scientific investigations yet.

The contribution of this work is the design and implementation of a flexible simulation model capable of evaluating distributed SDN controller architectures within the OMNeT++ framework. Furthermore, we present an exemplary evaluation demonstrating the capabilities of the implemented framework by analysing the impact of distributed controller architectures on the offered traffic of the individual controllers.

The remainder of this work is structured as follows. Section 2 summarizes relevant background and related work on SDN, controller architectures, OMNeT++ and the performance evaluation of SDN. The implemented framework is introduced in Sect. 3. The impact of physically distributing the control plane on the offered control plane traffic is illustrated in Sect. 4. The paper is concluded in Sect. 5.

2   Background

This section summarizes relevant background and related work on SDN, OMNeT++, as well as controller architectures and their performance evaluation.

2.1   SDN and OpenFlow

The concept of Software-defined networking (SDN) has been introduced to achieve a higher configuration flexibility as well as a reduction in the complexity of modern network architectures. To accomplish this task, SDN is driven by four core principles, i.e., separation of control and data plane, a logically centralized controller, open standards and a programmable interface [11].

The communication between the SDN controller and the switch, which reflects the separation of the control and data plane is defined by a particular protocol i.e., OpenFlow. Whereas the SDN enabled switch is often a dedicated networking device, the SDN controller is implemented as software and is usually deployed on a standard server component.

Whenever an OpenFlow enabled switch receives a packet from the data plane it first performs a lookup in its flow table to determine if a matching rule is already existent. In the case no rule is found the switch extracts the header fields of the packet and creates a Packet-in message, which is sent to the controller asking for further instructions on how to handle the received packet. Once the Packet-in message is received and processed by the SDN controller it responds with a Packet-out message, which details how the switch should forward the packet. In addition the controller may send a Flow-mod message, which installs a rule into the switch's flow table and handles future matching packet without controller intervention.

2.2 OMNeT++ and INET

OMNeT++ [2] is a discrete event based network simulation framework which follows a component based design pattern and therefore makes it easy to be extended by third party modules. At its core, the OMNeT++ network simulation framework features the concept of *simple* and *compound* modules, which represent the individual entities of a simulation. To enable the exchange of information during the simulation, the modules need to encode the relevant data into Messages, which are then sent through gates to other connecting modules. The INET Framework [1] is a third party extension to OMNeT++ and provides the most common protocols used in the Internet. In particular, protocols such as TCP, UDP, IPv4, IPv6, FTP and many more have been implemented. In addition, INET also provides simple applications and entities, which make use of the underlying protocols and which can be reused within custom simulations.

2.3 Distributed Controller Architectures

To mitigate the drawbacks of the single point of failure and scalability limitations imposed by the SDN controller, the logically centralized control plane has to be physically distributed. This results in fundamental trade-offs like staleness of information vs. optimality of decisions [14]. Distributed controller algorithms, e.g., following a horizontal or a hierarchical architecture, allow to control this trade-off by adjusting their synchronization mechanism.

Relevant horizontally distributed controller implementations are HyperFlow [21] and OpenDaylight [17]. Whereas OpenDaylight uses a DHT which is accessible to all cluster nodes, HyperFlow stores state changing events to a distributed file system. Kandoo [6] follows the hierarchical approach by introducing local and root controllers. Local controllers handle all requests for which their local domain knowledge is sufficient and forward requests to the root controller, which require the global view of the network. In addition to Kandoo, the ONOS [3] controller also incorporates a hierarchical design. Onix [13] and Disco [18] differentiate between an intra and inter domain context and choose the method of synchronization accordingly. In this context, both controllers utilize a horizontal architecture for intra domain communication in form of a distributed data store and for inter domain purposes a hierarchical organization is created by only exposing aggregated information of an individual domain.

2.4 Performance Evaluation of SDN Architectures

One possibility to investigate the performance of distributed controller architectures is using a suitable test bed, e.g., Mininet [5] or DOT [20]. However, often access to existing OpenFlow test beds is limited or they do not feature the required network characteristics. Analytical approaches as presented in [10] presuppose a high abstraction level and neglect specific details, e.g., protocol behaviour on data link layer. Hence, another possible approach is to create a simulation model featuring the desired level of detail, e.g., using OMNeT++.

A detailed implementation of the OpenFlow protocol together with an investigation of the controller placement problem is provided in [12]. Although the investigated research question is closely related to the investigation of distributed controller architectures, the provided source code could not be extended due to a tight integration of the main controller and application responsibilities.

3   OpenFlow OMNeT++ Suite

To provide the tools needed to investigate the performance and impact of different SDN controller architectures in large scale networks, we implemented the OpenFlow OMNeT++ Suite, which extends the OMNeT++ framework with OpenFlow capabilities. For this, the OpenFlow OMNeT++ Suite provides an SDN controller and an OpenFlow enabled switch module, which communicate via the OpenFlow protocol. Furthermore, the suite features a variety of common controller applications such as topology discovery, different forwarding mechanisms and an ARP proxy. In addition to the common single controller approach, the package also features a horizontally and a hierarchically distributed controller architecture. The implementation of the OpenFlow OMNeT++ Suite is based upon OMNeT++ and INET in version 4.6 and 2.5.0 respectively. The OpenFlow OMNeT++ Suite's content is grouped into six packages, illustrated in Fig. 1.

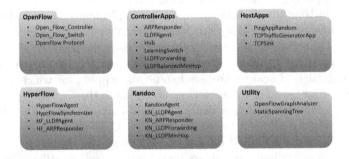

Fig. 1. OpenFlow OMNeT++ suite packages.

In the following, we describe the main modules in detail. The source code of the OMNeT++ Suite is publicly available [1] and is published under GPL v3 license.

3.1   OpenFlow

The OpenFlow package holds the main components, which consist of the OpenFlow protocol implementation, as well as the OpenFlow enabled switch and controller compound module.

---

[1] https://github.com/lsinfo3/OpenFlowOMNeTSuite.

OpenFlow Protocol. The communication between the SDN controller and the switch is enabled by the OpenFlow protocol, which defines a variety of messages. For the implementation of the supported OpenFlow messages, we reused the exact same message definitions as detailed by the OpenFlow Switch Specification [16] in version 1.3 as far as applicable, to model the protocol as close as possible. Since the implementation of every single OpenFlow message would be beyond the scope of this work, we focused on messages providing the main functionality of the protocol. At the current state, the suite supports *hello, Feature-request* and *Feature-reply* messages to initiate the OpenFlow channel as well as *Packet-in* and *Packet-out* messages to control the forwarding of data plane packets. At last, *Flow-mod* and *Port-mod* messages can be used to modify the flow or port table of an individual switch. All implemented messages are derived from the *Open_Flow_Message* class, which merely holds the OpenFlow header. Following this approach, additional message classes can be easily created if the necessity arises.

OpenFlow Switch. An implementation of the OpenFlow enabled switch is represented by the *Open_Flow_Switch* compound module. As displayed in Fig. 2, the module is composed from multiple components, which are organized in three groups.

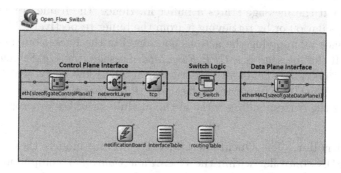

Fig. 2. Open_Flow_Switch compound module in OMNeT++.

Whereas the right group consists of a single gate named *gateDataPlane* and acts as the interface to the data plane, the group on the left is responsible for the communication with the control plane. Since this communication is handled via TCP, additional modules are required. The first module is a gate which functions as an interface and allows connections to and from other modules. The *networkLayer* and *tcp* modules are both provided by the INET framework and mimic the functionality of their real world counterparts. The *OF_Switch* module implements the main logic of the OpenFlow switch and thus is connected to both groups. This module is responsible for the connection initiation to the OpenFlow controller as well as managing packets received from the control and data plane.

The switch can be configured with a service time, which is used to simulate the time needed to process a packet received from the data plane. In addition, the controller's IP address and port as well as the time at which the switch should initiate the connection to the controller can be set. The OpenFlow connection is then established, by first completing the TCP 3-Way-Handshake which is followed by the initiation of the OpenFlow Channel. For this the controller and the switch first exchange *hello* messages. The controller then sends an *OFP_Feature_Request* message, to which the *OF_Switch* module responds with an *OFP_Feature_Reply*.

Once a packet originating from the data plane is scheduled for execution, the *OF_Switch* module first checks if the *flowTable* property can match the received packet. If a matching entry is returned, the packet will be handled according to the contained instructions. Otherwise, the *OF_Switch* module extracts the header fields of the received packet and builds an *OFP_PacketIn* message. It then tries to store the packet into its *buffer* property and, if successful, updates the Packet-in message with the appropriate identifier. In the case that the buffer has reached its full capacity, the entire packet is encapsulated into the Packet-in message. Finally, the Packet-in message is sent to the controller.

Whenever the *OF_Switch* receives a packet from the control plane, it casts the received packet to an *Open_Flow_Message* and then uses the OpenFlow header to determine the type of the OpenFlow message. In case of an *OFP_Packet_Out* message, the *OF_Switch* module first checks if the message contains the original frame or if the message states a buffer id. Hence, the frame is restored by either decapsulation or by retrieving it from the buffer respectively. The module then continues by applying the actions contained in the Packet-out message to the frame. If the message is a *OFP_Flow_Mod* message, the *OF_Switch* module extracts the necessary fields for constructing a new Flow entry, which is then stored by the *flowTable* property. At last *OFP_Port_Mod* messages are processed by updating the corresponding entry in the module's *portVector* property.

SDN Controller. The OpenFlow OMNeT++ Suite models the functionality of the SDN controller within the *Open_Flow_Controller* compound module, which is illustrated in Fig. 3. As OpenFlow is the de-facto standard southbound API protocol currently in use, we will utilize the term openFlow/SDN controller interchangeably through out this paper. The individual components can be categorized into three groups according to their functionality as depicted in Fig. 3.

Similar to the *Open_Flow_Switch* module, the category on the right is composed of three modules and functions as an interface to the control plane. The *controllerApps* and *tcpControllerApps* are used as slots, which enable the user to load different applications to the controller. The individual applications can extend or alter the behaviour of the controller. The *OF_Controller* module implements the main logic of the controller and is responsible for establishing and maintaining the communication to the OpenFlow switches as well as interacting with the assigned controller applications. Following the design architecture of most real-world controllers, the *OF_Controller* module can support an

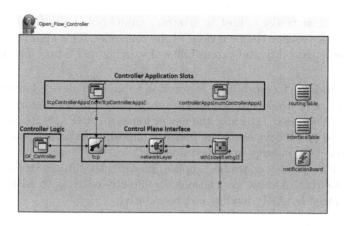

Fig. 3. Open_Flow_Controller compound module.

arbitrary number of applications which run on top of the main controller process. The communication between the controller and its applications is realized by a producer/consumer design pattern provided by OMNeT++ called signals.

Prior to the start of the simulation, the *Open_Flow_Controller* can be configured with an IP address and port to listen for active OpenFlow connections. Furthermore, a service time can be set which is applied to all received packets to simulate the time needed by the controller to process a request from the switch. At last, the module emits a signal at the beginning of the simulation to inform the controller applications that it has booted and is now fully operational.

Once a packet is received from the data plane and scheduled for execution, the module checks if it has been received from an open connection or if a new connection has to be established. If the message is sent by an unestablished connection, the controller forks the initial connection and initiates the OpenFlow Channel as specified by the OpenFlow protocol. Yet, if the packet has arrived via an existing connection, the *OF_Controller* module emits a Packet-in signal with an attached reference pointer to the packet. This signal is then examined by the individual controller applications, which determine the further course of action.

Following this design pattern, a unique signal is used to inform the applications of received and sent OpenFlow messages. Each of these signals provides a pointer to the original message which triggered the signal. This message can then be examined by the application for further processing. At last, the *OF_Controller* module provides an interface to the controller applications for sending OpenFlow messages to its managed switches.

3.2 Controller Applications

The *OF_Controller* module is intentionally kept simple and only manages the connection to the switches. Hence the controller applications are required to handle more complex processes. In this context, the suite allows the user to configure each individual controller to host an arbitrary number of applications, which can extend, alter or redefine the behaviour of the controller. This approach provides a high interchangeability and extensibility of existing and future modules.

ARPResponder. To establish a connection to another device located on the same network, a device has to first determine the MAC address associated to the destination IP address. Typically, the device issues an ARP [19] Request, which is broadcasted to all devices on the network imposing additional load onto the network, especially in large broadcast domains.

The *ARPResponder* controller application tries to mitigate this effect, by caching IP-to-MAC address associations. By directly replying to ARP requests, the load induced by ARP flooding can be reduced.

LLDPAgent. SDN controllers often rely on the Link Layer Discovery Protocol (LLDP) to build a map of the network topology [8]. To bring this functionality to OMNeT++ the OpenFlow OMNeT++ Suite provides the *LLDPAgent* controller application and a *LLDP* message class. Whereas the *LLDP* message reflects the structure of its real world counterpart, the *LLDPAgent* module sends these messages in regular time intervals.

Hub. The *Hub* controller application is the simplest forwarding mechanism provided by the OpenFlow OMNeT++ Suite. It implements a hub behaviour, in which the switch is instructed to flood every data plane packet on all active ports except for the ingress port.

Learning Switch. The second forwarding mechanism is implemented by the *LearningSwitch* controller application. In comparison to the *Hub* module, this controller application maps the observed MAC addresses to the respective ingress port and is thus able to directly forward data plane packets towards their destination.

LLDP Forwarding. The *LLDPForwarding* controller application makes use of the topology information provided by the *LLDPAgent* module to forward packets along the shortest path from source to destination. The shortest path is computed by Dijkstra's algorithm and the hop count is used as cost function. Since the information of the network topology might be outdated or incomplete, no route to the destination may be found. In this case, the module can be either configured to drop or flood the packet. Yet, if a path is returned, the *LLDPForwarding* controller application sends a Flow-mod message to every switch along the path to establish the forwarding route. Once all Flow-mod messages have been sent, the module proceeds by sending a Packet-out message to the switch which originally triggered the request, to forward the packet to the next hop. From there on, all switches along the path have already executed the Flow-Mod instructions and are now able to directly forward the packet to its destination without any further controller intervention.

LLDP Balanced Min Hop. The last forwarding mechanism featured by the OpenFlow OMNeT++ Suite is implemented by the *BalancedMinHop* module and forwards packets along the shortest path towards the destination. Whereas the *LLDPForwarding* controller application always uses the same deterministic route, the *BalancedMinHop* module tries to balance the load among several shortest paths. This not only makes better use of the provided bandwidth but also spreads the load among the intermediary network devices, thus making this forwarding mechanism especially beneficial for network topologies containing numerous redundant paths to a single node.

3.3 Host Applications

Host applications are similar to the controller applications, except that they are running on the *StandardHost* module, which is included in the INET framework. In total, the OpenFlow OMNeT++ Suite features three host applications which are presented in the following.

Ping App Random. The *PingAppRandom* module extends the standard ping application provided by the INET framework. Whereas the base module sends a ping request to a preconfigured IP address, the *PingAppRandom* application selects a random host by an uniform distribution as destination.

TCP Traffic Generator. The *TCPTrafficGeneratorApp* module provides the possibility to generate a realistic TCP traffic pattern. For this, the module can be configured with an arrival rate, at which it establishes a TCP connection to a random host in the network. Once the connection is established, the module starts by sending an amount of data according to a flow size value which is randomly selected from an input file.

TCP Traffic Sink. The *TCPTrafficSinkApp* host application is used in combination with the *TCPTrafficGeneratorApp* module and serves as communication partner. Once the connection is established, the *TCPTrafficSinkApp* module accepts all incoming packets, but does not process them any further. In contrast to the TCPSink module provided by OMNeT++, our implementation actively closes the TCP connection on reception of the last packet. This has been done to correctly record the timestamps of the individual connection phases.

3.4 HyperFlow

In addition to a centralized controller, the OpenFlow OMNeT++ Suite provides a HyperFlow implementation, which realizes a horizontally distributed controller architecture [21]. The implementation consists of a *HyperFlowAgent* and a *Hyper_Flow_Synchronizer* compound module as well as custom messages which establish the communication between these two entities. Furthermore, selected controller applications have been expanded to denote and replay events which need to be synchronized. In the following we give details about the interior working of these modules and state the changes we made to port HyperFlow to the OMNeT++ framework.

HyperFlow Agent. The *HyperFlowAgent* module is implemented as controller application and is modelled according to the original HyperFlow design [21], despite some minor differences discussed in Sect. 3.4. It provides an interface to the controller applications to replicate state changing events as well as synchronizing the local view in regular time intervals. Furthermore, it implements a failure discovery of controller instances.

HyperFlow Synchronizer. The original HyperFlow implementation uses a distributed file system as synchronization mechanism, which is not available in OMNeT++. Thus, we created the *Hyper_Flow_Synchronizer* module, which functions as master node during the synchronization process.

In comparison to the distributed file system, the *Hyper_Flow_Synchronizer* module needs to be placed in one fixed location in the network and imposes a higher delay to nodes having a physical greater distance to this module. The distributed file system handles this issue more efficiently by distributing the information from nodes which are located in closer proximity to each other. Thus, the original HyperFlow implementation is able to distribute the information more quickly and hence can provide a smaller window of inconsistency among all nodes. Yet, the *Hyper_Flow_Synchronizer* module provides the unique ability to simulate the performance of different synchronization mechanism by setting the service time parameter to reflect the capabilities of the system of interest. Since the overall performance of HyperFlow is decisively determined by the underlying synchronization mechanism as stated in [21], the *Hyper_Flow_Synchronizer* module enables an extensive analysis of different synchronization technologies.

HyperFlow Controller Applications. As HyperFlow requires a modification of the controller applications to signal state changing events, this also applies to the applications provided by the OpenFlow OMNeT++ Suite. Currently, the suite provides two controller applications, which have been adapted to work in combination with the *HyperFlowAgent* module, i.e., the *HF_ARPResponder* and *HF_LLDPAgent* module. Each of these modules are derived from their respectively named parent module and feature the same core functionality. In addition to the functionality provided by the base class, the modules have been extended to use the *HyperFlowAgent* module to denote state changing events and to synchronize their own state by listening to emitted signals from this module.

3.5   Kandoo

In addition to HyperFlow, the OpenFlow OMNeT++ Suite features a hierarchical distributed controller architecture, which is modelled after Kandoo.

Here, two distinct hierarchies of controllers are utilized to balance the load inflicted onto the control plane. For this, the *KandooAgent* controller application module can be configured to either run as local or root controller. In addition, the suite provides a variety of controller applications, which have been expanded for their use with Kandoo. In the following, we outline the implementation details of these modules and describe their interactions.

Kandoo Agent. The *KandooAgent* module provides the core functionality and is modelled in similarity to the original Kandoo implementation [6]. As Kandoo differentiates between local and root controllers, the module can be configured with the according mode of operation. If the application runs in local mode it provides interfaces to other controller applications to forward requests to the root controller. In case the *KandooAgent* module is set to root mode, it maintains the global view of the network and handles requests from local controllers.

Kandoo Controller Applications. As stated in [6], a modification of the controller applications is required to enable the communication between the local and root controller instances. In addition, each application has to respect the mode of operation in which the controller is currently running and has to behave accordingly. In this context, we have adapted a total of four controller applications to function properly in combination with the *KandooAgent* module. Namely, these four modules are the *KN_ARPResponder*, *KN_LLDPAgent*, *KN_LLDPForwarding* and *KN_LLDPBalancedMinHop*, which are all derived from their respective base classes and feature the same core functionality.

3.6 Utility

The utility package of the OpenFlow OMNeT++ Suite contains two modules, i.e., *StaticSpanningTree* and *OpenFlowGraphAnalyzer*, which assist in constructing and analysing an OpenFlow enabled simulation network.

Static Spanning Tree. The *StaticSpanningTree* module constructs a spanning tree on the data plane of the switches and thus enables simulations of network topologies containing loops. This is achieved by setting the *OFPPC_NO_FLOOD* flag on all ports, which are not part of the spanning tree.

OpenFlow Graph Analyzer. The *OpenFlowGraphAnalzer* module can be placed within an OpenFlow network and extracts several graph characteristics, i.e., the minimum, maximum and the average path length.

4 Evaluation of Distributed Controller Architectures

To analyse the offered traffic of distributed controllers architectures, we modelled a topology after the Advanced Layer 2 Services (AL2S) test bed in the OpenFlow

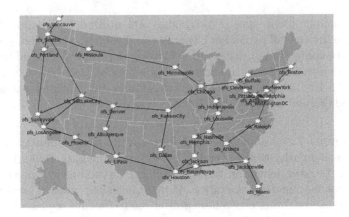

Fig. 4. Subset of the AL2S test bed in OMNeT++.

OMNeT++ Suite as illustrated in Fig. 4. The AL2S test bed is comprised of multiple sites distributed throughout the United States, which are interconnected and enable researchers to investigate different configuration mechanisms by using Software-defined networking technologies such as OpenFlow.

In total the modelled topology features 34 *Open_Flow_Domain* nodes which reflect the individual sites. Each domain features one OpenFlow switch module as well as a configurable number of *StandardHost* modules, which has been set to two for our investigations. The connections between the sites have been realized in the OMNeT++ simulation framework through the use of the *DistanceChannel*, which imposes a delay on every message according to the physical length of the channel at a data rate of $10Gbps$. We used POCO [7] to compute the controller placements based on the minimum controller to switch latency. The individual placements are detailed in Table 1.

In our scenario, the controllers are set to run the *ARPResponder, LLDPAgent* and the *LLDPForwarding* module in addition to the respective distributed controller agents. The LLDPAgent module is configured to send LLDP messages every 30 s, which is the default value of the Cisco IOS Operating System. The StandardHost modules are all equipped with the PingAppRandom application, which is configured to send one ping request per second to a random host in the network.

Table 1. AL2S controller placement for a varying number of k controllers

Controller/k	1	2	3	4	5
Controller 1	Kansas City	Louisville	Denver	Seattle	Seattle
Controller 2	-	Salt Lake City	Portland	El Paso	El Paso
Controller 3	-	-	Atlanta	Chicago	Atlanta
Controller 4	-	-	-	Atlanta	Houston
Controller 5	-	-	-	-	Cleveland

Furthermore, ARP responses are cached for 60 s to represent the default value of the Linux Mint Operating System. To conclude, the service time of each Open-Flow switch is configured to 0.035 ms, which is the average processing delay per packet as observed in [4]. For the following results we simulate a time span of 30 min and each configuration is repeated 4 times. In this configuration, a single simulation run is completed within approximately 12 min when executed on an Intel(R) Core(TM) i7-2600 CPU @ 3.40 GHz having 16 GB memory.

To quantify the impact of the individual controller architectures, we investigate the offered load, which is derived by dividing the number of packets per second at the individual control plane interfaces by the controller's service time per packet.

4.1 HyperFlow

We start our evaluation of the offered load for the horizontal controller architecture by configuring all controllers with the *HyperFlowAgent* module. Here, the placement of the synchronization module resides in Kansas City. For our investigations, we vary the number of controllers from 1 to 5 as shown in Table 1 and for each configuration repeat the simulation with a deterministic message service time ranging from 3 to 7 ms. In Fig. 5a, the y-axis states the offered load and the x-axis groups the varying number of controllers by the configured service time. Within one group the red, brown, green, blue and purple bar relate to the scenario in which 1, 2, 3, 4 or 5 controllers are used respectively and the error bars represent the 95% confidence interval.

For a service time of 3 and 4 ms, the offered load increases with a rising number of controllers with the exception of the 5 controller scenario. The increased

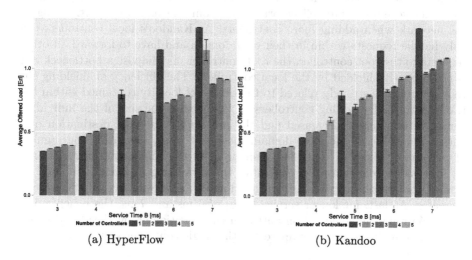

(a) HyperFlow   (b) Kandoo

Fig. 5. Offered load for a varying number of controllers using (a) Hyperflow and (b) Kandoo. (Colour figure online)

load for the multi-controller scenarios is influenced by several impact factors in a non-intuitive manner. This is due to the induced synchronization load, which is augmented with each additional controller. The slight exception for 5 controllers results from a more efficient and balanced controller placement within the AL2S topology. Starting with a service time of 5 ms, the single controller scenario produces the highest offered load for a given service time. This results from a single controller no longer being able to handle the traffic in a timely manner. Thus TCP timers of the host applications expire and force a retransmit, hence causing more offered load. In the case of a service time of 7 ms, this effect can also be observed for the two controller scenario.

4.2 Kandoo

We continue our investigation by analysing the impact of a hierarchical controller architecture on the offered load. For this all controllers are configured with the *KandooAgent* module and an additional root controller is placed in Kansas City. Figure 5b displays the results. As described previously, the y-axis denotes the offered load, whereas the individual service times are plotted on the x-axis. The number of configured controllers is represented by the bar color and the error bars depict the 95% confidence intervals.

Overall, the figure shows a general increase on the offered load with rising service times. For a service time of 3 ms and 4 ms, the offered load is augmented with additional controllers, which is caused by the synchronization overhead. Starting with a service time of 5 ms, the single controller scenario induces more load into the system compared to when using 2 or 3 controllers. Again, this is caused by the resource limitation of a single controller and its incapability to handle the offered traffic. Yet, a similar trend is observed for the 4 and 5 controller scenarios. This effect originates from the increased partitioning of the network when adding more controllers. As Kandoo's local controllers can only handle requests within in their own domain and have to forward all other requests to the root controller, the root controller may impose a bottleneck if it is not properly shielded by the local controllers. The efficiency of shielding the root controller is strongly related to the degree of locality contained within the traffic pattern. By adding controllers to the cluster, the size of the individual controller domains is decreased and the probability that the destination of a packet is outside of the local domain increases. Thus, increasing the number of requests to the root controller. Similar as in the single controller scenario, an overloaded root controller may stall the processing of packets to such an extend, that retransmissions are triggered and therefore the overall offered load increases. At last, for longer service times of 6 ms and 7 ms, the benefits of a multi controller implementation outweigh the partitioning overhead and hence the offered load is lower as compared to the single controller scenario.

5 Conclusion

In this paper we present the OpenFlow OMNeT++ Suite, which enables the simulation of distributed SDN controller architectures within the OMNeT++ framework. In addition to a single controller approach, the suite provides a horizontal and a hierarchical distributed controller architecture, which are modelled in resemblance to HyperFlow and Kandoo respectively. To demonstrate the suite's capabilities, we perform an exemplary evaluation highlighting performance influence factors of these controller architectures. The results show how partitioning, instance placement and service times may affect the offered control plane load. Furthermore, a greater synchronization overhead is observed for a larger number of distributed controller instances. HyperFlow achieved a better efficiency than Kandoo in the investigated scenario. This is mostly due to the chosen traffic pattern featuring a low degree of locality. Yet, further investigations have to be conducted to determine the exact degree of locality needed by Kandoo as well as to determine further key performance indicators impacting the individual controller architectures. For these and future evaluations, the OpenFlow OMNeT++ Suite offers the necessary level of detail and flexibility to provide a solid foundation.

Acknowledgment. This work has been performed in the framework of the CELTIC EUREKA project SENDATE-PLANETS (Project ID C2015/3-1), and it is partly funded by the German BMBF (Project ID 16KIS0474). The authors alone are responsible for the content of the paper.

References

1. INET framework. http://inet.omnetpp.org/. Accessed 01 Sep 2015
2. OMNeT++: OMNet++ network simulation framework. http://www.omnetpp.org/. Accessed 01 Sep 2015
3. Berde, P., Gerola, M., Hart, J., Higuchi, Y., Kobayashi, M., Koide, T., Lantz, B., O'Connor, B., Radoslavov, P., Snow, W., et al.: ONOS: Towards an open, distributed SDN OS. In: Proceedings of the Third Workshop on Hot Topics in Software-defined Networking. ACM (2014)
4. Dürr, F., Kohler, T., et al.: Comparing the forwarding latency of openflow hardware and software switches. Technical report Computer Science 2014/04. University of Stuttgart, Faculty of Computer Science, Electrical Engineering, and Information Technology. University of Stuttgart, Germany (2014)
5. Handigol, N., Heller, B., Jeyakumar, V., Lantz, B., McKeown, N.: Reproducible network experiments using container-based emulation. In: Proceedings of the 8th International Conference on Emerging Networking Experiments and Technologies, pp. 253–264. ACM (2012)
6. Yeganeh, S.H., Ganjali, Y.: Kandoo: a framework for efficient and scalable offloading of control applications. In: Proceedings of the First Workshop on Hot Topics in Software-Defined Networks. ACM (2012)
7. Hock, D., Hartmann, M., Gebert, S., Jarschel, M., Zinner, T., Tran-Gia, P.: Pareto-optimal resilient controller placement in SDN-based core networks. In: 25th International Teletraffic Congress (ITC). IEEE (2013)

8. IEEE Standards Association: IEEE standard for local and metropolitan area networks-station and media access control connectivity discover. http://standards. ieee.org/getieee802/download/802.1AB-2009.pdf. Accessed 01 Sep 2015

9. Jain, S., Kumar, A., Mandal, S., Ong, J., Poutievski, L., Singh, A., Venkata, S., Wanderer, J., Zhou, J., Zhu, M., et al.: B4: Experience with a globally-deployed software defined wan. In: ACM SIGCOMM Computer Communication Review, vol. 43. ACM (2013)

10. Jarschel, M., Oechsner, S., Schlosser, D., Pries, R., Goll, S., Tran-Gia, P.: Modeling and performance evaluation of an openflow architecture. In: Proceedings of the 23rd International Teletraffic Congress, pp. 1–7. International Teletraffic Congress (2011)

11. Jarschel, M., Zinner, T., Hossfeld, T., Tran-Gia, P., Kellerer, W.: Interfaces, attributes, and use cases: A compass for SDN. IEEE Commun. Mag. **52**, 210–217 (2014)

12. Klein, D., Jarschel, M.: An openflow extension for the OMNet++ INET framework. In: Proceedings of the 6th International ICST Conference on Simulation Tools and Techniques, pp. 322–329. ICST (Institute for Computer Sciences, Social-Informatics and Telecommunications Engineering) (2013)

13. Koponen, T., Casado, M., Gude, N., Stribling, J., Poutievski, L., Zhu, M., Ramanathan, R., Iwata, Y., Inoue, H., Hama, T., et al.: Onix: A distributed control platform for large-scale production networks. In: OSDI 2010 (2010)

14. Levin, D., Wundsam, A., Heller, B., Handigol, N., Feldmann, A.: Logically centralized?: state distribution trade-offs in software defined networks. In: Proceedings of the First Workshop on Hot Topics in Software Defined Networks, pp. 1–6. ACM (2012)

15. McKeown, N., Anderson, T., Balakrishnan, H., Parulkar, G., Peterson, L., Rexford, J., Shenker, S., Turner, J.: Openflow: enabling innovation in campus networks. ACM SIGCOMM Comput. Commun. Rev. **38**(2), 69–74 (2008)

16. Open Networking Foundation: Openflow switch specification. https://www. opennetworking.org/. Accessed 01 Sep 2015

17. OpenDaylight foundation: Opendaylight. https://www.opendaylight.org/. Accessed 01 Sep 2015

18. Phemius, K., Bouet, M., Leguay, J.: DISCO: Distributed multi-domain SDN controllers. In: 2014 IEEE Network Operations and Management Symposium (NOMS), pp. 1–4. IEEE (2014)

19. Plummer, D.: Ethernet address resolution protocol: Or converting network protocol addresses to 48. bit ethernet address for transmission on ethernet hardware. Request For Comments 826 (1982)

20. Roy, A.R., Bari, M.F., Zhani, M.F., Ahmed, R., Boutaba, R.: Design management of DOT: a distributed openflow testbed. In: 14th IEEE/IFIP Network Operations and Management Symposium (NOMS), May 2014

21. Tootoonchian, A., Ganjali, Y.: Hyperflow: A distributed control plane for openflow. In: Proceedings of the 2010 Internet Network Management Conference on Research on Enterprise Networking. USENIX Association (2010)

22. Yazici, V., Sunay, M.O., Ercan, A.O.: Controlling a software-defined network via distributed controllers. CoRR (2014)

Estimation of Synchronization Time in Cloud Computing Architecture

Fidan Kaya Gülağız[✉] and Onur Gök

Department of Computer Science, Kocaeli University,
Umuttepe, 41380 Izmit, Kocaeli, Turkey
{fidan.kaya, ogok}@kocaeli.edu.tr

Abstract. Size of the electronic data is constantly increasing with today's technology. Distribution of this data is provided via servers or cloud servers. There are some restrictions caused by network traffic and network infrastructure between these servers. Some of these restrictions can be listed as bandwidth, packet transmission rate, number of users that can be simultaneously answered. These are cause problems about data traffic and efficient transfer of data. In this thesis study, it is aimed to develop an efficient data synchronization system architecture that is compatible with distributed proxy server/cloud server architectures. Thus, it is aimed to optimize the traffic of created by data synchronization.

Keywords: Distributed systems · Data synchronization · Nosql · CouchDB · Cloud computing

1 Introduction

Along with the developments in technology, data is transferred to electronic environment. The size of the data transferred to electronic environment is increasing day by day. The increasing size of data causes traffic in the some network architectures. In case of the increased traffic, delays take place between the ends where data is transmitted and re-transmissions take place because of the delays. There is a need for proxy server based studies in order to overcome this problem or decrease the effect of this problem.

In this thesis, a synchronization method which based on proxy server/cloud server architecture is suggested. In this architecture, proxies does not contain same data. Each proxy server contains information belonging to its subnet and only synchronize its data with cloud server not other proxies. However, the problem of consistency arises in such architectures due to the storage of data in different servers (proxy and cloud servers). In order to ensure the consistency of data, mechanisms of data synchronization is needed. For this purpose, the synchronization traffic that will emerge between proxy servers and cloud servers should be optimized. In the architecture to be developed, a dual synchronization process is needed. A dual synchronization will be conducted both from cloud server to proxy server and from proxy server to cloud server. In these architecture cloud server will collect whole data which stored each proxy and proxies will store their specific data.

In order to store the data, a noqsl database CouchDB will be used. It is aimed to increase the speed of access to the data by using a noqsl database. CouchDB database

© ICST Institute for Computer Sciences, Social Informatics and Telecommunications Engineering 2017
R. Agüero et al. (Eds.): MONAMI 2016, LNICST 191, pp. 19–30, 2017.
DOI: 10.1007/978-3-319-52712-3_2

architecture has a synchronization module in itself. With this module, it conducts the synchronization process via multi-master computing, which is a subtype of master-master replication. However, the mapping process here can be conducted either on-demand (instant) or in permanent mode. In case of the preference of permanent synchronization mode, dual synchronization of the selected servers is carried out in one minute intervals. However, in case of an increase in the number of data and proxy servers to be synchronized, this process will cause a serious load on the system.

A system should be developed that will carry out the synchronization process by determining the most proper timing and without increasing the load on the system. In this thesis, it is aimed to develop a flexible architecture that is compatible with distributed proxy server- cloud server architectures and will provide the synchronization of data as frequent as possible.

The rest of the article is structured as follows. In the second section, proposed method is given. In the third section, the effect of background traffic is given for proposed distributed network architecture. Fourth section explains the selected parameters for network analysis. Fifth section explains the simple network architecture formed by OPNET. Conclusion and some future enhancements are given at the conclusion section.

2 Proposed Method

The main objective of the method to be developed is to create an architecture that will be alternative for current synchronization methods in the CouchDB database. In CouchDB database, there are three different type synchronization methods. These are can be listed as long polling, triggered mode and continuous mode. We want to develop a new and intelligent polling architecture to CouchDB database. This architecture will also determine the timing of synchronization according to network congestion in the application layer. This architecture will detect the appropriate polling period for each subnet according to their historical data. Also these data will give information about user behavior in related subnet and intelligent polling method will detect synchronization time according to user's behavior. The steps to be followed for the development of the system can be listed as below;

- Establishment of a network to simulate the distributed network architecture
- Obtaining network parameters to be used for analysis during a specific time period
- Using profile hidden markov model to analyze the obtained parameters
- Processing a synchronization control algorithm to detect synchronization time
- Repeating the second and third steps until all network is being modeled

As it can be understood from the steps, the method to be developed has two basic modules. These are the construction of distributed network architecture and determination of mapping time. A detailed description of these modules is given in Sects. 2.1 and 2.2.

2.1   Distributed Network Architecture

The overall view of distributed network architecture to be designed is presented in Fig. 1. In the architecture, N number of proxy servers communicates with the cloud server. This communication is carried out via an internet cloud. The architecture seen in the figure is giant network architecture and it is difficult to be designed in real life. Therefore the architecture will be modeled in OPNET environment. To be compatible with real life, after the model is set up, packet size, packet transmission frequency and packet delay values will be determined according to the appropriate probability distributions. Then, background traffic at different rates will be added to the link between cloud server and internet cloud. In this way, all probable situations of the network will be tried to be modeled. When all the processes are carried out, the network architecture to work on will be obtained.

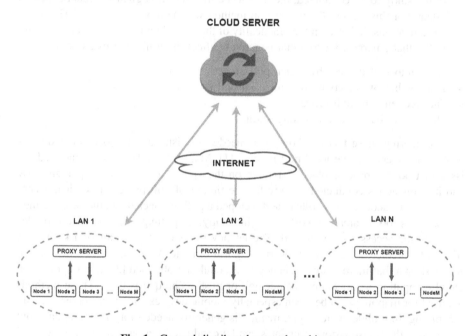

Fig. 1. General distributed network architecture

After the architecture is designed, different data sets that model different congestion situations in the network will be obtained. Via these data sets, an architecture that will instantaneously model the situation of the network in a specific time will be designed. Profile Hidden Markov Model will be used for the learning process on the obtained data sets. In this way, the most appropriate times of the network for synchronization will be detected by using the previous periods.

2.2   Detecting Synchronization Time

There are two main methods for data transmission in the given internet environment. These are poll and push techniques. In the poll technique, requests are sent to server from client and information as an answer is taken from server. Poll method is a more traditional method than push method. It is generally used to carry out planned tasks in a time slot. As an example for the uses of the poll method, applications in which delays in data can be neglected and data transfers in giant sizes can be given. In the push technique, the server informs the client about the changes in information. At the same time, the transfer of the updated information can also be carried out as a part of the informational message. Push method is more often used for real time applications. The loading of updates in mobile phone applications or applications in which data is processed in only one.

In the study to be conducted, the data to be transferred is giant size data called as bulk data. For this reason, the use of poll method will be more appropriate. However, there is a relationship between the practicality of the data obtained in poll technique and the traffic that emerges. Factors that negatively affect the traffic are listed below.

- The number of devices by which poll process is conducted.
- The number of objects needed for each poll process.
- The frequency of poll process.
- The current bandwidth and congestion.

Considering these factors above, it is needed to distribute the load for wide networks and categorize the local poll process [1]. Many researchers have examined the issue that polling process places a burden on the system and it requires planning. Lv and his colleagues conducted a study for the timing of poll process in optical access networks [2]. Jacob and his colleague developed a polling mechanism that was planned for wireless body area networks. In the study, a polling method that provides discrete-time access was suggested. The latency times of the transmission knots was tried to be predicted according to Karn's algorithm logic. With the method developed, it was shown that more realistic latency times could be obtained [3]. It is important in cloud computing architecture whether poll or push technique is used. These methods are used for mapping data between especially mobile devices and cloud server in cloud computing. In mobile devices, poll method is generally needed for the first update, but afterwards, the transmission of updates can be conducted via push method. In a study carried out by Carvalho and his colleagues, evaluation of the use of poll and push methods between cloud server and mobile devices was conducted. At the end of the study, it was found that if the application doesn't have to send more than one request in 40 min, it is appropriate to use the poll technique [4]. Li and colleagues stated that Android applications in mobile devices use traditional poll methods. They found that when the data draining frequency of the applied poll method is not detected accurately, problems such as information delays, unnecessary consumption of network traffic or unnecessary battery consumption in mobile devices may emerge [5]. Similarly, Fang and colleagues also suggested an architecture that provided the timing of broadcast poll approach fixed on mobile devices [6]. Saxena and colleagues suggested a hybrid method in order to shorten the access time to data in mobile devices. They provided a probability based approach that tried to predict the next poll time or push time separately. With the method developed, access time to data under high system load was shortened. Therefore, they showed that scheduled mechanisms are very useful for access to data [7].

The CouchDB database that will be used in the suggested architecture carries out the synchronization process via three different mechanisms. These can be listed as continuous, triggered and long polling.

Continuous mechanism, as it can be understood from its name, runs on a permanently open connection. This open connection continuously listens to CouchDB's Changes API, which is the modified API of CouchB. When a modification takes place in any of databases that will be synchronized, it automatically starts the synchronization process. When this method is conducted, real time synchronization is provided.

The second mapping mechanism, long polling, is the most effective way of polling process. The server waits for a fixed time before it sends the response in case there will be a modification. Therefore, it eliminates the unnecessary polling processes when there is no modification. The method to be used before long polling is short polling method. In the short polling process, polling is continuously carried out in fixed intervals. Long polling has a longer poll time and aims to send modifications collectively. However, short polling mechanism causes congestions in traffic. In this method, there is a certain pre-scheduled transmission time between the transferred packets and if there are delays in the network, the time between two control periods will be insufficient for transmission [8].

Triggered method is an alternative method for continuous and long polling methods. CouchDB runs on triggered mode as default. This system also works with short polling logic; however it is the type of short polling that is triggered at a time. Only the CouchDB administrator can carry out the poll process on demand. The disadvantage of this method is that it requires constant triggering. Mapping will not be carried out without being triggered even if there is a modification.

In this thesis study, a different method that will be an alternative for the three synchronization mechanisms in the CouchDB structure is suggested. This method will be a smart poll method. The frequency period of poll time will be modified according to the situation of network by the use of this method. For this process, data that is saved from the network at different periods and Profile Hidden Markov Model will be utilized. Therefore, no time will be spent for synchronization when traffic or packet transfer to cloud server is condensed.

3 Effect of Background Traffic on Network

In the suggested system, data to be sent has to transmit via internet cloud in order to reach the server after leaving from LAN (Local Area Network) environment. Considering that internet is a giant environment and it is shared by a lot of different networks, the background traffic will have a serious effect on the application. Therefore, it is necessary to consider the effect of background traffic in the design process of the distributed system architecture to be developed.

Several researchers have studied how and to what extent the background traffic has an effect while developing distributed architecture systems. In a study conducted by Venkatesh and Vahdat [9], it was shown that the traffic stream in the background affects the service and protocol behaviors. They showed that synthetic traffic models that were used previously don't represent the effect of the traffic that is seen in real life, and therefore, sufficient congestion sampling cannot be obtained. Applications behave differently when they have to compete with the background traffic. Therefore, they carried out behavior analysis for both synthetic background traffic and real background traffic of different applications. As a result, they found out that every application is affected by traffic congestion to some extent depending on the type of the application. Venkatesh and Vahdat [10], tried to conduct a new research with software called Swing to obtain a more realistic traffic in the following years. In this study, they showed that structural traffic models special to applications can be created successfully with Swing software. It was proved that the traffic created by Swing is a realistic traffic under different application, network and user circumstances. In another study carried out by Nahum and colleagues [11], it was shown that WAN conditions have a serious effect on servers' performances. In this study, they showed that lost packets decrease the performance of servers by 50% and increase the response time at the same rate. In real life, every server in a WAN environment faces problems such as packet losses and delays. For this reason, while evaluating the performances of servers, WAN characteristics should also be considered. In the study, it is stated that packet losses take place more often when the internet is burst. Eylen and Bazlamaçı [12] attempted to develop a system to be able to measure unicast delays without the need for clock mapping. In this study, they stated that background traffic is needed to obtain traffic similar to real life traffic. Therefore, random delays were added to trial packages used in the study. In this way, three background traffics at different rates were created by using Poisson distribution. The aim here is to provide congestion at different rates. The first situation is a high loaded traffic situation called as "heavy load/high load". In this situation, the link via which the transmission will be done is overloaded. In other words, more background traffic is injected to the network than the capacity of the link. There will be congestion in this situation and queue size will increase. The second situation is "low load" situation. In this situation, packet transmission was tried to be done with a null transmission queue. The density of background traffic is much less than the capacity of the link. The aim of creating traffic at this rate is to catch instant modifications in delays. The third situation is the traffic rate called as "silence rate". In this situation, the rate of the traffic created equals to half of the capacity of the link. The reason for creating this situation is to determine the presence of packets that aren't delayed. Real traffic was modeled with the three types of traffic created. The analysis of the developed method was carried out more accurately under background traffic in this way. In another study conducted by Levesque and Tipper [13], background traffic was created to provide accurate predictions of point-to-point mapping time under asymmetric delay conditions. The main reason for queue delays in the network is the general traffic load of the network. If traffic load is considerably low, mapping errors will decrease at the same rate. Mapping errors will increase along with the increase in traffic load. The analysis of the developed method has been tested in different traffic conditions and the effect of background traffic is clearly shown.

In these studies, it has been found out that background traffic has a serious effect on both applications and servers. The dimension of the effect depends on several parameters. Therefore, in order to conduct analyses of applications realistically, background traffic should certainly be taken into consideration.

4 Determination of Parameters for Network Analysis

Packet losses and re-transmissions take place when the traffic is condensed. Congestions occur in the points where the traffic is too condensed. Different versions of current TCP transmission protocols can detect congestion situations with different ways [14]. TCP Reno, New Reno, Tahoe and SACK versions use packet losses as congestion signals. However, noticing a packet loss can take a very long time for congestion. During this time, more packet losses may occur due to filling of router's buffer. TCP Vegas, which is the last version of TCP, tries to do congestion control relying on round time value. In TCP Vegas, pending throughput and real throughput computations are done relying on RTT. The frame size is calculated according to results obtained from this process. However, the inappropriate choice of parameters in frame size calculation results in packet losses. TCP Vegas allows packet retention between 1–3 intervals in congestion queue. When background traffic increases, this situation causes an unnecessary obstruction.

Mechanisms that can produce a solution before congestion occurs by detecting the congestion situation in application level are needed for congestion detection and more effective use of congestion prevention mechanisms in TCP. Solutions for congestion situations in application layer can be listed as three items [15]. Response packets that servers send to clients can be sent in big sizes. In this way, the number of packets to be sent can be decreased. Data transmission should be schedulable so as not to collide with each other and users who carry out simultaneous transmissions can be restricted.

The congestion situations should be detected before occurring or shortly after occurring for the application of solutions suggested in this part. For this reason, the parameters to be used for accurate detection of congestion situations should be determined appropriately. There are software such as Netflow [16] and Sfolw [17] developed by Cisco for congestion management in the application level. These software use the following items as parameters for congestion control:

- Response time,
- Accessibility of network resources,
- Application performance,
- Jitter for video data transfer,
- Connection time,
- Throughput and
- Packet losses

In addition to these, parameters to be used in networks with a heterogonous structure for detection of congestion are listed by Floyd as following [18].

- Throughput
- Delay
- Lost packets
- Response time

These parameters are common parameters that are used for congestion detection and congestion prevention [19]. After background traffic at different rates is created in our study, the required congestion detection parameters of transmitted trial packages must be registered. Four different parameters will be used in this step. These are throughput, delay, re-transmission numbers and response time. These parameters are standard parameters used by Cisco for congestion detection. In this step, the number of packets pending in the queue, pending time of packets in the queue and the numbers of re-transmission of packages are aimed to be decreased in the analysis conducted with congestion parameters.

5 Forming Network Using OPNET

A WAN network has to be set up in order to obtain the data to be used for the study. The screenshot of the network set up is given in Fig. 2. In the figure, we gave sample architecture. After we obtained first results, subnet count will be increased and method will be tested in more realistic conditions. There are four subnets in the sample network. These are named as Subnet Istanbul, Test Subnet, Samsun and Erzurum. The subnet in Istanbul stands for the subnet where the cloud server exists. Test Subnet stands for the subnet where the network's values of throughput, delay, response time and re-transmission number will be registered. There is a proxy server here. The four parameters mentioned were registered via the probe packets sent from this proxy server.

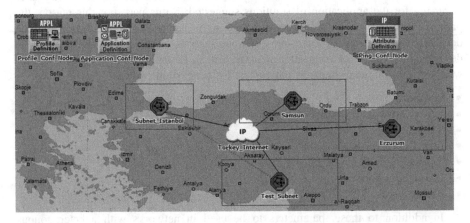

Fig. 2. Sample network architecture that is built using OPNET

The IP Cloud in Fig. 2 stands for the internet in Turkey. In order to make the simulation realistic, latency at different rates was added to the IP cloud and data was obtained according six different latency values. Packet discard ratio value was determined as 0.1. This value equals to loss ratio in cabled networks [20]. These two parameters should appropriately be modeled in order to model the real traffic accurately [21, 22]. In order to add random latencies to probe packets to be sent, random latencies were added to the link via which the server is connected to the IP cloud. These latencies were added according to Poisson distribution and implemented at three different ratios. The reason for adding latencies is to create congestion and then, solve the congestion situation [12]. The first one of the three ratios stands for high load case when the link is overloaded. In this situation, more background packet than the capacity of the link was injected to link. The second situation stands for low load case. In this situation, the traffic created is much lower than the capacity of the link. The third situation is silence rate situation. In the third situation, the traffic rate is half of the capacity of the link [23].

These three traffic ratios were applied with round bin logic during the simulation process. In the first situation, the situation in which the transmitter queue size increases was modeled by the application of high load situation. Then, low load situation was applied as the second step. The transmitter queue was decreased in this way. Silence rate situation was applied as the last step. Therefore, these three situations were modeled under the conditions of different latencies that may occur in IP cloud. The matlab code that was created in order to add traffic to the link is given in Table 1.

Table 1. Matlab code to generate background traffic

High Load	Low Load	Slience Rate

x=0;
A=poissrnd(50000000,1,60);
yaz=fopen('dosya','w+');
fprintf(yaz,'seconds bits/second\n');
for i=1:60
    t = num2str(A(i));
    t2=num2str(x);
    t3='\t';
    t5='\n';
    t4 = strcat(t2,t3,t,t5);
    fprintf(yaz, t4);
    x=x+60;
end
	B= poissrnd(900000,1,60);
	for i=1:60
	    t = num2str(B(i));
	    t2=num2str(x);
	    t3='\t';
	    t5='\n';
	    t4 = strcat(t2,t3,t,t5);
	    fprintf(yaz, t4);
	    x=x+60;
	end
		C=poissrnd(30000000,1,60);
		for i=1:60
		    t = num2str(C(i));
		    t2=num2str(x);
		    t3='\t';
		    t5='\n';
		    t4 = strcat(t2,t3,t,t5);
		    fprintf(yaz, t4);
		    x=x+60;
		end

After the background traffic is added, it is necessary to determine according to which distribution the packets to be sent from subnets in Samsun and Erzurum will be transmitted. There are several probability distributions in literature for modeling different situations of the network. However, the appropriate parameters for these distributions vary along with developments in technology. Distributions that can be appropriate for different web packets and different traffic densities were determined by Garsva and colleagues in a study in 2014. According to the study, it was found out that the use of Pareto distribution when the traffic is condensed and the use of Weibull or Lognormal distributions when density is low are appropriate for sizes of transmitted data [24]. For this reason, three different packet transmission applications that were appropriate for the three different background traffics created were designed.

After the packet sizes mentioned above were applied to the subnets in Samsun and Erzurum, load, throughput, response time and re-transmission number parameters of probe packets sent from test subnet were saved in a text document. A sample screenshot of the data obtained is given in Table 2.

Table 2. A part of obtained dataset

Time (sec.)	Response time (sec.)	Delay (sec.)	Load (bytes/sec.)	Retransmission count
0.0	#N/A	#N/A	0	#N/A
1.2	#N/A	#N/A	0	#N/A
2.4	#N/A	#N/A	0	25
3.6	#N/A	#N/A	0	50
4.8	#N/A	#N/A	0	50
6.0	#N/A	#N/A	0	75
7.2	#N/A	#N/A	0	51
8.4	#N/A	#N/A	0	100
9.6	#N/A	#N/A	0	100
10.8	#N/A	#N/A	0	100
12.0	0.128293420847	0.063659785183	32000.000000000018	150
13.2	0.154222547248	0.071516954689	67840.000000000044	101
14.4	0.188230963541	0.083656841361	67413.333333333372	150
15.6	0.221081878731	0.115675131047	69119.999999999942	53
16.8	0.247895827499	0.115175899488	46080.000000000029	51
18.0	0.272231176872	0.130691457222	46080.000000000029	51
19.2	0.294266277436	0.113949038065	25173.333333333347	#N/A
20.4	0.307123112638	0.11617685566	26453.33333333335	26

6 Results

In this thesis proposal, a new method is suggested in order to solve the synchronization problem in distributed network architectures. The main aim of the method is to add an adaptive poll to CouchDB database, which is a noqsl database.

With the architecture to be developed, it is aimed to decrease the unnecessary delays and re-transmissions of packets that may occur in proxy server- cloud server architectures that require dual synchronization. In this part of the study, distributed network architecture is implemented with low server numbers on OPNET. In this way, data sets belonging to different time periods are obtained considering the different situations of the network.

In the second part of the study, firstly, it is aimed to obtain the missing values in the obtained data with statistical methods. Then, by using the Profile Hidden Markov Model, different models will be designed for data belonging to different periods. The congestion situations in OPNET environment will be detected from the application layer via these models. Therefore, the synchronization time will be planned adaptively according to the situation of the network.

References

1. Kenyon, T.: Data Networks: Routing, Security and Performance Optimization. Digital Press, Newton (1960)
2. Lv, Y., Jiang, N., Xue, C.: Energy-efficient load adaptive polling sequence arrangement scheme for passive optical access networks. IEEE/OSA J. Opt. Commun. Networking **7**, 516–524 (2015)
3. Jacob, A.K., Jacob, L.: A discrete time polling protocol for wireless body area network. In: IEEE International Advance Computing Conference, pp. 294–299. IEEE Press, India (2014)
4. Carvalho, S.A.L., Lima, R.N., Silva-Filho, A.G.: A pushing approach for data synchronization in cloud to reduce energy consumption in mobile devices. In: Brazilian Symposium on Computing Systems Engineering, Brazil, pp. 31–36 (2014)
5. Li, P., Chen, Y., Li, T., Wang R., Sun, J.: Implementation of cloud messaging system based on GCM service. In: IEEE International Conference on Computational and Information Sciences, China, pp. 1509–1512 (2013)
6. Fang, Q., Vrbsky, S.V., Dang, Y., Ni, W.: A pull-based broadcast algorithm that considers timing constraints. In: International Conference on Parallel Processing Workshops, Canada, pp. 46–53 (2004)
7. Saxena, N., Pinotti, C.M., Das, S.K.: A probabilistic push-pull hybrid scheduling algorithm for asymetric wireless environment. In: IEEE Global Telecommunications Conference Workshops, USA, pp. 5–6 (2004)
8. Aron, W., Druschel, P.: TCP implementation enhancements for improving webserver performance. Technical report TR99-335, Rice University (1999)
9. Venkatesh, K., Vahdat A.: Evaluating distributed systems: does background traffic matter? In: USENIX Annual Technical Conference, Boston, Massachusetts, pp. 227–240 (2008)
10. Venkatesh, K., Vahdat, A.: Swing: realistic and responsive network traffic generation. IEEE/ACM Trans. Networking **17**, 712–725 (2009)
11. Nahum, E.M., Roşu, M.C., Seshan, S., Almedia, J.: The effects of wide-area conditions on www server performance. In: ACM Sigmetrics Conference on Measurement and Modelling of Computer Systems, USA, pp. 16–20 (2001)
12. Eylen, T., Bazlamaçı, C.F.: One-way active delay measurement with error bounds. IEEE Trans. Instrum. Meas. **64**, 3476–3489 (2015)
13. Levesque, M., Tipper, D.: Improving the PTP synchronization accuracy under asymmetric delay conditions. In: IEEE International Symposium on Precision Clock Synchronization for Measurement, Control, and Communication, Germany, pp. 11–16 (2015)
14. Venkataramani, A., Kokku, R., Dahlin, M.: TCP nice: a mechanism for background transfers. In: 5th Symposium on Operating Systems Design and Implementation, Boston, pp. 329–343 (2002)
15. Ren, Y., Zhao, Y., Liu, P., Dou, K., Li, J.: A survey on TCP incast in data center networks. Int. J. Commun. Syst. **27**, 1160–1172 (2014)

16. Cisco Systems: NetFlow Configuration Guide, Cisco IOS Release 12.4, San Jose, USA (2011)
17. Cisco Systems: Cisco Nexus 9000 Series NX-OS System Management Configuration Guide, Release 7.x, San Jose, USA (2015)
18. Floyd, S.: Metrics for the evaluation of congestion control mechanisms, RFC5166 (2008)
19. Mathis, M.: A framework for defining empirical bulk transfer capacity metrics, RFC3148 (2001)
20. Isobe, T., Ito, D., Akashi, D., Tsutsumi, S.: RADIC-TCP: high-speed protocol applied for virtual private WAN. In: 18th International Conference on Telecommunications, Cyprus, pp. 505–510 (2011)
21. Kang, S., Prodanoff, Z., Potti, P.: Performance model of a campus wireless LAN. In: Sobh, T., Elleithy, K., Mahmood, A., Karim, M.A. (eds.) Novel Algorithms and Techniques in Telecommunications, Automation and Industrial Electronics. Springer, Dordrecht (2008)
22. Lee, J., Payandeh, S., Trajkovic, L.: Performance evaluation of transport protocols for internet-based teleoperation systems. In: OPNETWORK 2010, Washington DC, USA (2010)
23. Narula, R.: Performance analysis and evaluation of hybrid network using different integrated routing protocols. Int. J. Comput. Technol. **11**, 3090–3100 (2013)
24. Garsva, E., Paulauskas, N., Grazulevicius, G., Gulbinovic, L.: Packet inter-arrival time distribution in academic computer network. Elektron. IR Elektrotechnika **20**, 87–90 (2014)

A Novel Signaling Protocol (ARCSPXP): Case Study on Synchronization of Educational Data

Süleyman Eken[1], Fidan Kaya Gülağız[1(✉)], Ahmet Sayar[1],
Adnan Kavak[1], Umut Kocasaraç[2], and Zana İlhan[2]

[1] Computer Engineering Department, Kocaeli University,
Umuttepe Campus, 41380 Izmit, Turkey
{suleyman.eken,fidan.kaya,ahmet.sayar,
akavak}@kocaeli.edu.tr
[2] Ardıç Arge Bilgi ve Teknoloji Cozumleri, Tübitak TEKSEB,
41470 Gebze, Kocaeli, Turkey
{umut.kocasarac,zana.ilhan}@ardictech.com

Abstract. To define the state of communication, a lot of signaling protocol has been studied by many researchers. In this paper, we firstly focus on a new hybrid optimized signaling protocol, ARCSPXP (ARDIC Cloud Service Platform Extension Protocol), which is specialized to mobile devices which are communicating with cloud based services via its internet connection. Then, we test usability and feasibility of ARCSPXP signaling protocol on synchronization of educational data (text, images, media, etc.) stored tablets, proxy servers, and cloud servers which are system actors of the most important educational project in Turkey. Experimental results show that ARCSPXP provides a more manageable and easy to use integration structure for mobile devices.

Keywords: ARCSPXP · Data synchronization · Machine-to-cloud signaling · M2M signaling · Proxy server

1 Introduction

Depending on cloud-based services, a lot of new technologies have begun to emerge. The basic need is to track mobile devices using services and provide access to these devices if necessary. With these needs, importance of signaling protocols has increased day after day. A signaling protocol is really just any protocol that can send a signal or message from one specific computer to another specific computer. The aim of our study is to evaluate the feasibility and efficiency of ARCSPXP signaling protocol on synchronization of educational data. Architecture, communication primitives and usage areas of ARCSPXP will be explained in the following sections.

Turkish Ministry of Education has recently launched FATIH (Movement to Increase Opportunities and Technology) project that is primarily based on employing tablets and smart boards in classes for students and teachers and using educational data stored in centralized cloud based servers. Currently, there are three main actors of the ecosystem within the scope of this system: (i) a cloud-based SaaS services, (ii) the smart boards in classes, and (ii) tablets at students and teachers/educators. These actors

© ICST Institute for Computer Sciences, Social Informatics and Telecommunications Engineering 2017
R. Agüero et al. (Eds.): MONAMI 2016, LNICST 191, pp. 31–43, 2017.
DOI: 10.1007/978-3-319-52712-3_3

are foreseen to actively exchange data with cloud services within the project ecosystem. However, there exist limitations due to network traffic and infrastructure between the tablet clients and cloud servers that store educational data. Many schools have limited internet infrastructure. The limited network infrastructure and increase in educational data size, which are two major parameters affecting the system performance, cause increase in network delays and degradation of system performance in case of that a user in school network wants to access to the cloud servers to download educational data. FATIH project does not have school level (client-side) proxy servers. To solve these limitations and problems, a school level client-side proxy server and an extension framework for integrating it into the cloud system are proposed. This framework includes cloud signaling and synchronization functionalities in tablet client and proxy server. Cloud signaling module enables tablet-proxy-cloud communication. Synchronization module guarantees to keep the same data (i.e. educational files) at different locations in a consistent manner. So, proxy server is a solution approach to both decreasing network traffic and increasing the efficiency in data transfers between the end users (tablets) and cloud servers in FATIH project [1].

In this paper, we focus on cloud signaling module of the proxy server-based solution, especially ARCSPXP signaling protocol. Signaling module is developed by adapting ARDIC's ArCloud platform according to our requirements. ArCloud (ARDIC Cloud Services Platform) [2] is a high performance, extensible cloud platform designed for mobile devices to provide user, application, device and security management.

The remainder of this paper is organized as follows. Section 2 presents relevant research on mostly used signaling protocols. Section 3 introduces the architecture of ARCSPXP protocol. In this section, its communication primitives and application areas are also mentioned. Section 4 presents building an ARCSPXP application for data management and synchronization. Section 5 draws a conclusion and suggests some future works.

2 Related Works

With needs for tracking mobile devices and providing access to these devices if necessary, importance of signaling protocols has increased day after day. Three different types of signaling protocols are the most widely used signaling protocols in communication: H.323, SIP (Session Initiation Protocol), XMPP (Extensible Messaging and Presence Protocol). Detailed information about these protocols will be given in next paragraphs. H.323 is developed to enable multimedia communication over a computer network and to provide audio and video transmission. H.323 protocol is defined as a binary. Message format of H.323 protocol is determined as ASN.1 (Abstract Syntax Notation One). PER (Packet Encoding Rules) procedures are used for message encryption. These encoding rules belong to ASN.1 message format. ASN.1 is a standard that responsible for determining rules for preparing, transmitting, encrypting and decrypting data during the telecommunications on the computer network [3].

H.323 protocol has too many protocols except its components. These protocols have different processes like control of the record situation, control of the search signal, real time transfer etc. Some of these protocols are H.225 Registration, Admission and

Status, H.225 Call Signaling, Audio Processing, H.245 Control Signaling, Real Time Transport Protocol and Real Time Transport Control Protocol. A various applications of H.323 exist in corporate and home user environments such as IP Telephony, video conferencing, multimedia call centers, and telecommuting. Disadvantage of H.323 is to be VOIP (Voice over Internet Protocol) oriented. Its main task is to provide messaging before transferring audio and video, so it has limited messaging infrastructure.

The second communication protocol is SIP. It creates, sets up and finishes VOIP phone calls and has a text-based message structure and defines messages which will be sending between couples during a call. Also SIP can be used in many areas such as video conferences, fax transmission, file transfer and transferring status information [4]. Elements of the SIP protocols are defined by RFC 3261, which are divided into two types: user agents and servers. User Agents define endpoints, which are responsible for managing a SIP session and transmission of SIP messages. There are also four different server types in SIP protocol: redirect server, proxy server, registrar server, and location server [5]. Besides being a text-based, SIP is also http-like protocol. Its messages are similar to http messages. Request and response messages defined by RFC3261 are the two types of messages in SIP. An example of a SIP request message is below [6]. SIP also provides services for media and VOIP oriented, so it has limited messaging infrastructure.

The third one is XMPP (Whitepaper), originally named Jabber. It is an XML based signaling protocol for message oriented middleware. It enables two endpoints on the Internet to mutually transfer any structural information. Also, it allows message, file, and status transfer among more than one unit (user, device, etc.). Although XMPP is first intended for instant messaging, its XMPP has been improved for larger systems such as cloud computing in parallel with an increase in human requests for communication [7]. XMPP finds large areas of application such as instant messaging [8], interactive social media [9], and collective work flow [10], internet of Things, multi-agent systems, and cloud computing [11]. It conveys not only text or status information, but also voice and video messages in real-time is transmitted between users.

XMPP has three basic XML elements: status (presence), messages and iq (info/query). Notification mechanism that allows entities to acquire network usability information is provided by <presence> element from an entity which the other entities are member of it. An entity sends information to other entities by means of <message> element asynchronously. Request and responses are carried by <iq> element.

The fourth signaling protocol is MQTT [12, 13], a lightweight application layer protocol designed for processing and memory constrained devices. It utilizes topic-based pub/sub architecture allowing multiple clients can establish a connection. MQTT supports three QoS levels. QoS level 0 guarantees best-effort delivery service. No retransmission or acknowledgment is defined. QoS level 1 means that every message is delivered at least once and acknowledgement is required. In QoS level 2, a four-way handshake mechanism is used to ensure the delivery of a message exactly once.

The fifth one is WebSocket that lets clients and servers to communicate over the same TCP connection bi-directionally. Clients and servers can initiate a message and exchange any messages in any format such as JavaScript Object Notation (JSON) [14]. The last one is that SSE enables efficient server-to-client streaming of text-based event data generated on the server. In this approach, servers send event data to clients using regular HTTP [15].

H.323 and SIP was wide widely used as the foundation to build VoIP services on desktops. XMPP, MQTT, WebSocket, SSE have been adopted to create the communication infrastructure between mobile devices and cloud services.

Besides the above-mentioned protocols, some researchers have studied on communication protocols and developed new ones to provide cloud based services. Bertacchi [16] proposed a method and system for providing compatibility between telecommunication networks using different transmission signal systems. Pospischil et al. [17] dealt with push location-based applications and therefore users need to explicitly subscribe to services which take advantage of location information. Their push service architecture is SMS, WAP (Wireless Application Protocol) and SIP based solution. Protocols such as SMTP, SMS and WAP have not extensible signaling infrastructure for cloud-based services, because they are acting independently of the message content. Similar architectures is developed using protocols such as H.323 and SMTP, but they are media and VOIP oriented.

ARCSPXP is a hybrid protocol and not a standard. Features of ARCSPXP, XMPP, SIP, and H.323 protocols are summarized by Kaya et al. [18]. However, we give all things about ARCSPXP in detail in this paper. If we compare the semantic structures and functional messaging background of protocols that are examined in our study, ARCSPXP signaling protocol has a significant difference in terms of integration support of SaaS services. This difference provides flexibility to ARCSPXP protocol's SaaS services for expanding message scale. XMPP and SIP protocols are general purposed protocols and these protocols try to solve the security problems at transport layer except protocol messaging. In addition to supporting functionalities of SIP, H.323 and XMPP, ARCSPXP also provides enhanced security solution with Authentication, Authorization and Accounting (AAA) support. ARCSPXP protocol is not a general purposed protocol so today's clients are not use this protocol widely, But ARCSPXP is specialized about large scale service layer signaling. So that ARCSPXP provides a more manageable and easy to use integration structure for mobile devices. H.323 was designed with a good understanding of the requirements for multimedia communication over IP networks, including audio, video, and data conferencing. SIP protocol is specialized in audio/video communication. It specialized about definition of VoIP session and life cycle of VoIP session. XMPP protocol is different from SIP protocol and care about the semantic message structure and offline state of client. XMPP has better message support for instant messaging and state communication. Nevertheless, XMPP uses too many port ranges so this may cause security vulnerabilities [19]. There is a possibility of contamination harmful files, viruses, trojan etc. during file sharing and data transfer between clients. Many advanced communication and collaboration system contains some of these protocols in itself. ARCSPXP cares about the lifecycle of message and related task that we want to monitor. ARCSPXP has ability to deliver the same message to multiple clients with structured data types using streaming structure.

3 Basics of ARCSPXP

ARCSPXP is an optimized signaling protocol that is specialized to mobile devices which are communicating with cloud based services via its internet connection. ARCSPXP is also used service level signaling for cloud internal signaling processes in the ArCloud. In this chapter, ARCSPXP's architecture, communication primitives and application areas are also mentioned. This structure consists of four layers: security layer, signaling layer (ARCSPXP), service layer and data layer.

- Security Layer: This layer obliged to provide necessary security infrastructure for ArCloud services. This security layer provides some security mechanisms for ArCloud's threats that are coming from internet. Some of these threats are Access Throttling, Deterrent Controls, Preventative Controls, Corrective Controls and Detective Controls etc.
- Signaling Layer: This layer enables the execution of ARCSPXP protocol and ArCloud signaling.
- Service Layer: This layer allows realize the ArCloud's services for mobile devices. Data synchronization and backup service that is provided for student's tablets will be implemented in this layer. Also this layer provides services such as detecting device location (at school or outside the school) etc. This layer inherently has a scalable architecture. Also the status and usage statistics of a service is provided by this layer. This layer allows use of more than one client simultaneous with Multi-Tenant architecture and this property provides isolation between clients in terms of data and service usage
- Data Layer: Services provided by ArCloud and mobile user data are stored at this layer. This layer is provided with the combine of different technologies data storage system to keep user and service data together. Many control processes are made at this layer. Some these controls are data storage, data analysis, data integrity and data information. The control operation is performed by this layer at periodic intervals.

ARCSPXP is a protocol created for facilitating communication between "client-server" and "server-to-server" and monitoring the connection between the client-server. Detailed information about this protocol will be given in following subtitles.

3.1 ARCSPXP Architecture

ARCSPXP is a hybrid protocol and it has improved in terms of the data representation. The semantic structure of XMPP protocol is preserved. Also XMPP uses XML data structure for data representation but ARCSPXP uses encapsulated JSON for data representation. With this data structure a new data structure oriented protocol is created, so XMPP protocol is optimized without changing the specific partitions of XMPP protocol. The critical part of XMPP optimization is expensive parsing cost of XML, which has been optimized with the defined JSON data structure.

ARCSPXP supports the plain text structure and Simple Authentication and Security Layer (SASL) authentication standards of XMPP. Clients are being included to authentication process by ARCSPXP protocol with the approach of hard ware root of trust. Protocol is extended with using structures of hardware based such as MAC address and DMI (Desktop Management Interface) for hardware root of trust.

ARCSPXP protocol needs two types of server to run. The first of these is the server named as ARDIC Cloud Service Platform Database Management System (ARCSP DMS). This server makes the authentication process of between client and server and then manages connections and forwards the message to the clients. The second server is the server named as Message Server. This server is responsible for sorting server's messages and sending messages to client. ARCSPXP uses certificate which is generated with public-key infrastructure (PKI) for Authorization and Communication Security. ARCSPXP uses parameters such as user name, password, certificate and the identity of the client device for client authentication. However, certificate and device id are enough for a limited authentication at the first installation for the client.

3.2   Communication Primitives

The message format in ARCSPXP consists of two parts. Mandatory fields of message are available in the first part, and they are XML-based. In the second part has a parametric type of message. These sections are filled through Cloud APIs which are open to the outside and JSON format. An example of a message belonging to ARCSPXP protocol is following:

```
<message id="12-123" from="caller" to="callee">
  <command>
    <JSON AREA>
  </command>
</message>
```

Due to the fact that XML is powerful structurally (structure and namespace are extendible easily), the main structure of the message is expressed in XML. To take advantage of the ease of JSON data presentation, contents of the command is sent in JSON format.

It is necessary three types of processes to work ARCSPXP protocol: The process of verifying the identity of clients, management of connections and forwarding of messages to clients. There are three different types of message on ARCSPXP: (i) Simple Message, (ii) Mandatory Delivery Message (MD), and (iii) Hybrid Message.

3.2.1   Simple Message
This messaging is used for the management of "client-server" connection. In this type of messaging, when the client sends a message to the server or vice versa, delivery and receipt status of the message is important and is confirmed automatically.

3.2.2   Mandatory Delivery Message
In this type of messaging, the status of message transmission is important and the protocol guarantees that the message has been transmitted, parsed and processed as expected. Commands used for client management and policy management use this message type.

When a Mandatory Delivery message is sent to a device, the message is recorded into message server firstly. After processing and queuing the message, it is sent to the client through ARCSPDMS. After the message is sent, message server is waiting ACK message from the client. Message server waits the answer for over a predetermined time-out. If ACK message is received, next message to be sent to the client starts processing. If the message sending process fails, the message server signs this message to send later and it takes care of other client's messages. As the client and the server is working on independent networks in this type, the possibility of sending the same message more than one arise in some extreme cases. As a solution to this problem, ArCloud is designed the messages to support "Idempotent Message Pattern". Also, command has been in the message reports about their own status (the status of operation, what stage operation is, and etc.) asynchronously. Figure 1 shows that flow diagram of MD message.

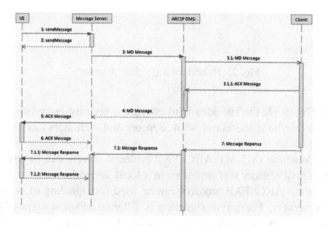

Fig. 1. MD message flow diagram

3.2.3 Hybrid Message

Hybrid message is a type that HTTP and ARCSPXP protocols are used together. These message types are derived from MD, so that it is guaranteed delivery status of message. Sync commands are sent with this message. It works same principle with the MD message, but information about-how to ensure binary data communication-exists in commands. When the client receives these messages, it does some of the operations related to the commands via the HTTP protocol. Flow diagram of hybrid message type is as shown in Fig. 2. Other messages can be concealed in ACK message in ARCSPXP protocol.

3.2.4 Application Areas

ARCSPXP has four main different application areas. These areas are Internet Enabled Sensors & Service Communication Signaling, Machine to Machine Communication Signaling (Tablet to IoT GW), Cloud Internal Server Signaling and Mobile OS to Cloud (Mobile to Cloud).

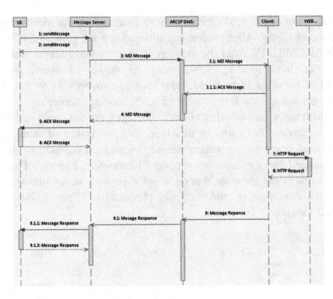

Fig. 2. Hybrid message flow diagram

- Internet of Things (IoT): The idea is to provide a security layer helping to define who can talk to whom and about what. Sensors and Actuators can talk each other and IoT gateways.
- Machine to Machine (M2 M): ARCSPXP protocol servers can be used as an IoT gateway to signal sensors and actuators in a local network.
- Server to Server: ARCSPXP protocol can be used for signaling of communication between the servers, The server signaling is different in some ways of the clients, these are relevant to theirs life cycles, ARCSPXP can be used as an abstract life-cycle management protocol to manage and monitor lifecycle of the servers and server clusters.
- Mobile to Cloud: In today's world the most critical thing is the presence/activity of the mobile clients which is using cloud based services. This approach is followed by many global service providers.

4   Building an ARCSPXP Application for Data Management and Synchronization

This section explains overall structure of proxy server-based approach as shown in Fig. 3. Tablets are connected with cloud from school or outside of the school. Tablets which are outside of the school access cloud server directly to access educational data. Tablets which are in school access data via proxy server. Educational data will be shared among tablets, will be organized according to the following scenarios with proxy server:

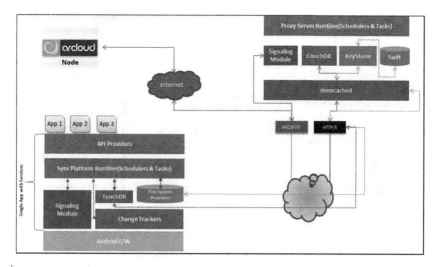

Fig. 3. High level communication between inter-components

- Getting the educational data that published via cloud server.
- Getting educational data from cloud server when the network traffic is low.
- Organizing the educational data that will be shared among student's tablets.
- Organizing the data requests when the network traffic is high at school.
- Transmitting the educational data updates from proxy server to cloud server.

Proxy server-based approach has generally two types of communication: (i) tablet-cloud server communication and (ii) tablet-proxy server communication. Tablet-cloud server communication scenario includes situations when tablet is used outside of the school or inside of the school without connected with proxy servers. If tablets are connected with the internet will also be connected to cloud, it does not matter whether tablets are in school or outside of the school. Cloud server always determines whether tablets will access educational data from cloud server or proxy server by identifying from where the tablet is connected. In other words, cloud server is decisive actor.

Figure 4 shows a flow diagram depicting that a tablet is connected to cloud server from outside of the school and accessing educational data from cloud server. Communication between tablet and cloud server will be provided via ARCSPXP protocol in this scenario. If tablet has internet connection, this communication would always be active. Downloading data from cloud server would be active only during content transfer, and the system has a structure that does not require continuous connection between cloud server and tablet.

The tablets which are connected with internet first time would be connected directly to the cloud server. For each new connection, a control will be started via cloud server. With this control, cloud server will decide whether tablet is an educational tablet or not. The cloud server will also decide whether tablet needs any adjustment or not. If a tablet wants to get any service from cloud server, it must be defined on cloud server with the following information before connection:

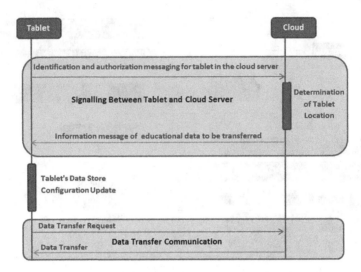

Fig. 4. Flow diagram of cloud signaling and data transfer when tablet is outside of the school

- Tablet's unique identity,
- User information assigned to the tablet,
- If the tablet assign a pre-defined group (e.g. group Istanbul), group assignment must be done,
- School ID, class and so on, which the tablet belonged.

After definition of required information, cloud server controls the tablet whether tablet is an educational tablet or not. If tablet is an educational tablet, cloud server will progress predefined operations. These operations are shown in Fig. 5. Detecting the location of the tablet (in school or outside of school) is one of these predefined operations. Later, if the tablet is in school, cloud server sends signaling message, including information about its proxy server to be able to upload and download data to this tablet.

It is possible minimizing the bandwidth usage between client-server and removing overload for creating message at client side and sending it. We can see the impact of this method to ARCSPXP bandwidth usage. Suppose that, a status message (ARCSPXP protocol monitors the activities of the clients via status messages) is transmitted at an average of 10 min and also a command message (ARCSPXP protocol transmits operations about functionality of ArCloud SaaS via command type messages) is transmitted at an average of 60 min. 168 ($1 \times 24 + 6 \times 24$) message per day are send with XMPP protocol for such communication. However, these status messages can conceal in ACK messages in the architecture developed for ARCSPXP. In other words, when the command message was sent to the client machine, status message have been cancelled in ACK messages arrived from client. So, it avoids the necessity to be sending some status messages at server side and to receive response from client. Thanks to this structure, this corresponds to possibility of eliminating 24 status messages to be sending and be received response daily. This provides decreasing bandwidth usage at server side by up to 14%. Also, Fig. 6 shows sync operation time according to document type and size depending on the number of users.

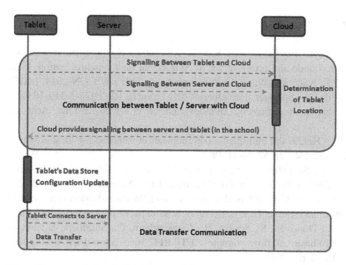

Fig. 5. Flow diagram of cloud signaling and data transfer when tablet is in the school

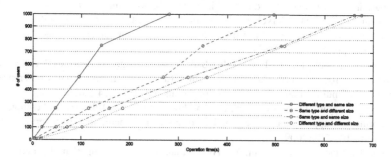

Fig. 6. Processing syncronization time depending on the number of users

5 Concluding Remarks

Currently due to the need of tracking mobile devices and providing access to these devices the importance of signaling protocols has also increased. In this paper, we explain a new hybrid optimized signaling protocol, ARCSPXP. It is specialized to mobile devices communicating with cloud based services by means of its internet connection. Results show that ARCSPXP provides a more manageable and easy to use integration structure for mobile devices. In the future, we will study optimization of messages sending and receiving between communication nodes.

Acknowledgments. This work is supported by the TUBİTAK under grant EEEAG 113E033 within 1003 Fatih Project Call.

References

1. Eken, S., Kaya, F., Sayar, A., Kavak, A., Şahin, S.: A method for localization of computational node and proxy server in educational data synchronization. In: Mumtaz, S., Rodriguez, J., Katz, M., Wang, C., Nascimento, A. (eds.) WICON 2014. LNICSSITE, vol. 146, pp. 180–190. Springer, Heidelberg (2015). doi:10.1007/978-3-319-18802-7_26
2. ArCloud. http://www.ardictech.com/indexphp/tr/cozumlerimiz/arcloud. Accessed 15 March 2015
3. Thom, G.A.: H.323: the multimedia communication standard for local area network. IEEE Commun. Mag. **34**(12), 52–56 (1996)
4. Rosenberg, J., Schulzrinne, H., Camarillo, G., et al.: SIP: Session Initiation Protocol. IETF RFC 3261. http://www.ietf.org/rfc/rfc3261.txt. Accessed 15 March 2015
5. Whitepaper, SIP Server Technical Overview. http://www.radvision.com/radvision/PDF/sip-server-platform/SIPServerTechnicalOverviewWhitepaper.pdf. Accessed 15 March 2015
6. Johnston, A., Donovan, S., Sparks, R., Cunningham, C., Summers, K.: Session initiation protocol (SIP) basic call flow examples. IETF RFC 3665. http://www.ietf.org/rfc/rfc3665.txt. Accessed 16 March 2015
7. Hornsby, A., Walsh, R.: From instant messaging to cloud computing, an XMPP review. In: IEEE 14th International Symposium on Consumer Electronics, pp. 1–6 (2010)
8. Saint-Andre, P.: Jingle: jabber does multimedia. IEEE Multimedia **14**(1), 90–94 (2007)
9. Hoekman, K., Ide, M., Deryckere, T., Martens, L.: XMPP and iDTV or how to make television a social medium. In: IEEE 4th Consumer Communications and Networking Conference, pp. 686–690 (2007)
10. Roczniak, A., Melhem,, J., Lévy, P.E., Saddik, A.: Design of distributed collaborative application through service aggregation. In: IEEE 10th International Conference on Distributed Simulation and Real-Time Applications, pp. 165–174 (2006)
11. Wagener, J., Spjuth, O., Willighagen, E.L., Wikberg, J.E.S.: XMPP for cloud computing in bioinformatics supporting discovery and invocation of asynchronous web services. BMC Bioinform. **10**, 279 (2009)
12. Dinesh, T., Xiaoping, M., Alvin, V., Hwee-Xian, T., Colin Keng-Yan, T.: Performance evaluation of MQTT and CoAP via a common middleware. In: IEEE Ninth International Conference on Intelligent Sensors, Sensor Networks and Information Processing (ISSNIP) Symposium on Sensor Networks, pp. 1–6 (2014)
13. Niccolò, D., Walter, C., Kris, S., Giuseppe, M., Gianluca, R.: Comparison of two lightweight protocols for smartphone-based sensing. In: IEEE 20th Symposium on Communications and Vehicular Technology in the Benelux, pp. 1–6 (2013)
14. RFC 6455. http://tools.ietf.org/html/rfc6455. Accessed 17 March 2015
15. Vinaski, S.: Server-Sent events with yaws. Internet Comput. **16**(5), 98–102 (2012)
16. Bertacchi, L.: Method and system for providing compatibility between telecommunication networks using different transmission signal systems. Patent no: 6625461 (2003)
17. Pospischil, G., Stadler, J., Miladinovic, I.: A location-based push architecture using SIP. In: IEEE 4th International Symposium on Wireless Personal Multimedia Communications (2001)

18. Kaya, F., Eken, S., Ilhan. Z., et al.: A comparative study of signaling protocols for data management and synchronization in fatih project with school level cloud proxy server deployment. In: IEEE 3rd Symposium on Network Cloud Computing and Applications, pp. 133–136 (2014)
19. Saint-Andre, P.: Extensible Messaging and Presence Protocol (XMPP): Core. http://xmpp. org/rfcs/rfc6120.html. Accessed 18 March 2015

Novel Core Network Architecture for 5G Based on Mobile Service Chaining

Dinand Roeland[(✉)] and Zhang Fu

Ericsson Research, Stockholm, Sweden
{dinand.roeland,zhang.fu}@ericsson.com

Abstract. A key requirement for the next generation mobile networks is flexibility to support multiple use cases with different network requirements. In this article, we focus on this challenge and propose a novel mobile core network architecture for 5G. We advocate an approach based on Software Defined Networking (SDN) that enables a solution without the need for centralized user plane nodes and with a strict division between control plane and user plane. This allows for flexibility to rapidly deploy network service functions in different deployment setups, supporting multiple use cases. The proposed architecture supports traffic aggregation on multiple granularities, not only per-device tunnels. This allows for efficiency and scalability required to support the massive amount of devices in the 5G time frame.

Keywords: Core network · Architecture · Mobility · Service chain · SDN · 5G · De-composition · CP/UP split · Anchorless

1 Introduction

In the last years a number of activities have defined requirements on the next generation mobile network. One effort is the 5G White Paper by the Next Generation Mobile Networks (NGMN) Alliance [1], which lists a very diverse set of use cases, including IoT (Internet of Things), vehicle-to-vehicle communications, controlling industrial robots, high quality media delivery, etc. These use cases define the requirements for the next generation of mobile networks, flexibility being one of the key requirements. For each use case user plane packets should traverse a different sequence of network service functions. A 5G core network architecture should offer an infrastructure to support flexibility of organizing such service chains. The 3rd Generation Partnership Project (3GPP) is currently running a study for such new 5G core network architecture [2, 3].

The current Evolved Packet Core (EPC) [4] architecture is optimized for the mobile broadband use case where traffic for an end user passes a Packet Data Network Gateway (P-GW) acting as mobility anchor point. It is limited in its flexibility to support new use cases due to the time consuming standardization process. E.g., adding network functionality to support an interface between P-GW and Wireless Local Area Network (WLAN) access [5] took more than a year of standardization, even though all new functionality was fully contained within an operator's network and had no impact on the user device. Furthermore, it is envisioned that the 5G core network architecture

© ICST Institute for Computer Sciences, Social Informatics and Telecommunications Engineering 2017
R. Agüero et al. (Eds.): MONAMI 2016, LNICST 191, pp. 44–57, 2017.
DOI: 10.1007/978-3-319-52712-3_4

will have to handle many more devices, which may make EPC inefficient since it maintains at least one tunnel per device.

The need for a new mobile core network architecture has been identified in several articles in literature with a variety of solutions proposed [6–9]. Briefly, most of the proposals leverage the Software-Defined Networking (SDN) paradigm to the architecture of the core network, in order to achieve the aforementioned flexibility by separating the user plane and the control plane. The flexibility can be further enhanced with Network Function Virtualization (NFV).

However, adopting SDN into the design is just the very beginning. Work is already ongoing to further separate control plane from user plane in EPC [10]. However, incorporating SDN in the current EPC architecture this way still uses per-device General Packet Radio Service Tunneling Protocol (GTP) tunnels via a P-GW anchor. In a 5G time frame, we will likely see an increase in use cases like, e.g., device-to-device communication or edge computing [1], where routing via a central P-GW is not preferred. Thus, we should allow an end-to-end SDN-based service deployment from base station to peering point. This goes beyond today's typical service chain deployments with SDN introduced above the P-GW anchor point [8, 11].

In this article we propose a novel mobile core network architecture for the 5G time frame. The architecture is based on mobile service chaining which is the ability of the network to combine service chaining with mobility handling. We advocate an all-SDN approach with a strict division between control and user plane. We abandon the limitation of using only a single mobility anchor point per user connection, allowing for a flexible deployment strategy. The architecture gives a flexibility to support multiple use cases, and rapid deployment of network service functions for various use cases. Regarding the packet forwarding within a service chain, we propose to use tags, allowing to aggregate traffic on different granularities than the GTP per-device tunnels. Furthermore, the approach does not require reconfiguration of user plane switches as a result of mobility events. This allows for an efficiency and scalability required to support the massive amount of devices in the 5G time frame.

The rest of this article is organized as follows. First we give a brief overview of today's EPC architecture in Sect. 2. In Sect. 3, we outline the components of the novel architecture and how service chaining is supported. Section 4 describes how to implement a number of use cases in the proposed architecture, followed by a comparison between the novel architecture and EPC in Sect. 5. We give a brief overview of our prototype in Sect. 6. After that we discuss a number of scalability aspects of the novel architecture in Sect. 7. We briefly review related work in Sect. 8. Finally, we draw our conclusions and point out some further investigations in Sect. 9.

2   EPC Architecture

As background, we provide a brief overview of the EPC architecture [4] in Fig. 1.

A mobile device, called UE for User Equipment, connects to a Base Station (BS). In EPC terminology the BS is called evolved Node B (eNB) and resides in the

E-UTRAN (Evolved Universal Terrestrial Radio Access Network). The BS is connected to the Mobility Management Entity (MME) which controls the network upon mobility of the device. In particular, the MME controls the setup and maintenance of GTP user plane tunnels between BS and P-GW via a Serving Gateway (S-GW). The P-GW acts as a global mobility anchor point and includes functions like Quality-of-Service (QoS) handling and charging support. The S-GW acts as a local mobility anchor point and includes functions like idle-mode buffering. Policy and charging is governed from the Policy and Charging Rules Function (PCRF). The Home Subscriber Server (HSS) is the prime database for subscription-related information.

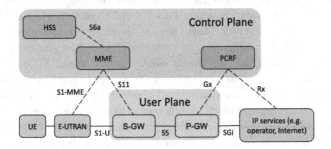

Fig. 1. Current EPC architecture

There is a standardized mechanism for flexible service function chaining above the P-GW on the SGi interface. Traffic steering control towards those service functions is performed from the PCRF [11]. The functions themselves are not standardized, but may include, e.g., a parental control function, a Transmission Control Protocol (TCP) proxy, etc. Note that in this solution the rest of the EPC architecture remains unchanged. In other words, the flexible chaining is not end-to-end down to the BS.

3   Proposed Novel Architecture

Figure 2 shows the proposed novel architecture. Note that this is a functional architecture; the relation to a product implementation is not shown. The functional architecture may run on a platform that may be distributed over multiple sites in the operator's network, like a distributed cloud. In an implementation different components could be virtualized and may be combined.

As EPC, the architecture is divided into a control plane and a user plane. A device communicates with the control and user plane via one or more Access Networks (AN). The concepts described in this article are equally applicable to all accesses. The AN could, e.g., be a novel 5G radio, E-UTRAN or even a fixed access. In this article we assume re-using the S1 interface from EPC.

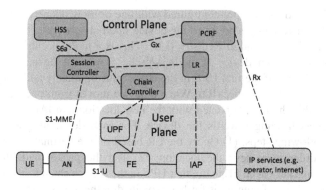

Fig. 2. Proposed generic functional architecture

3.1 Control Plane

The control plane (CP) contains all control plane logic, allowing for a strict separation between control and user plane. The Session Controller includes an access management function for each access. For an LTE access, this would include the access-specific functions of the MME. The Session Controller further deals with user session management and the creation of the service chain for the user. The Chain Controller deals with the setup and maintenance of the service chain in the user plane. Besides this, the CP contains the PCRF and HSS. The LR is explained in the next section. This article does not go further into the specifics of the CP. Instead it focuses on the user plane and the signaling between user plane and control plane.

3.2 User Plane

The user plane contains three types of function nodes: Forwarding Element (FE), User Plane Function (UPF) and Internet Protocol (IP) Advertisement Point (IAP).

An FE forwards each packet to one of its ports based on rules it has received from the CP. An FE may forward a packet through one or more UPFs. An FE is only concerned with the actual forwarding; it does not classify or modify a packet.

A UPF is a service function that processes user plane packets. Processing may include altering the packet's payload and/or header. UPFs are not expected to know topological information regarding the chain, including which other UPFs are in the chain and how to reach them. A UPF may serve multiple users, and may or may not keep user-specific data. We call such data for context in this article.

The IAP is a key component to achieve an anchorless network; i.e. a network without a mobility anchor point. Just like a plain IP router, an IAP advertises a range of IP addresses/prefixes towards an outer IP network. This may be Internet or an operator-internal network. A single IP address/prefix may be advertised by multiple IAPs. If the IP address of a specific device is advertised by multiple IAPs, then packets for that device can enter the network via any of those IAPs. Similarly, an anchored approach can be achieved by allowing only a single IAP to advertise the IP address for that device. Each IAP is thus pre-configured with one or more address ranges. It is the CP that assigns an IP address/prefix to the device upon attachment.

The CP contains a Location Registry (LR). This is a table of entries, where each entry is a mapping from device IP address/prefix to current device location. The location is the address of the first UPF in the chain, plus optionally additional location information, e.g., a BS Identifier (ID). When a device moves from one BS to another, the CP ensures that the LR is updated with the new location. An IAP is only used for downlink packets heading towards the device. For each downlink packet, the IAP performs the following steps: (1) Query the LR based on the destination IP address of the packet in order to retrieve the location; (2) Tag the packet with the location; (3) Forward the packet via an FE to the first UPF in the service chain as indicated in the LR reply. The concept of tagging is further explained in the next section. Note that the LR can be implemented in an optimized fashion. E.g., the IAP query may be performed towards an IAP-internal cache. Only if no entry is found in that cache, the LR is queried. For non-mobile devices, implementing the query is simplified as the entry in the LR for that device will not change.

3.3 Service Chaining

FEs forward packets to different UPFs and BSs according to which service chain the packets need to traverse and where the corresponding devices are located. Such information is added to the packet as tags by the classifiers.

A classifier (CL) is a UPF that determines which service chain a packet takes based on the packet header and rules it has received from the CP. A CL may change the packet's header, e.g., adding a tag to indicate which service chain the packet traverses. A CL may contact the CP when a packet cannot be classified, or it may drop such packet. The classifier can be configured by the CP with rules at several occasions:

- Before a device attaches; for generic rules that apply to multiple devices.
- When a device attaches; for rules that apply to the specific user that attaches.
- After the device has attached. These updates might originate from user-specific real-time events that are reported to the CP from, e.g., a UPF performing Deep Packet Inspection (DPI), or an external application that requests the CP for a specific QoS treatment.

We assume that there is at least one uplink and one downlink CL in the network which classify the traffic from the devices and to the devices, respectively. Classifiers could be placed early in the chain; e.g., uplink CL co-located with BS and downlink CL co-located with IAP, or could be placed at every branch point.

FEs forward packets according to tags in the packets. Tags are logically expressed with a name/value pair. A packet may have one or more tags. There are multiple ways to carry tags in packets. E.g., Q-in-Q [12] where tags are encoded as Virtual Local Area Networks (VLANs), or a tunneling protocol where a variable number of tags can be carried as metadata [13], or even an evolution of GTP. In certain cases, an existing protocol element can act as tag value; e.g., an IP address can act as device ID. Regarding the implementation, the FEs may be implemented as OpenFlow switches, given that OpenFlow [14] supports multiple tags and also multiple flow tables. We have followed an approach were the FEs and UPFs are be implemented as virtualized network entities running on general-purpose hardware; see Sect. 6.

A UPF handles a collection of flows. The definition of flows is kept flexible and can be configured by the CP depending on the use case. Examples of flows include: packets with the same IP 5-tuple, all packets to/from a specific BS.

Putting it all together, an uplink packet would traverse the BS and one or more FEs. Each FE may forward the packet via one or more UPFs. Similarly, a downlink packet would traverse the IAP, one or more FEs and a BS. In both uplink and downlink, at least one UPF acts as CL.

The next sections describe how to implement a number of use cases in the proposed architecture.

4 Implementing Use Cases

The most important use case for many mobile network operators today is the mobile broadband offering. Given that a large portion of the mobile broadband traffic can typically be cached [15], let us assume that the operator has deployed a number of Content Delivery Networks (CDNs) to reduce peering cost. In a typical EPC deployment, such CDNs would reside in a central site together with P-GWs and other EPC components. With our novel architecture, EPC's P-GW and S-GW would be de-composed into multiple smaller UPFs. In this specific use case, there may be one chain of functions for traffic towards the CDNs and one chain for traffic towards Internet. Both chains may have segments in common. The functions may be deployed across the network topology. Figure 3 shows an example of a simplified deployment. The Internet chain consists of F1–F2. F1 could, e.g., be a bandwidth limiter, and F2 could, e.g., be a DPI, or a complex charging function. The CDN chain consists of F1–F3, where F3 may perform simple charging. The peer in the CDN chain is the actual CDN and is deployed in the IP services network of the central site. Note that the chains in the figure are simplified with regards to uplink and downlink symmetry. The chaining concept itself allows certain UPFs only to be traversed in one direction; e.g., the uplink classifier only in the uplink.

In some use cases it may be beneficial to perform processing in a local site or base station site instead of in a central site which is far away from the device. E.g., the CDN from the use case above may be placed in a local site in order to save bandwidth between local and central site. Or, a base station site may host a specific application that requires very low latency; e.g., an industry application where the device is a factory robot. In Fig. 3 such use case is shown as a third chain F1–F4. The peer in the IP services network of the local site acts as industry application.

Note that the use cases above are just examples. They can also easily be combined; e.g., a device may access Internet but at the same time access the peer in the local site. The use cases above are used in the following sections as a guiding example to explain data exchange and mobility handling.

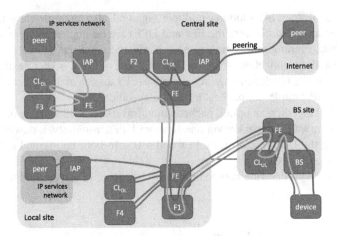

Fig. 3. Example of a deployment and three chains: (1) device-BS-CL_{UL}-F1-F2-CL_{DL}-IAP-peer, shown in red; (2) device-BS-CL_{UL}-F1-F3-CL_{DL}-IAP-peer, shown in yellow; (3) device-BS-CL_{UL}-F1-F4-CL_{DL}-IAP-peer, shown in green. (Color figure online)

4.1 Data Exchange

Figure 4 illustrates a packet exchange between a mobile device connected to a BS and the CDN in the central site. This is the yellow CDN chain from Fig. 3. FEs are not shown in this call flow. The text below each arrow lists a subset of the packet's header fields. The uplink classifier CL_{UL} classifies the packet (step 2) based on rules it has received from the CP. In this example, the CL_{UL} has a rule "if destination IP address is x then set $Tag_C = y$", where x is the address of the CDN and Tag_C indicates that this is a CDN chain. There may be multiple types of CDN chains, and the value y indicates the type. Eventually the packet reaches the CDN (step 4). Note that the CDN is on its own IP network and may be a third party product not aware of service chaining. In this example, the IAP on that IP network may announce the complete IP address range used for the operator's mobile devices. The IAP performs the lookup to the LR and tags the packet with the BS ID (steps 6–7). The IAP then forwards, via an FE, to the first UPF in the chain based on information received from the LR (steps 7–8). The first UPF is here the downlink classifier CL_{DL}, which marks the packet with $Tag_C = y$ to denote that this is a specific type of a CDN chain (step 9). In the downlink towards the device, the FEs use Tag_C to forward the packets through the right UPFs and Tag_{BS} to forward the packet to the current location of the device (steps 10–11).

Note that the call flow assumes that the CLs and FEs have been provisioned with rules before the packet exchange starts. These rules may have been provisioned when the device attached to the network. At that point in time, certain UPFs may also need to be provisioned with context for the particular device. E.g., the bandwidth limiter F1 may be informed about the maximum bandwidth for this specific subscriber. Many rules may also be common to a group of devices. In this example, forwarding rules for Tag_{BS} and Tag_C can all be provisioned to the FEs once for many devices.

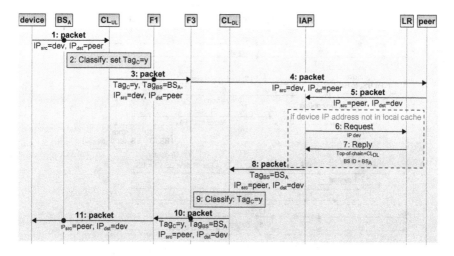

Fig. 4. Exchange of a packet between device and peer over the CDN chain

For the Internet chain and the local processing chain, the call flow is the same except that a different tag will be set at classification. This causes a different set of UPFs to be traversed. Note that the IAPs for these chains may all announce the IP address of all the operator's mobile devices. The device uses only a single IP address and is not aware of the chaining infrastructure and where its packets gets routed in the operator's network.

4.2 Dealing with Mobility

Handling mobility is remarkably simple in the proposed architecture. Figure 5 gives a call flow for a handover from BS_A to BS_B. BS_A is connected to a first local site and BS_B to a second local site. In this example we assume that both local sites are connected to the same central site.

After the actual handover (step 4) the target BS sends a "path switch request" to the CP (step 5) as in EPC's eNB handover procedure [4]. After this BS handover, parts of the chain may also need to be moved. In this particular example, CL_{UL} and F1 need to move from the first local site A to the second local site B. The CP provisions the target UPF instances $CL_{UL,B}$ and $F1_B$ (steps 6 and 8). This step may involve copying device-specific context from source to target UPF instance (steps 7 and 9), similar to copying, e.g., keying context in EPC's eNB handover procedure. The CP stores the new location of the device in the LR (step 10). It informs any IAP that recently has queried the location of the device (step 11), such that the IAP-internal cache has the up-to-date information. After this the handover can be acknowledged (step 12). Finally, resources that are no longer needed are released (steps 13–15). After this user packets can be exchanged again (steps 17–18). Such packet exchange is as in Fig. 4, with the difference that a new value for Tag_{BS} will be set.

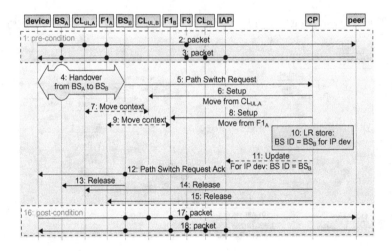

Fig. 5. Handover between base stations

Note that it is possible to change forwarding rules in the FEs as part of the procedure. However, in the example this is not required as all FEs can be pre-provisioned with rules for Tag$_{BS}$ and the chain tags. Also note that the IAP in the target site will simply perform the query to the LR to retrieve the current location of the device. There is no change of IP address needed due to the handover. This also means that the UE is not impacted.

5 Comparison to EPC

The proposed architecture imposes a number of advantages compared to EPC. These advantages are in particular important to fulfill the expectations on a 5G core network.

The architecture allows for a de-composition of functions and a flexible composition of these functions. As shown in the example, not all UPFs need to be involved in all service chains. This is difficult to achieve in EPC's P-GW and S-GW where all functions are specified by standards.

The strict separation of control plane and user plane in the proposed architecture allows them to scale independently. This is only partly possible in EPC where the P-GW consists mainly of user plane functionality but also contains control plane functionality, limiting independent scaling of those planes. E.g., the P-GW deals with GTP tunnel setup handling based on commands received from the PCRF over the Gx interface.

The above mentioned advantages also imply that it is easier to distribute the user plane to, e.g., local sites. If needed, the control plane can remain in a central site. In EPC it would be possible to place the P-GW in a local site. However, that causes inefficient routing after a handover, since the P-GW anchor function requires the traffic to be routed back to the source site. In our proposed architecture routing can be kept optimal due to the anchorless concept. An example of this was provided in Fig. 5 where the packets after handover go via the target local site without passing the source local site.

The de-composition and strict separation of user plane also allows us to place different UPFs on different processing platforms. In the example of Fig. 3, the UPFs in the local site are fairly simple functions and could together with the FE be implemented on a high-performance packet processing environment. Service functions such as DPI and parental control that require complicated processing may require a general-purpose processing environment like a complete virtual machine. The next section gives a brief overview of how we have implemented FEs and UPFs in a prototype.

6 Prototyping

A preliminary prototype has been implemented by our colleagues in order to investigate the performance [16]. The user plane is implemented in servers with moderate configuration (3.5 GHz 6-core Intel Xeon E5-1650 CPUs and 32 GB RAM). In the prototype, the FEs and the UPFs are realized as Click elements in a Click modular router [17]. There are three types of UPFs in the prototype: counter, traffic-rate limiter and header compressor. All of the UPFs require packets modifications, e.g. adding counter values in the payload, adding markers in the packet headers and compressing packets. Three types of UPFs were added incrementally into the chain, and the resulted throughput varied from around 5 Mpps to around 2 Mpps. Note that the UPFs are also elastic, meaning that there could be multiple instances of the same type of UPF, thus user plane packets can be processed in parallel resulting higher aggregated throughput.

7 Scalability Discussion

In the 5G time frame, data rates, data volumes and number of devices are expected to increase drastically [1]. This places high demands on the scalability of a 5G core network.

In the proposed architecture, each IAP may announce the complete IP address range of the operator's devices. In the uplink, once the last UPF of the chain has been traversed, the packet can leave the mobile core network at any place. This offers the opportunity for traffic to use an optimal route.

As explained in Fig. 4, when an IAP receives packets for a specific device it performs a query to the LR and stores an entry for the current location of the device in its local cache. We define active time of a device as the time the device keeps sending or receiving packets. The IAP may remove the entry when it does not receive any packets for that device for a predefined time period. So, after the active time plus this timeout, the entry in the local cache is removed. Assume we model the devices becoming active as a Poisson process with arriving rate λ. Further assume that the active time of the devices follows an exponential distribution with the mean τ. We can then compute the probability that there are n entries in the IAP using the formula for M/M/∞ queue [19], that is $P_n = \rho^n/n! \cdot e^{-\rho}$, where $\rho = \lambda(\tau + \text{timeout})$. Figure 6 shows

P_n with different λ values. We can see that at most of the time the number of entries in the IAP is around $\lambda(\tau + \text{timeout})$ which is typically much less than the number of IP addresses that IAP announces.

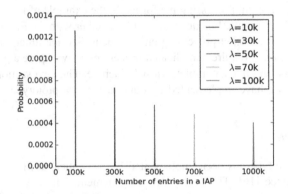

Fig. 6. We choose λ as [10k..100k], so on average [10k..100k] devices become active every second; τ as 5, so on average each device is active 5 s; and timeout as 5 s.

Suppose the users are active for a long time; e.g., they are watching a live video, which may cause the number of entries in the IAP to accumulate to a high number. In such case, we believe that the performance of the IAP will not be a problem, since much work has already been done on high performance switches, e.g., CUCKOOSWITCH [18], which combines high performance lookup table with highly-optimized I/O engine (e.g., Intel DPDK). The IAPs can be implemented as such switches and can achieve tens of millions pps throughput, even if there are a billion of entries.

For scalability reasons, it is of course possible to duplicate the number of IAPs where each pair announces half of the address range thus handling less traffic then before. Furthermore, network-wide mobility would likely only be needed for very few devices; e.g., a device that acts as hotspot in long-distance trains or a device in an entertainment system of a car. The majority of devices will be less mobile. Their addresses only need to be announced by a subset of the IAPs, accepting a less optimal routing if they move. Or, alternatively, accepting an IP address change when they move, e.g., to a new central site.

Regarding the signals exchanged between the IAPs and the LR, we argue that it is mainly affected by three factors: the active time of each device, the handover frequency of the devices, and the timeout for location entries in the IAP's cache. In the active time, the IAP will perform an LR query when the first downlink packet for the device arrives. Upon every handover, the IAP will receive an update as long as the location entry is active. Once the entry times out, no more updates will be sent.

The proposed architecture does not mandate any specific tagging scheme. Instead, we give the control plane the freedom of deciding the scheme, e.g., how many tags are used, what their meaning is, and how to encode them in the packet header. By using the proper tagging scheme, we can reduce the signals from the LR to the IAPs. As an example, assume a deployment as in Fig. 3 with a strict hierarchical setup; many BS sites to one local site, many local sites to one central site, and vice versa. In such setup, the IAP of the Internet chain in the central site would be updated upon every mobility event happening for one of the devices underneath that site (step 11 in Fig. 5). In order to reduce that update rate, it is fully possible to use a different tagging scheme. E.g., the LR may store not only a BS ID, but also a local site ID. The IAP in the central site would only query the local site ID from the LR. Consequently, it would only get updates (step 11 in Fig. 5) for devices moving between local sites. Forwarding to the local site would be based on a local site tag. Once in the local site, a second LR query would be performed to find the BS ID.

The tagging scheme can also be used for load balancing purposes. Take, e.g., Fig. 3 where F2 is a complex UPF like a DPI engine. To accommodate scaling, F2 may come in multiple instances at that site, where the FEs select an instance based on, e.g., Tag_{BS} or the device IP address. Similarly, the FEs can be scaled this way. Taking the example of Fig. 3 again, there may be multiple FEs in the central site connecting to local sites. Each such FE would only handle a subset of the local sites.

An important scalability aspect is the aggregation of devices. In EPC, every device has at least one GTP tunnel. This tunnel needs to be setup at attachment time and changes at every mobility event. In our proposed concept this is possible but not required. As shown in the example of Fig. 4, FEs can be pre-provisioned with aggregate rules for multiple devices. These rules do not need to change upon mobility events.

8 Related Work

Solutions for mobile service chaining were proposed in a number of articles.

MobileFlow [6] proposes an architecture based on SDN technology. However, the solution is still based on per-device GTP tunnels and re-use of EPC reference points. The article opens up for novel mobility handling that does not rely on GTP tunneling, but no comprehensive solution is described.

SoftCell [7] focuses on a scalable architecture that does not require centralized nodes like P-GW. It proposes an access switch in each BS that performs packet classification. The switch acts as a Network Address Translator (NAT) for uplink traffic, where the new source IP address and port denote not only the location of the switch but also the required network service for that packet. Such approach may induce a number of problems. For example, encoding the required service in IP address and port fields only works for flows that originate from the mobile device. Because the peer is not aware of any encoding scheme, the approach does not work for flows originating from the peer. This implies that no mobile device can act as server. Furthermore, after a mobile device has moved to a new BS, existing flows are still routed via the switch associated with the old BS, which introduces sub-optimal routing. This is in particular a disadvantage for long-lasting flows.

In [9] an all-SDN network architecture is proposed. The article focuses on the control plane aspects and proposes a hierarchical set of controllers instead of a single one. An underlying assumption is made that mobility handling always leads to a reconfiguration of the user plane switches, which is not necessary in our architecture.

OpenBox [20] proposes highly de-composed UPFs and a means to re-compose them in an efficient way. Besides this, there are other efforts on implementing a service chain in an efficient way; for example, FD.io [21]. However, neither [20] nor [21] address mobility.

9 Conclusions and Future Work

In this article, we presented a novel core network architecture based on mobile service chaining. The architecture provides flexibility to support multiple use cases. The flexibility is end-to-end, from BS to peering point. De-composing into user plane functions allows for a more flexible composing depending on the specific use case. The architecture provides a strict separation between user plane and control plane. These merits allow for easier introduction of new functions supporting faster time-to-market. It also allows for greater flexibility in the choice of execution platform and the deployment of the network; e.g., a distributed deployment. The architecture is efficient as no central nodes like P-GW are required. Instead, an anchorless approach is used allowing for shortest path routing. Furthermore, tags are used for maximum traffic aggregation given the assumption that many devices follow the same service chain. Service chains on a per-device granularity, or even per-device-and-flow granularity, can still be supported. Furthermore, the architecture is scalable as forwarding tables in FEs and classifier rules in CLs can be pre-configured for most of the traffic. There is no need for re-configuration due to mobility events. Tags can be organized in any hierarchy, e.g., depending on the size and topology of the network. This allows limiting the table sizes and the table update rates. Lastly, the architecture works with both anchorless and anchored setups.

Regarding future work, we are currently extending our data plane prototype [16] with control plane aspects. The flexible architecture we propose also requires a large flexibility in the setup and management of the network. We are currently integrating our prototype with orchestration and life-time management handling.

References

1. NGMN 5G White Paper. https://www.ngmn.org
2. 3GPP TR 22.891: Feasibility Study on New Services and Markets Technology Enablers
3. 3GPP TR 23.799: Study on Architecture for Next Generation System
4. 3GPP TS 23.401: General Packet Radio Service (GPRS) Enhancement for Evolved Universal Terrestrial Radio Access Network (E-UTRAN)
5. Roeland, D., Rommer, S.: Advanced WLAN integration with the 3GPP evolved packet core. IEEE Commun. Mag. **52**(12), 22–27 (2014)
6. Pentikousis, K., Wang, Y., Hu, W.: Mobileflow: toward software-defined mobile networks. IEEE Commun. Mag. **51**(7), 44–53 (2013)
7. Jin, X., Li, L.E., Vanbever, L., Rexford, J.: Softcell: scalable and flexible cellular core network architecture. In: Proceedings of CoNEXT (2013)

8. Zhang, Y., et al.: StEERING: a software-defined networking for inline service chaining. In: ICNP (2013)
9. Kozat, U.C., Sunay, M.O.: A new control plane for 5G network architecture with a case study on unified handoff, mobility, and routing management. IEEE Commun. Mag. **52**(11), 76–85 (2014)
10. 3GPP TS 23.714: Study on Control and User Plane Separation of EPC nodes
11. 3GPP TS 23.203: Policy and charging control architecture
12. IEEE Std 802.1Q-2005: IEEE Standard for Local and metropolitan area networks, Virtual Bridged Local Area Networks
13. IETF: Network Working Group, Internet-Draft, draft-ietf-sfc-nsh
14. OpenFlow Switch Specification. https://www.opennetworking.org
15. Ramanan, B., et al.: Cacheability analysis of HTTP traffic in an operational LTE network. In: Wireless Telecommunications Symposium (WTS), 2013. IEEE (2013)
16. Pinczel, B., et al.: Towards high performance packet processing for 5G. In: IEEE Conference on Network Function Virtualization and Software Defined Networks, pp. 67–73 (2015)
17. Kohler, E., Morris, R., Chen, B., et al.: The click modular router. ACM Trans. Comput. Syst. **18**(3), 253–297 (2000)
18. Zhou, D., Fan, B., Lim, H., et al.: Scalable, high performance ethernet forwarding with CUCKOOSWITCH. In: Proceedings of CoNEXT (2013)
19. Adan, I., Resing, J.: Queuing systems (2002)
20. Bremler-Barr, A., Harchol, Y., Hay, D.: OpenBox: a software-defined framework for developing, deploying, and managing network functions. In: SIGCOMM, pp. 511–524 (2016)
21. FD.io. https://fd.io/technology

Internet-of-the-Things and Vehicular Networks

RF-based Monitoring, Sensing and Localization of Mobile Wireless Nodes

Marco M. Carvalho$^{(\boxtimes)}$, Bereket M. Hambebo, and Adrian Granados

School of Computing, Harris Institute for Assured Information,
Florida Institute of Technology, Melbourne, FL 32901, USA
mcarvalho@fit.edu
http://www.fit.edu

Abstract. Spectrum sensing and characterization play a very important role in the implementation of cognitive radios and adaptive mobile wireless networks. Most practical mobile network deployments require some level of sensing and adaptation to allow individual nodes to learn and reconfigure based on observations from their own environment. Spectrum sensing can be used for detection of a transmitter in a specific band, which can help cognitive radios to detect spectrum holes for secondary users and to determine the presence of a transmitter in a given area. In addition to determining the existence of a transmitter, information obtained from spectrum sensing can be used to localize a transmitter. In this paper, we focus in oner particular aspect o that problem: the distributed and collaborative sensing, characterization and location of emitters in an open environment. Thus, we propose a software defined radio (SDR)-based spectrum sensing and localization method. The proposed approach uses energy detection for spectrum sensing and fingerprinting techniques for estimating the location of the transmitter. A Universal Software Radio Peripheral (USRP) managed via a small, low-cost computer is used for spectrum sensing. Results obtained from an indoor experimental setup and the K-nearest neighbor algorithm for the fingerprinting based localization are presented in this paper.

1 Introduction

Spectrum sensing in cognitive radios is becoming a widely researched area these days for two reasons. First, spectrum is a limited resource and is even becoming scarce. Wireless service providers buy a chunk of spectrum for various purposes and at times they use all their resource, while other times it remains under-utilized [1]. Cognitive radios alleviate this problem by being able to sense the environment and exploit information to find if a user is present in a specific spectrum [2]. This allows secondary users, with lower propriety than primary users, to use the band that is not used by primary licensed networks. Second, spectrum sensing can be used in cognitive networks to detect, indicate and localize a target or an intruder in a given area [3]. For this work, we will use spectrum sensing to determine a presence of a transmitter in a given indoor environment,

© ICST Institute for Computer Sciences, Social Informatics and Telecommunications Engineering 2017
R. Agüero et al. (Eds.): MONAMI 2016, LNICST 191, pp. 61–71, 2017.
DOI: 10.1007/978-3-319-52712-3_5

and then determine the location. Various approaches have been proposed for spectrum sensing in literature such as, matched filter detection, and cyclostationary feature detection, energy detection [4–6]. Energy detection method is chosen for this work due to its less implementation complexity and due to the assumption that there is no prior knowledge of the transmitted signal. Once a presence of a transmitter is determined, the location can be estimated using signal measurements obtained from receivers. In this research, we use fingerprinting based localization technique to estimate location of a transmitter. This technique is chosen because we are dealing with indoor environment, and its model free nature makes it efficient to be implemented in highly multipath environment.

The goal of this work is to show that a transmitter operating in a given frequency band, can be detected and be localized using n receivers. Software defined radios are a good candidate to implement these features. In this work we use a set of small computers (Banana PIs) to serve as hosts to software defined radios. These computers will perform spectrum sensing after receiving streams of data from the radios. Using these computers to control SDRs is cost effective and provides portability. A central controller connected to the Pis will perform the localization. We use USRPs, Ettus researches SDRs, together with the UHD C++ API to implement the sensing and localization of a transmitter in an indoor environment.

This paper is organized as follows. Section 2 presents background on software defined radios, and UHD C++ API package. In addition, Sect. 2 also discusses available sensing and localization schemes in the literature. In Sect. 3, experimental setup of our work is presented. Our results are presented in Sects. 4 and 5 concludes the paper.

2   Background

2.1   Software Defined Radio (SDR)

SDR is a reconfigurable radio system where its components are implemented by means of software on embedded devices. Its reconfigurability allows easier implementations of various radio functions instead of redesigning radio hardware for the same purpose. Its flexibility and cost has made it very popular in current wireless researches. For this work we use the Universal Software Radio Periferal (USRP).

USRP. The Universal Software Radio Peripheral (USRP) is a low-cost hardware platform developed by Ettus Research that enables users to design and implement a broad range of research, academic, industrial and defense applications [7]. The radio has a modular architecture that includes a motherboard and a set of optional daughterboards to provide different configuration and operational capabilities.

The USRP motherboard provides basic components for signal processing, such as clock generation, synchronization, ADCs, DACs, FGPA, host processor interface (USB 2.0 or Ethernet), and power regulation. The daughterboards are the modular front-ends used for up/down-conversion and filtering, and are selected based on the application requirements for frequency coverage, bandwidth, number of channels.

The USRP can be controlled by a host computer through the use of the USRP Hardware Driver (UHD) software package, also developed by Ettus Research. UHD provides a host driver and API for standalone or third-party applications, such as GNU Radio, Simulink, etc.

UHD API. The UHD API is a C++ set of libraries that provides basic peripheral configuration functions and enables applications access to the USRP hardware. Its purpose is to ease the configuration of the radio front-end as well as transfer of data between the host application and the USRP. It can be used on Linux, Windows and Mac OS. It implements a full network stack, which makes the UHD routable and requires no custom driver.

2.2 Spectrum Sensing

For spectrum sensing, primarily the following three techniques are proposed in literature:

Cyclostationary feature detection: This technique exploits the cyclostationarity of modulated signals to differentiate between random signal with particular modulation type in a background of noise and modulated signals [6]. Cyclostationarity features can be used to distinguish a signal from noise and other modulated signals.

Matched filter detection: Matched filter is a filter designed to maximize the SNR of a given signal. Matched filter detection performs coherent detection where a received signal is convolved with a filter whose impulse response is the time shifted version of the reference signal. This technique requires a prior knowledge of the received signal.

Energy detection: This type of detection is done by comparing the energy of a received signal with a predetermined threshold [8]. If the energy of a signal in a specific frequency band is greater than the threshold, then there is a signal present in the environment in that band. Otherwise, a signal is not present. It can be implemented in both time domain and frequency domain as shown in Figs. 1 and 2. It is less complex and requires no prior knowledge of the signal. Due to that, it is the most popular sensing technique used.

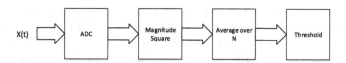

Fig. 1. Energy detection in time domain

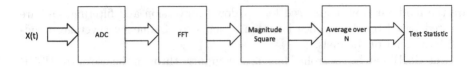

Fig. 2. Energy detection in frequency domain

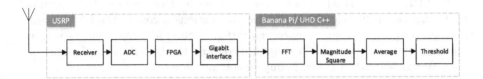

Fig. 3. Energy detection at the receiver

2.3 Indoor Localization

Most localization and tracking systems use GPS information to determine a location of a user. However, GPS information is only reliable when there is direct line of sight communication between the user and satellites in space which makes it impossible to use for indoors [9–11]. Examples of the localization techniques that can be used for indoor environments are TOA, TDOA, AOA, and fingerprinting appcoachers. In ToA, the emitter transmits time stamped signals so that the receivers calculate the distance between the emitter and themselves from the transmission delay. This requires synchronization of the transmitter with the receivers and it is not a viable choice when transmit signal is not time stamped. Instead of measuring time measurements at receivers, Time Difference of Arrival (TDOA) techniques use relative time measurements. Hence, only receivers require time synchronization [12]. Other systems use the angle of arrival (AoA) of a transmitter signal to determine location [13]. This technique's accuracy is negatively affected by the existence of multipath and non light of sight propagation of signals in the indoor environment. Localization and positioning in indoor environment using the aforementioned is a challenging task mainly because the propagation of wireless signal is highly affected by multipath components created from the environment. For that reason, it is difficult to mathematically model the wireless propagation in indoor setting. Therefore, fingerprinting localization approach is considered. When using this approach, a radio map of a given area is created based on signal strength measurements from several access points for a given location [14–16]. A mobile user at an unknown location then infers its location through comparing signal strength measurements to the map to estimate the location. Most indoor localization techniques are concerned with the user finding its own location based on received power it collects from a number of stationary access points. In those techniques, the user first trains itself by building an RSSI map. Then it uses the map to find a

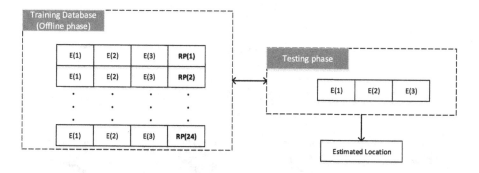

Fig. 4. Fingerprinting method

current location. In this work, however, the stationary access points operating in different spectrum collect received energy from a transmitter and estimate the location of the transmitter.

3   Experimental Setup

The experiment was designed to evaluate spectrum sensing and localization of a single transmitter using energy detection techniques. We used three USRPs acting as energy detectors and a USRP acting as the transmitter to be localized. The four USRPs were deployed in a medium-size conference room of the Harris Institute for Assured Information at the Florida Institute of Technology in Melbourne, FL (Fig. 7).

Each of the USRPs is connected to a host Banana Pi, which is a credit card-sized and low-power single-board computer that includes a 1 GHz ARM Cortex-A7 dual-core processor, 1 GB DDR SDRAM, SATA 2.0 and Gigabit Ethernet. The Banana Pi can run the Android, Ubuntu and Debian operating systems. It was chosen as the host computers for the USRPs because it is low cost, portable, and provides the required Gigabit Ethernet port to interface with the USRPs.

Each Banana Pi is connected to a central controller through a switch. We used SBX daughterboards for this experiment, which can cover frequencies from 400 to 4400 MHz. Each receiver senses presence of a transmitter in a specified frequency band and a bandwidth set to 5 MHz. The transmitter USRP is also configured to use a bandwidth of 5 MHz. The transmit frequency is set to 910 MHz. Figure 5 illustrates the configuration of the test network, including the four Banana Pi/USRP units and the controller computer that performs the localization of the transmitter based on energy measurements reported by three sensors.

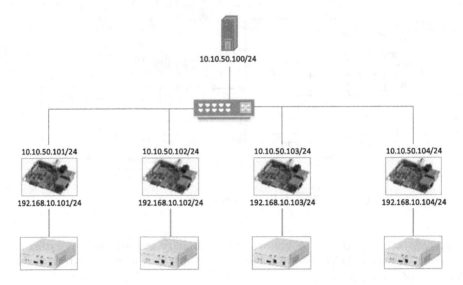

Fig. 5. Experimental setup

Energy detection technique was used for the spectrum sensing part. This kind of technique does not require prior knowledge of other users signals. The energy of a received signal is compared to a threshold to determine the presence of a signal in a band. Energy detection is based on two hypotheses:

$$H_0 : y(n)\& = w(n) H_1 : y(n)\& = w(n) + x(n), n = 1, 2, 3, ...N \qquad (1)$$

where $y(n)$ represents the received signal, $w(n)$ represents noise signal, and $x(n)$ represents a transmitted signal. Hypothesis H_0 defines that there is no transmitter present in a specified frequency band, and H_1 defines there is a transmitter in the band. The goal of the energy detection algorithm is to compute a test statistic T and compare it with a given threshold γ. The hypothesis selection can be determined by comparing the decision statistic T as follows:

$$T < \gamma \rightarrow H_0 T \geq \gamma \rightarrow H_1 \qquad (2)$$

Figure 3 represents a block diagram of a receiver that uses energy detector in this study. The USRP receiver captures analog signal and first converts it to digital signal then passes it to the computer through a gigabit interface. The FFT coefficient values were then calculated and squared. The squared FFT coefficients are averaged over observation interval. The final output is used to make decision on whether a signal is present or not by comparing it with a threshold γ.

After the presence of a transmitter is confirmed, the next step is to localize the transmitter. Each Pi connected to the USRP receivers send their measured energy value to the central controller using UDP sockets. The central controller receives energy measurements to perform the localization. The localization method used in this work is RF fingerprinting approach. There are two phases in location fingerprinting technique, offline phase also known as training phase, and online phase also known as localization phase. In the offline phase, the goal is to create a database for each reference or known locations from the energy of a signal captured by each stationary receiver. In the online or localization phase, the training database is used to determine the location of a transmitter with a given energy from the captured signal. The layout for the location fingerprinting technique used in this work is shown in Fig. 4.

As shown in the figure, in the offline phase, the signal energy fingerprints $E(1), E(2),$ and $E(3)$ from the receivers are associated to their corresponding reference positions $RP(i)$ to create a training database.

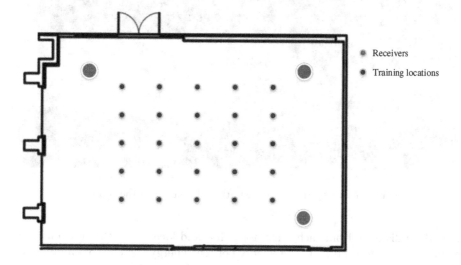

Fig. 6. Training locations with receivers positions

Figure 6 shows a layout of the training locations or reference points used in this work. For building the energy map, the area was divided into grids of 50 in. between them. They are denoted by the blue circles in the figure. Energy of a signal from each of the 25 reference positions is obtained from three receivers. For each position, we collected 50 energy measurements at 5 different times. Therefore, we will have a total of 250 energy measurements for each position from the three receivers. The difference of measurements from each receiver for each sets of samples is calculated. This is because energy received at different times might change. However, the difference of the measurement from each of the receivers is assumed to stay relatively constant. Each of the 5 sets of measurements, are averaged. The average of the averages of the difference in measured energy is used to construct our training data set. Therefore we have 25 samples corresponding to the reference points.

In the online phase, energy values at an unknown location measured by the three receivers is compared with the training database by measuring the

Fig. 7. Receivers and transmitter placement in the room

Euclidean distance from each reference point, and location of the transmitter is estimated. Euclidean distance in energy between energy vector E of an unknown position U and energy vector of reference point RP is given as:

$$E = \sqrt{\sum_{i=1}^{3}(U_i - RP_i)^2} \qquad (3)$$

Then the weighted k-nearest neighbor algorithm is used to find the unknown location of the transmitter. K smallest Euclidean distances which correspond to k-nearest reference points are evaluated. To find the coordinates of the estimated location of the unknown signal point, each of the k-distances are given weights as follows:

$$w_k = \frac{\frac{1}{E_k}}{\sum_{i=1}^{k} \frac{1}{E_i}} \qquad (4)$$

The estimated coordinates are then calculated using the weighted k-NN as:

$$(x, y) = \sum_{i=1}^{k} w_i(x_i, y_i) \qquad (5)$$

4   Results

The measurement taken from the sensing and localization system built were analyzed and the results are presented here. The training data is composed of reference points (reference locations), where reference point has signal energy level from each of the stationary receivers. From the test data, distance from each reference point to test point is calculated to find the nearest neighbor. Here, by distance we mean signal distance. Then, k reference points which have minimum distance are selected to estimate location. As mentioned in the previous section, we averaged the energy over the samples to obtain a row vector for both the training and testing phases. That is because there could be variations in energy measurement that can be corrected when averaged over a period or sample number.

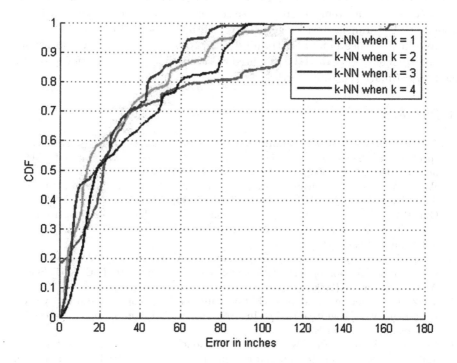

Fig. 8. CDF of estimation error

The results of the experiments using weighted k nearest neighbor algorithm are presented in Fig. 8. As a measure of performance, the Euclidean distance error was used, which represents the distance between the estimated location and true location of the transmitter. The cumulative distribution function (CDF) describes the estimation characteristics. Figure 9 shows the CDF of error depending of k-nearest neighbors used to estimate the location. From the figure, we can see that 90th-percentile error distance for k = 3 is 60 in.. That means about 90% of the time, the error was below 60 in.. The average of the error distance is 24.7 in., and the standard deviation is 22.5. For the 90-th percentile error distance, the average of the error distance is 20.86 in. and the standard deviation is 18.37. For the 90-th percentile, the 95% confidence interval (min, max) is (19.82 in, 21.9 in) with margin of error (ME) of 1.04 in.

5 Conclusion

In this paper we presented a SDR-based spectrum sensing and localization method using energy detection techniques for spectrum sensing and Euclidean distance-based nearest neighbor method for localization. We demonstrated our approach using a set of USRP radios, each of them connected to a small, low-cost computer to act as sensors for energy detection. A central controller was used to receive energy measurements from these sensors and perform the localization of a single USRP transmitter. Fingerprinting method was used to map the energy received at reference points for training, then to test using unknown locations. Test results has shown that the weighted 3-NN method for localization provides the best estimation distance error.

References

1. Akyildiz, I.F., Lee, W.-Y., Vuran, M.C., Mohanty, S.: Next generation/dynamic spectrum access/cognitive radio wireless networks: a survey. Comput. Netw. **50**(13), 2127–2159 (2006)
2. Wang, W.: Spectrum sensing for cognitive radio. In: Intelligent Information Technology Application Workshops, pp. 410–412 (2009)
3. Qiu, R.C., Zhang, C., Hu, Z., Wicks, M.C.: Towards a large-scale cognitive radio network testbed: spectrum sensing, system architecture, and distributed sensing. J. Commun. **7**(7), 552–566 (2012)
4. Sahai, A., Hoven, N., Mishra, S.M., Tandra, R.: Fundamental tradeoffs in robust spectrum sensing for opportunistic frequency reuse. Submitted IEEE. J. Select. Areas Commun. **1** (2006)
5. Ye, Z., Grosspietsch, J., Memik, G.: Spectrum sensing using cyclostationary spectrum density for cognitive radios. In: 2007 IEEE Workshop on Signal Processing Systems, pp. 1–6. IEEE (2007)
6. Kim, K., Akbar, I., Bae, K., Um, J.-S., Spooner, C., Reed, J.: Cyclostationary approaches to signal detection and classification in cognitive radio. In: 2nd IEEE International Symposium on New Frontiers in Dynamic Spectrum Access Networks, DySPAN 2007, pp. 212–215. IEEE (2007)
7. Ettus, M.: Universal software radio peripheral (USRP). Ettus Research LLC http://www.ettus.com
8. Digham, F.F., Alouini, M.-S., Simon, M.K.: On the energy detection of unknown signals over fading channels. In: IEEE International Conference on Communications, ICC 2003, vol. 5, pp. 3575–3579. IEEE (2003)
9. Sayed, A.H., Tarighat, A., Khajehnouri, N.: Network-based wireless location: challenges faced in developing techniques for accurate wireless location information. IEEE Signal Process. Mag. **22**(4), 24–40 (2005)

10. Fang, S.-H., Lin, T.-N.: Indoor location system based on discriminant-adaptive neural network in IEEE 802.11 environments. IEEE Trans. Neural Netw. **19**(11), 1973–1978 (2008)
11. Pahlavan, K., Li, X., Makela, J.-P.: Indoor geolocation science and technology. IEEE Commun. Mag. **40**(2), 112–118 (2002)
12. Zhang, D., Xia, F., Yang, Z., Yao, L., Zhao, W.: Localization technologies for indoor human tracking. In: 5th International Conference on Future Information Technology (FutureTech), pp. 1–6. IEEE (2010)
13. Liu, H., Darabi, H., Banerjee, P., Liu, J.: Survey of wireless indoor positioning techniques and systems. IEEE Trans. Syst. Man Cybern. Part C: Appl. Rev. **37**(6), 1067–1080 (2007)
14. Ciurana, M., Barcelo-Arroyo, F., Izquierdo, F.: A ranging method with IEEE 802.11 data frames for indoor localization. In: Wireless Communications and Networking Conference, WCNC 2007, pp. 2092–2096. IEEE (2007)
15. Ladd, A.M., Bekris, K.E., Marceau, G., Rudys, A., Wallach, D.S., Kavraki, E.: Using wireless ethernet for localization. In: IEEE/RSJ International Conference on Intelligent Robots and Systems, vol. 1, pp. 402–408. IEEE (2002)
16. Narzullaev, A., Park, Y., Jung, H.: Accurate signal strength prediction based positioning for indoor WLAN systems. In: Position, Location and Navigation Symposium, 2008 IEEE/ION, pp. 685–688. IEEE (2008)

A Solution for Tracking Visitors in Smart Shopping Environments: A Real Platform Implementation Based on Raspberry Pi

Juan R. Santana[✉], Juan Carrasco, Jose A. Galache, Luis Sanchez,
and Ramón Agüero

Universidad de Cantabria, Santander, Spain
{jrsantana,jgalache,lsanchez,ramon}@tlmat.unican.es,
jca37@alumnos.unican.es

Abstract. In parallel to the explosion of the use of wireless technologies to connect devices, the scientific community is continually aiming to take advantage of such technologies to provide new services. In this sense, there have been many attempts to exploit the information provided by IEEE802.11 and Bluetooth interfaces, commonly found in most of the smartphones that are being used at the time of writing. In this paper we describe a novel deployment that fosters such approach. Furthermore, the measurements that are gathered are made available, thanks to its integration within the SmartSantander testbed, and to the federation with complementary testbeds. The federation platform and the described deployment are outcomes of the FESTIVAL collaborative project (Europe-Japan). Besides depicting the corresponding software architecture, the paper also discusses some preliminary results that are used to assess the feasibility of the proposed scheme.

Keywords: IEEE802.11 · Indoor localisation · Federation · Testbed · Experimentation facility · EaaS · Smartsantander · Smart Shopping

1 Introduction

During the last decade, the penetration of smartphones in the global market has strongly increased, providing a larger number of features for the users. Among all these features, connectivity is seen as one of the most relevant ones. Hence, most of the smartphones that are nowadays sold include wireless technologies such as 802.11 or Bluetooth. Furthermore, according to some usage statistics, three-quarters of smartphones users employ location-based services [1]. Although location technologies such as GPS or Glonass are well established, they cannot provide localisation information in indoor scenarios. Nowadays, there are many alternatives for indoor localisation that leverage existing Wi-Fi, FM, TV and GSM signals sent by the surrounding devices to localise themselves; as well as RF-beacons, RFID, infrared, ultrasound, Bluetooth, short-range FM transmitters or magnetic signal modulators to perform indoor localisation with a wide range of results [2].

© ICST Institute for Computer Sciences, Social Informatics and Telecommunications Engineering 2017
R. Agüero et al. (Eds.): MONAMI 2016, LNICST 191, pp. 72–87, 2017.
DOI: 10.1007/978-3-319-52712-3_6

Despite these multiple attempts that have been carried out for providing indoor positioning, there are no existing solutions yielding accurate results. This paper describes a novel testbed that would allow experimentation of radio technologies, such as 802.11 or Bluetooth, for indoor localisation in a real scenario. The approach followed in this infrastructure is to deploy a set of SSH-accessible devices with the appropriate sensors, including IEEE802.11 and Bluetooth 4.0 interfaces, as well as complementary sensors, such as humidity and temperature. Its flexible design would allow the integration of more sensors in the future.

The infrastructure deployed for experimentation has been built under the framework of the FESTIVAL project [3], a European and Japanese collaborative project that aims provide a federation platform for external experimenters, where the focus is on three domains: Smart Energy, Smart Building and Smart Shopping [4]. In this regard, within the framework of the Smart Shopping domain, the infrastructure is integrated within the SmartSantander testbed [10], which will be federated in the EaaS FESTIVAL platform. Hence, the deployment follows a two-fold approach. On the one hand, to provide external experimenters with a set of measurements to perform experiments to improve indoor localisation techniques based on radio technologies. On the other hand, the implementation of a localisation service that can be exploited by end-users.

The paper is structured as follows. Firstly, Sect. 2 presents the FESTIVAL initiative for the creation of an intercontinental federation platform, namely EaaS (Experimentation as a Service). This section also includes the description of the SmartSantander testbed, that will be federated in FESTIVAL. Secondly, Sect. 3 describes the infrastructure deployment, including the different sensors that have been installed and the localisation of the devices in the deployment area. Afterwards, Sect. 4 describes the system design, conceived to retrieve the measurements, as well as its integration within the SmartSantander platform at the server side. Section 5 discusses a first analysis of the measurements gathered from the deployment, as an assessment of the feasibility of the platform for experimentation. Finally, Sect. 6 presents the conclusions derived from the work carried out, as well as the next steps to be performed in the next years of the FESTIVAL project.

2 FESTIVAL Intercontinental Federation and SmartSantander

As described in the introduction, one of the main goals of FESTIVAL is to provide an EaaS platform for external experimenters that will federate a set of facilities from Europe and Japan. The EaaS platform will provide a single API to access a highly heterogeneous set of resources. This API will enable the rapid deployment of experiments based on the required services in some of the most demanded domains for experimentation: smart energy, smart building and smart shopping. Moreover, the EaaS platform provides easy repeatability and traceability of experiments in different testbeds, as well as resources for conducting any experiment. The facilities federated in FESTIVAL can be divided in four groups, depending on the resource type:

- **IT testbeds**, which embrace those facilities that provide virtual resources for computation. These cope with the computing power requirements of applications for smart services.
- **Open Data platforms**, providing a SPARQL query languages to perform semantic searches in heterogeneous smart city platform on a uniform way. These platforms provide large datasets from several cities, such as Lyon or Santander.
- **IoT testbeds**, these are related with the Internet of Things domain, where multiple sensors and actuators are made available to the experimenter. The data gathered from these sensors is provided in real time, and there are many of them from the smart city, industry or building automation domains.
- **Living labs**, which are composed of open spaces where the experimenters can include prototypes or gather the opinion from the end users. For instance, they can take advantage of the living labs to perform surveys or focus groups about the developed applications or services.

Following the aforementioned division, the federation is composed by four gateways, which manage the testbeds. The gateway in charge of IT resources is based on SFA (Slice based Federation Architecture) [5], as it is already used in other FIRE projects such as FED4Fire [6]. The IoT gateway is implemented through the sensiNact platform [7], while the Open Data and Living Lab gateways are ad-hoc developments. Furthermore, on top of the gateways, FESTIVAL implements a logic for provisioning the EaaS RESTful APIs, the security layer, implemented using the IdM Generic Enabler from FIWARE [8], and the KPI (Key Performance Indicators) monitoring. Finally, a web portal is offered to the experimenters, to ease the experimentation. Figure 1 shows the logic architecture of FESTIVAL.

Among others, one of the testbeds that is being federated in the EaaS is the SmartSantander testbed [9, 10]. SmartSantander was conceived as an urban laboratory, which provides a unique infrastructure to experiment with the Internet of Things sensors, such as traffic, environmental or mobile sensors, and their communication protocols, including exclusive native IEEE802.15.4 interfaces for experimenting purposes. Additionally, SmartSantander also envisions the provision of services for the citizen, easing their daily life.

The SmartSantander's deployment size involves more than 12000 IoT devices, which can be divided, depending on the sensor type, as follows:

- **Static environmental monitoring**: these devices are the core of the SmartSantander testbed, and are composed by around 2000 IoT devices with several sensors, including: temperature, luminosity, CO or noise sensors.
- **Mobile environmental monitoring**: deployed to extend the static sensors, these nodes have been deployed in around 150 public vehicles, such as buses and taxis, able to retrieve information from the CO, NO2, O3, particle matters, temperature and humidity sensors included in each module. Other driving parameters are also gathered from 10 of them, including position, altitude, speed, course or the odometer.
- **Parks and gardens irrigation**: with 50 nodes deployed in three parks in Santander, these sensors are able to measure parameters such as temperature, humidity, ground temperature or soil moisture tension. All of them are irrigation-related parameters aim at improve its efficiency.

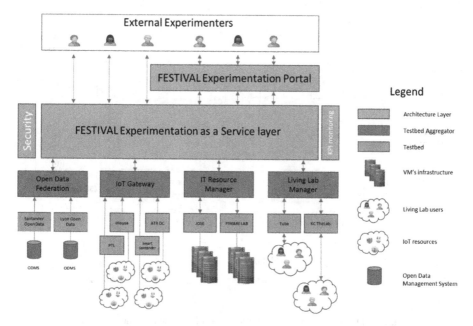

Fig. 1. EaaS FESTIVAL architecture overview

- **Outdoor parking management**: buried under the asphalt, almost 375 sensors are deployed in the city centre of the city to monitor existing parking spots.
- **Guidance to free parking lots**: deployed to provide the parking information to the drivers, 10 panels are available in some streets of the city centre, indicating the free spots in the area.
- **Traffic density monitoring**: are 60 sensors deployed in the main entrances of the city to measure the traffic parameters, including traffic volumes, road occupancy and the average and median speed of the vehicles.

In this sense, the infrastructure that is described in this paper can be seen as the first indoor deployment in the SmartSantander testbed.

3 Infrastructure Deployment

The chosen location to deploy the system and gather data about visitors is a well-known market in the city centre of Santander. The market is an old building that was restored in 2000 to make room for shops, restaurants, a regional tourist office and a museum. The market is called "Mercado del Este" and is a symmetric building of 60×40 m, with three entrance doors at each long side. The interior of the market is composed by a two aisles that cross the market side to side, and one long corridor surrounding its interior. The market map is represented in Fig. 2, which also highlights the location of the deployed devices, including its coordinates referenced in meters to the lower left corner.

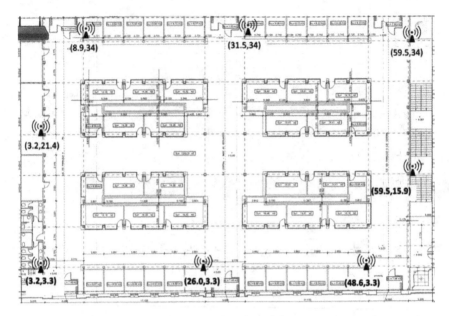

Fig. 2. Deployment site and the location of the measurement nodes.

The market location is optimal since, being at the downtown, lot of people visit it every day, guaranteeing enough measurements for future experiments. It counts with access to the municipality network, which provides 24 h of high speed connectivity. Finally, within the market, it also counts with a gateway from the SmartSantander network, providing connectivity through Digimesh, a proprietary protocol based on IEEE802.15.4. Hence, SmartSantander compatible repeaters can be installed.

To provide a great set of variable measurements, we have deployed 8 devices, configured for the IEEE802.11 based localisation.

The hardware platform chosen for the deployment is the Raspberry Pi. This is an ARM based platform that provides the required USB ports for the interfaces (IEEE802.11 and Bluetooth) plus a set of GPIO pins to support the extra environmental sensors. We have deployed 7 Raspberry Pi model 2 and 1 Raspberry Pi model 1 B+. The main technical specifications of the Raspberry Pi are described in Table 1.

Table 1. Technical specifications of the deployed devices.

Parameter	Raspberry Pi model B+	Raspberry Pi 2 model B
SoC	Broadcom BCM2835	Broadcom BCM2836
CPU	ARM 1176JZF-S a 700 MHz	900 MHz quad-core ARM Cortex A7
GPU	Broadcom VideoCore IV	Broadcom VideoCore IV
SDRAM	512 MiB	1 GB
USB ports	4	4
Energy consumption	3 W	4 W
Dimensions	85.60 mm × 53.98 mm	85.60 mm × 53.98 mm

The operative system used in both types of Raspberry Pi is a debian image named "Raspbian GNU/Linux 8 (jessie)". This operative system, along with the well-known Raspberry Pi hardware, has been chosen mainly due to the wide community supporting it. Additionally, it might be easily extended in the future thanks to the existing USB ports.

For this first deployment, we have integrated 3 types of sensors: two of them are based on radio technologies (localisation purposes), while the third one is devoted to environmental monitoring, providing measurements of temperature and humidity.

The radio interfaces are two: a Bluetooth radio interface and an IEEE802.11n radio interface. The former one is a generic Bluetooth chip that supports Bluetooth 4.0, whilst the IEEE802.11 interface uses the TP-LINK TL-WN722 N USB adaptor, with a 4 dBi antenna. This adaptor implements the ATHEROS AR9271 chipset, that is fully compatible with the selected linux distribution and provides the IEEE802.11n specification. Currently, the IEEE802.11n radio interface will be dedicated for experimenting purposes, while the Bluetooth interface would be later exploited to send real-time offers, being out of the scope of this paper.

Regarding the environmental monitoring, the sensor used is a DHT22, whose specifications are shown in Table 2, as described in its datasheet.

Table 2. Technical specifications of the deployed environmental sensors.

Parameter	DHT22
Power supply	3.3–6 V DC
Output signal	Digital signal via single-bus
Sensing element	Polymer capacitor
Operating range	Humidity 0–100%RH and temperature $-40°$–80 °C
Accuracy	Humidity ±0.1%RH and temperature ±0.5 °C
Resolution	Humidity ±0.1%RH and temperature ±0.1 °C
Repeatability	Humidity ±0.1%RH and temperature ±0.2 °C
Dimensions (mm)	$14 \times 18 \times 5$

All the devices are powered 24 h through Power Over Ethernet. This guarantees continuous data provision with configurable measurement rates.

4 Software Platform for Data Gathering

As mentioned earlier, the infrastructure deployment is able to gather several types of measurements that will enable the experimentation in the EaaS platform within the Smart City domain. The sensor information elements that will be captured are described below.

Firstly, the location data for experimentation is obtained using the IEEE802.11 interface. The IEEE802.11 protocol defines the two lower layers of the OSI model, the physical and link layers, within the open frequency range in the 2.4 GHz. At the time being, most common versions of the protocol are the IEEE802.11 g and IEEE802.11n, supported by the deployed devices in the infrastructure, while the last version in the market is the IEEE802.11ac. It is worth mentioning that all versions are backwards compatible and it is possible to capture frames from devices implementing a more recent version.

The IEEE802.11 protocol specifies two methods to find already known access points. The first method is the so called "passive scanning", in which the device is listening to Beacon messages that are periodically sent from routers. This is a high energy consuming method, as the devices must be continuously listening to beacons. On the contrary, the most common method is the "active search", in which the device periodically sends a so-called "Probe Request" frame, with the known access points in all the 802.11 channels, and waits for a reply from one of them. Due to the fact that this method is used by the client devices, and the frames are periodically sent, we will capture these data packets in order to gather the required features: the RSSI and a unique identifier.

Secondly, 4 of the deployed devices also integrates the DHT22 sensor described in the previous section. These data will be also sent to the SmartSantander, to provide extra measurements for experimentation.

Finally, we will also deploy a dosimeter, which will provide information regarding the electrical field inside the building, which could be therefore correlated with the data got by the 802.11 interface.

4.1   Software Controller for the Measurement Nodes

The software controller for data gathering has been implemented in python. The library used for parsing the 802.11 packets is pyshark [11], which takes advantage of the command-line utility of wireshark, named tshark. For the case of the environmental parameters, the measurement process has been made using the library provided by Adafruit, Adafruit_DHT [12].

The controller divides the gathering of sensor measurements into two processes, one for the environmental measurements, and another one to read the 802.11 probe request packets. Once the program is started, both processes are created. The process for measuring the environmental data is described below:

(1) The sensor is powered. Afterwards, a loop is initialised to measure the data provided by the sensor every 60 s.
(2) Within the started loop, every 60 s the sensor data is captured, by reading the GPIO pins where the sensor is connected, up to 5 times in a row. Then, we just consider the median of the five values.
(3) The measurement is sent through a TCP socket to the server, where it will be injected into the SmartSantander testbed. The data message sent to the proxy includes: the temperature with a precision of two decimals, the humidity with a precision of two decimals, and the time when the measurement was taken.

On the other hand, Fig. 3 shows the workflow of the software controller for the 802.11 radio interface, which is also described as follows.

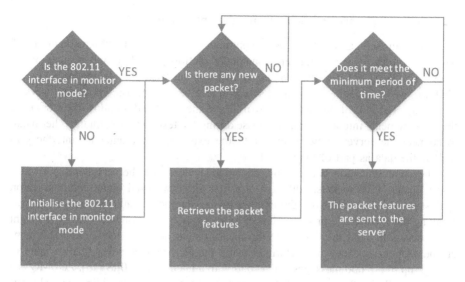

Fig. 3. Workflow of the software controller for measuring the RSSI from IEEE802.11 packets.

(1) Firstly, the process checks if the 802.11 interface has been initialised. If it is not the case, the interface is initialised with the monitor mode enabled. Using the monitor mode allow us to gather all the existing packets in the 802.11 wireless channels.

(2) Once the interface is up, the process start listening to the packets in the wireless channels, filtering them in order to retrieve the Probe Request packets.

(3) Every time a probe request is captured, the controller draws the main features of the packet for localisation and device counting: MAC address and the RSSI. So as to preserve the privacy of the users, the MAC is anonymised by means of a hashing function that implements SHA-1.

(4) Every time the probe request packet received is from a new device, the controller creates a new field in a local cache, storing the MAC address and the reception time. Hence, it is possible to set up a minimum period of time for each packet sending.

(5) Finally, the packet is sent to the server if there were not measurements sent during the last time period of 10 s (so as to get all the measurement nodes synchronised, all of them implements a network time protocol, and the periods are the result of dividing each minute in 6 periods of 10 s). The message is composed by the hashed MAC, the RSSI, the timestamp when the packet was received in the interface, and the timestamp when the measurement node sent the packet to the server.

4.2   Server Software and SmartSantander Integration

As was mentioned earlier, the measurement nodes deployed in the "Mercado del Este" have been integrated into the SmartSantander platform, so they will be part of the EaaS FESTIVAL platform. In order to forward the measurement gathered to the platform, we have deployed a central server to receive such measurements and work as a gateway. The aim of this server is twofold: on the one hand, to allow the storage of the measurements into an internal database during the testing phase; on the other hand, to connect the server software output to the existing SmartSantander interfaces to include the data as part of the testbed.

The communication between the deployed devices and the server has been performed using TCP sockets. Although at a first phase we used direct communication against a temporary database, the number of measurements gathered per second was delaying the file storage process. Hence, to avoid such situation, we used lightweight TCP sockets to send the data from the measurement nodes to the server. The management of the socket was performed using the ZeroMQ libraries, that are able to manage up to 500000 messages per second with a latency of 100µS [13]. ZeroMQ is a networking library that uses sockets to send atomic messages, providing several types of communication patterns, such as PUB/SUB, the sender (PUB) characterises the messages and any number of receivers (SUB) can subscribe to them, or PUSH/PULL, where the sender (PUSH) sends a message to a specific address created by the receiver (PULL). The communication diagram between the deployed devices and the server is depicted in Fig. 4.

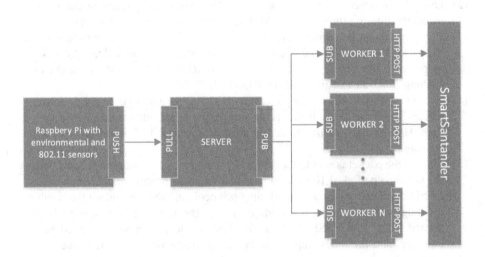

Fig. 4. Communication diagram of the deployed nodes and the server.

(1) The first step is to create the socket in both sides. In the server side, a PULL socket is bound to a port, and it start listening to a configured port for incoming

messages. In the measurement nodes, a connection with the IP and the port of the server is performed through a PUSH socket. Additionally, the server initialises a local PUB socket where it will publish all the incoming messages. At the execution time, the server will also create eight workers that will be subscribed to the PUB socket.

(2) Secondly, the measurement nodes will send a message through the PUSH socket including the parameters mentioned in the software controller description.

(3) The server that is listening for the incoming messages will forward every message to the PUB socket.

(4) Finally, the workers subscribed to the SUB socket will forward every message to the SmartSantander testbed with the appropriate message format. The interface used in SmartSantander is a web service interface, and we consider it as a black box.

5 Deployment Validation

We have performed several tests to validate the deployment carried out and confirm its appropriate behaviour. These tests can be divided in two different parts. Firstly, there is a comparison between the temperature, the number of people in the deployment site and the number of detected devices by the system. Secondly, the comparison is done between a set of known positions of a specific device and the estimated positions using a weighted centroid method.

5.1 Comparison Between the Devices Detected and the Environmental Measurements

The first comparison has been done between the detected devices using the IEEE802.11 interface and the environmental measurements. Additionally, we have also performed real measurements, by counting the number of people in the deployment site during two hours, with a six minutes' period of cadence. This is intended to assess the correct behavior of both type of sensors, as well as to get a first impression of the capacity of the system to count people based on the number of detected devices.

Figures 5 and 6 show the time series of the number of detected devices in the deployment site and the number of people present at that moment in the building. The number of the detected devices are considered obtaining the number of different hashed MACs detected during a period of 2 min, with a frequency of one measurement every 6 min.

In order to avoid the detection of devices that are from people walking outside the building, we consider that a device is within the building when a minimum number of measurement nodes have detected it. In the Fig. 5 we have considered that a device is within the building when, at least, 4 of the 8 IEEE802.11 sensors have indeed detected it. In the Fig. 6 the minimum of measurement nodes considered are 6.

As can be seen in both figures, the number of detected devices is always smaller than the number of people in the building. This could be happening because there are yet some people within the market that are not using smartphones with Wi-Fi

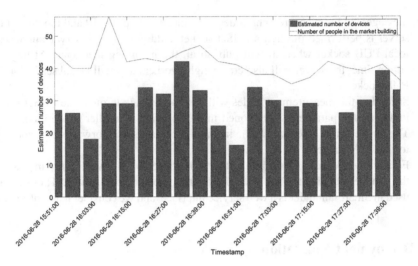

Fig. 5. The number of people counted in the market building and the estimated number of devices detected by the deployment, considering the detection of 4 measurement nodes.

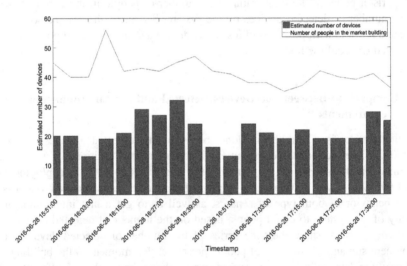

Fig. 6. The number of people counted in the market building and the estimated number of devices detected by the deployment, considering the detection of 6 measurement nodes.

capability. It is also possible that some people present at the building had the Wi-Fi connectivity switched off. Furthermore, the cadence of the probe requests sent by the mobile phones heavily depends on each manufacturer, and it can last for more than 15 min. Therefore, detecting the devices strongly depends on the sojourn time of the people in the building.

On the other hand, Figs. 7 and 8 show the temperature measured by the different sensors and the number of detected devices during one day. These graphs are shown to

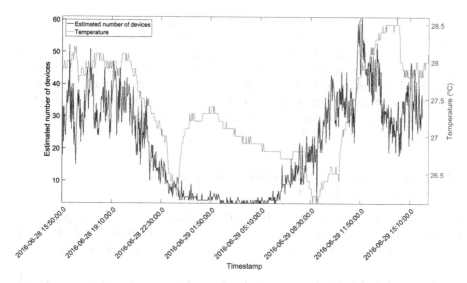

Fig. 7. Comparison between the measured temperature and the detected devices during 24 h.

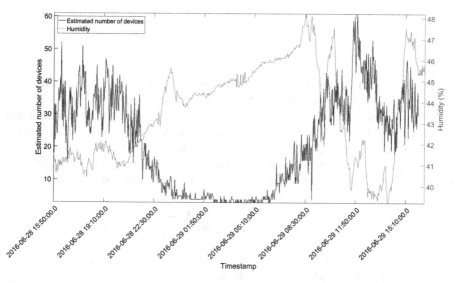

Fig. 8. Comparison between the measured humidity and the detected devices during 24 h.

assess the feasibility of the platform to measure and manage other type of parameters, such as environmental values. Therefore, to provide the possibility to carry out studies involving different domains which are not correlated a priori.

According to the figures, we can consider that the system is able to provide a good approximation of the occupancy state of the building, as the system detects the devices within the opening times of the building; and the hours with more visitors, lunch and dinner periods, match with the higher number of detected devices. Regarding to the environmental parameters, the correlation with the number of detected devices is different. Whilst the temperature seems to be higher when most of the devices are detected, the humidity seems to follows a different trend, being lower as more devices are detected. However, there are other factors that affect to the measurements of the environmental parameters and their relation with the number of people in the building, such as the air conditioners, ventilation or the external conditions, thus it is not possible to confirm the causality with the current data.

5.2 Location Estimation Using a Simple Weighted Centroid-Based Method

In order to test the behavior of the IEEE802.11 deployment for locating people, we have implemented a simple algorithm based on weighted centroids [14, 15]. This algorithm uses the RSSI to weight the coordinates of the measurement node that detects a device.

The centroid, or geometric centre, of a plane figure can be defined as the arithmetic mean position of all points in the shape. The calculation of the centroid can be done with (1).

$$\left(X_{target}, Y_{target}\right) = \left(\frac{1}{N}\sum_{k=0}^{N}X_k, \frac{1}{N}\sum_{k=0}^{N}Y_k\right) \tag{1}$$

Where X_k and Y_k are the coordinates of the deployed measurement nodes that detected the node K, being N the number of measurement nodes.

However, considering that the measuring devices are static, the centroid solution does not use the RSSI values and the results can be limited to a determined fixed position for each of the different combinations of measurement nodes, as it will consider only nodes that detect a signal from a device. Therefore, to get more accurate results, the coordinates of the measuring devices are weighted by the measured RSSI (2).

$$\left(X_{target}, Y_{target}\right) = \left(\frac{\sum_{k=0}^{n}X_k \cdot W_k}{\sum_{k=0}^{n}W_k}, \frac{\sum_{k=0}^{n}Y_k \cdot W_k}{\sum_{k=0}^{n}W_k}\right) \tag{2}$$

Where, considering the RSSI as proportional to the inverse square of the distance, W_k is the root of the RSSI detected by the node K.

In order to analyse the performance of the system, we have taken manually a set of 95 measurements for a given device in 13 known positions. Applying the Weighted Centroid formula to the gathered measurements, we obtained a root mean error square (3) of 5,7242 m. Figure 9 shows the histogram with the repeated square errors, yielding a reasonable approximation.

$$RMSE = \sqrt{\frac{\sum_{k=0}^{n}\left(X'_k - X_k\right)^2 + \left(Y'_k - Y_k\right)^2}{n}} \tag{3}$$

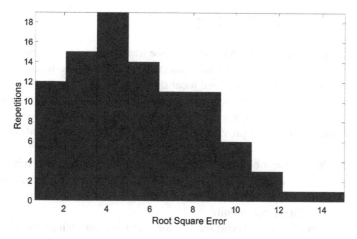

Fig. 9. Distribution of the detected root square error.

Finally, Fig. 10 depicts the real and the estimated positions of several measurements. It is clear that, in the case there are several measurements in a short period of time, we could avoid the results that are not grouped, which will reduce the variance error.

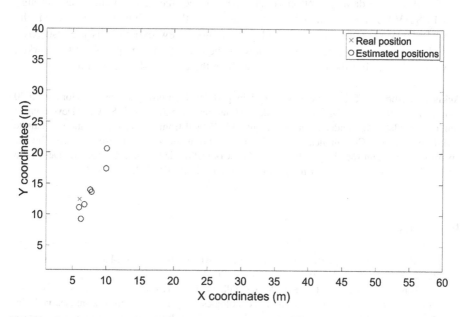

Fig. 10. One measurement of a real position and estimated position using the weighted centroid-based method.

6   Conclusions and Future Steps

Online shopping has taken a big proportion of the traditional market consumers during the last years, considerably reducing sale numbers for local shops. In that sense, with the aim of modernizing these traditional local shops, many attempts have been done to provide new elements for attracting new generations of customers. Among them, localisation in indoor scenarios has been proposed in previous works, with a two-fold objective: on the one hand, to provide information to the customers, and on the other hand, to analyse their behaviour so that shop owners can take appropriate actions to improve the sales. These objectives have been addressed within the framework of FESTIVAL, through the deployment of an open real indoor area for experimentation, that is integrated in the SmartSantander testbed and will be accessible through the EaaS platform for the scientific community.

Aiming at providing a powerful tool to the scientific community to continue the research within the Smart Shopping domain, a testbed deployment in a real scenario has been presented. The deployment characteristics, including the devices used and the sensors included have been described in detail, as well as the deployment location and the software platform developed to sustain the system. Additionally, the FESTIVAL federation initiative has been presented, along with the description of the SmartSantander testbed, where the deployment has been integrated.

A first analysis of the measurements has been performed to assess the feasibility of the proposed testbed, including the analysis of real measurements and the comparison with the obtained results. We checked the accuracy of the occupancy estimation, as well as a localisation method based on weighted centroids.

Finally, as the deployment phase has just finished, the deployment access through the FESTIVAL federation will be released in the coming months, when the EaaS FESTIVAL platform is finished. Furthermore, new experiments are also envisioned, such as the implementation of new methods for localising people in the market, as well as improving the existing ones, such as the centroid-based method.

Acknowledgments. This work was funded in part by the European Union's Horizon 2020 Programme of the FESTIVAL project (Federated Interoperable Smart ICT Services Development and Testing Platforms) under grant agreement 643275, and from the Japanese National Institute of Information and Communications Technology. This work has been also supported by the Spanish Government (Ministerio de Economía y Competitividad, Fondo Europeo de Desarrollo Regional, FEDER) by means of the project ADVICE (TEC2015-71329-C2-1-R).

References

1. Zickuhr, K.: Three-quarters of smartphone owners use location-based services. Pew Research Center's & American Life Project (2012)
2. Lymberopoulos, D., Liu, J., Yang, X., Choudhury, R.R., Handziski, V., Sen, S.: A realistic and comparison of indoor location technologies: experiences and lessons learned. In: Proceedings of the 14th International Conference on Information Processing in Sensor Networks, pp. 178–189. ACM (2015)

3. FESTIVAL project. http://www.festival-project.eu/
4. Santana, J.R., Galache, J.A., Akiyama, T., Gurgen, L., Matsuoka, M., Maggio, M., Murata, S.: FESTIVAL: towards an intercontinental federation approach. In: Agüero, R., Zinner, T., García-Lozano, M., Wenning, B.-L., Timm-Giel, A. (eds.) MONAMI 2015. LNICSSITE, vol. 158, pp. 269–280. Springer, Heidelberg (2015). doi:10.1007/978-3-319-26925-2_20
5. Slice-based federation architecture.: slice-based federation architecture (sfa). Ad Hoc Design Document (2010)
6. FED4Fire project. http://fed4fire.eu/
7. SensiNact platform. http://open-platforms.eu/library/sensinact-aka-butler-smart-gateway/
8. FIWARE initiative. https://www.fiware.org/
9. SmartSantander project. http://smartsantander.eu/
10. Sanchez, L., Muñoz, L., Galache, J.A., Sotres, P., Santana, J.R., Gutierrez, V., Ramdhany, R., Gluhak, A., Krco, S., Theodoridis, E., Pfisterer, D.: Smartsantander: IoT experimentation over a smart city testbed. Comput. Netw. J. **61**, 217–238 (2014)
11. Pyshark software. https://github.com/KimiNewt/pyshark
12. Arduino DHT library. https://github.com/adafruit/Adafruit_Python_DHT
13. ZeroMQ Measuring messaging performance. http://zeromq.org/whitepapers:measuring-performance
14. Kosović, I.N., Jagušt, T.: Enhanced weighted centroid localization algorithm for indoor environments. World Acad. Sci. Eng. Technol. Int. J. Comput. Electr. Autom. Control Inf. Eng. **8**(7), 1219–1223 (2014)
15. Dong, Q., Xu, X.: A novel weighted centroid localization algorithm based on RSSI for an outdoor environment. J. Commun. **9**(3), 279–285 (2014)

Intra-Vehicle Wireless Sensor Network Communication Quality Assessment via Packet Delivery Ratio Measurements

Stefan Reis[1(✉)], Dirk Pesch[1], Bernd-Ludwig Wenning[1], and Michael Kuhn[2]

[1] Nimbus Research Centre, Cork Institute of Technology, Cork, Ireland
stefan.reis@mycit.ie
[2] University of Applied Sciences Darmstadt, Darmstadt, Germany
http://nimbus.cit.ie/

Abstract. For the development of reliable intra-vehicle low power wireless communication protocols, realistic wireless channel models are required. In this article, we present measurements taken in two different vehicles (compact passenger cars), one with a petrol and the other with an electric engine, with the aim to develop such channel models. We measured the received signal strength indicator (RSSI) and packet delivery ratio (PDR) values for several channel and communication settings, e.g. varying IEEE 802.15.4 channels, transmit power levels, packet sizes and different levels of Wi-Fi interference. We observed several unique characteristics of the wireless channel behaviour, resulting in separate zones inside the vehicle with similar behaviour, effects due to different types of engines and observed the impact of charging the electric car.

Keywords: RSSI · SNR · PDR · Intra-vehicle low power wireless communication · Wireless channel behaviour · IEEE 802.15.4

1 Introduction

Recently, there has been increasing interest in intra-vehicle low power wireless communications. The benefits of wireless sensors inside the vehicle are to reduce weight due to reduced cabling, simpler installation (deployment) and easier replacement of the sensors. Additionally, it is possible to customize the sensor installations for individual preferences, such as adding temperature sensors or distance sensors to enhance the basic configuration of a vehicle. This interest in in-vehicle wireless sensor networks has resulted in the development of specialized MAC protocols for this area. In order to develop efficient MAC protocols, we need to be able to accurately simulate a realistic vehicle environment. The most critical requirements in the intra-vehicle environment are short communication delays and high reliability for safety critical applications such as tyre pressure sensing or distance measurements [1]. For this reason it is important to have a realistic channel model or at least a suitable probabilistic packet reception model for the proposed environment. Most of the published research in this area

© ICST Institute for Computer Sciences, Social Informatics and Telecommunications Engineering 2017
R. Agüero et al. (Eds.): MONAMI 2016, LNICST 191, pp. 88–101, 2017.
DOI: 10.1007/978-3-319-52712-3_7

has focused on characteristics of the intra-vehicle wireless channel for Ultra-Wideband (UWB) or frequencies higher than 2.4 GHz, see [2–6]. In this paper, we focus on the channel behaviour of intra-vehicle low power wireless communication for a range of different scenarios. The measurements were performed in two different car types, i.e. one with petrol and one with electric engine, and considering the presence of different levels of Wi-Fi interference. The remainder of this paper is structured as follows. The next section presents related work in the field of intra-vehicle wireless channel measurements. Then Sect. 3 presents the experimental deployment which includes the software and hardware platform being used. The experimental setup in Sect. 4 describes the different settings for the sensor communication and the different scenarios for the measurement campaign. The fifth section presents the experimental results and discussion of the observed channel behaviour. Finally, the conclusions provide a brief summary and critical discussion of the findings and give an outlook to future work.

2   Related Work

The intra-vehicle radio channel behaviour for the IEEE 802.15.4 standard in the frequency range of 2.4 GHz has been investigated to a lesser extent when compared to the study of UWB in intra-vehicle scenarios. In [7,8] the authors performed measurements of the channel behaviour inside the car for a small number of nodes with a fixed gateway position. Additionally, the measurements were carried out with a fixed topology and only for a single IEEE 802.15.4 channel with fixed packet size. Conclusions from this measurement configuration are limited to a specific application and cannot be adopted for a broader range of applications with different packet sizes or on different IEEE 802.15.4 channels. The authors in [9], who investigated the coexistence between Zigbee and Bluetooth devices inside a vehicle, also only focus on a small number of nodes to measure the interference. In their work, they consider the channel behaviour for different areas inside the vehicle such as the passenger area and the engine compartment. A broader range of measurement settings is used in [10] to observe the intra-vehicle channel characteristics, but only for one vehicle and without Wi-Fi interference. In [11] the authors measured the intra-vehicle channel characteristics at three positions only, which are not practical positions for wireless sensor nodes inside a vehicle. There is no observation of the different zones inside the vehicle such as the passenger area or the boot. The study [12], which observes the bit error rate (BER) against signal to noise ratio (SNR) performance of UWB systems applied in commercial vehicles includes similar measurements but with a smaller number of nodes and focused on the IEEE 802.15.3a frequency range of 3100–10600 MHz. Beyond these publications, to the best of our knowledge, there is no research that measured the intra-vehicle channel behaviour in the 2.4 GHz frequency band with a similarly wide range of measurement setups and different types of vehicles as presented here.

3 Experimental Platform

The measurements presented in this paper were carried out with the XM1000 wireless sensor node platform [13]. The XM1000 sensor node has an IEEE 802.15.4 compliant Texas Instruments CC2420 radio chip. All recorded Received Signal Strength Indicator (RSSI) and Link Quality Indicator (LQI) values are based on the technical description of the CC2420 radio chip. We programmed the sensor nodes with the "TRIDENT" [14] firmware, which is based on the "TinyOS" [15] operating system version 2.1.2. TRIDENT provides a fast and simple measurement setup without the need for individual programming of each sensor node for each measurement. In addition, TRIDENT supports over the air upload of the recorded packet information from the nodes onto a back-end server system. This prevents changes in the measurement environment through changing positions or/and antenna orientation of the nodes. In order to compare channel characteristics across different types of cars, we performed the experiments in a 2000 Hyundai Accent GLS (petrol engine) and in a 2011 Nissan Leaf (electric engine).

4 Experimental Setup

For the measurements we placed the wireless sensor nodes at different positions inside the vehicle. The measurements were carried out with a measurement time of up to 5 h for each setting. Figure 1 shows the wireless sensor node position schema inside the Hyundai.

To compare the effect of radio propagation with different types of engines, we carried out the same type of experiments also in a Nissan Leaf (see Fig. 2 for the schematic setup). The smaller number of nodes used for Nissan Leaf is a result of the observations from the Hyundai Accent measurements, which concludes that a reduced number of nodes provides sufficient results for certain measurements. The positions of the smaller number of nodes are based on the results of the measurements with higher number of nodes. It represents the same channel behaviour with a less complex measurement setup. The measured difference between the results from the 19 nodes and the 11 nodes is then 1.32% in the worst case. To observe the effect of the engine when driving, a smaller setup of wireless sensor nodes was used for these measurements (see Fig. 3). The positions of the nodes are chosen to represent different sensor applications: node ID 1 is at the rear view mirror for temperature sensing or light sensor for the auto dip function, node ID 2 and 3 are in the corners of the dashboard next to the wing mirrors for distance sensors or mirror adjustments. Node ID 4 is placed at the bottom of the dashboard for temperature sensing and node ID 5–8 are below or behind the passenger seats to represent the seat belt detection or passenger detection. The distance sensors for the rear are represented by node ID 9 and 10. The nodes ID 12–15 in the engine section represent different temperature sensors or washer fluid level sensor. The tyre pressure sensors are displayed by the nodes ID 16–19. The star mark of the Wi-Fi symbol represents the position of a laptop which generates the Wi-Fi interference by UDP broadcasts with fixed transmit power. All nodes are oriented orthogonally to the side of the vehicle, their USB ports pointing to the left side of the car. All nodes behind the driver door are oriented with the top to the engine section and all other nodes are oriented to the boot section. This setup ensure that the main beam of inverted F Antenna of the XM1000 sensor node is orientated to the middle of the vehicle to reduce the influence of external interference.

Transmit power: In order to distinguish between weak and strong links with varying transmit power settings, we choose a wide range of transmit power settings from 0, −5, −10, −15 to −25 dBm.

Transmission setup: Each node takes turns to broadcast a single packet, which is received by the other nodes. They then record the received packet information as shown in Table 1. This transmission cycle repeats until each node has sent 100 packets for each measurement configuration. The RSSI and LQI values are generated based on the technical description of the CC2420 radio chip.

Selected channel: The 2.4 GHz ISM band is the common frequency band for IEEE 802.15.4 Wireless Sensor Networks (WSN) and for IEEE 802.11 Wi-Fi. The IEEE 802.15.4 channels "11" and "12" overlap with Wi-Fi channel "1" and the IEEE 802.15.4 channels "15" and "20" are located between the typically used Wi-Fi channels "1", "6" and "11". This configuration allows us to measure the typical interference created by Wi-Fi traffic on the low power wireless communication. The selected IEEE 802.15.4 channels "15" and "20" are used as non-interfered reference for comparison of channel behaviour with and without the Wi-Fi interference.

Packet size: We varied the packet size of the experiment data from 14, 32 to 64 bytes plus 16 bytes IEEE 802.15.4 specific header data and 2 bytes cyclic redundancy check (CRC).

Packet structure: The packet structure can be seen in Fig. 4.

Wi-Fi interference setup: The Wi-Fi transmit power was varied from 10.0, 4.77, 3.01, to 0.0 dBm and the Wi-Fi traffic was UDP packet based.

Table 1. Recorded values

Recorded packet information	
Sender ID	Packet Sequence Number
Noise level [dBm]	RSSI [dBm]
Link Quality Indicator (LQI)	

4.1 Scenarios

We observed the wireless channel behaviour for different scenarios based on the experimental parameters listed above, e.g. different transmit powers, different

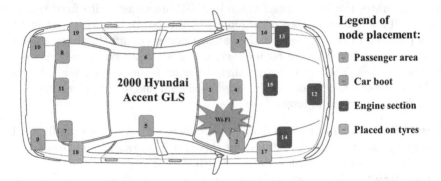

Fig. 1. Nodes placement inside the vehicle.

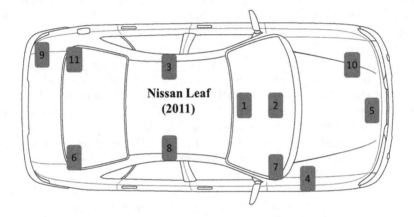

Fig. 2. Measurement setup for the 2011 Nissan Leaf.

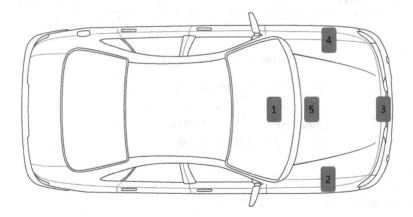

Fig. 3. Measurement setup to observe the influence of the engine types.

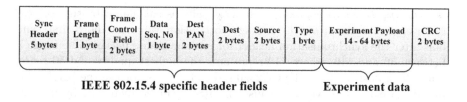

Sync Header 5 bytes	Frame Length 1 byte	Frame Control Field 2 bytes	Data Seq. No 1 byte	Dest PAN 2 bytes	Dest 2 bytes	Source 2 bytes	Type 1 byte	Experiment Payload 14 - 64 bytes	CRC 2 bytes

IEEE 802.15.4 specific header fields   Experiment data

Fig. 4. Packet structure

IEEE 802.15.4 channels, different packet sizes and different Wi-Fi interference level and additionally for the engine measurements the status of the car, such as parking, driving or specifically for the electric car the charging phase after driving. Tables 2 and 3 show the settings used for the different scenarios.

Table 2. Scenarios for the 2000 Hyundai accent GLS:

Scenario no	Driving	Dif. channels	Dif. Tx powers	Wi-Fi interference	Dif. packet size
1	No	Yes	Yes	Yes	Yes
2	Yes	Yes	Yes	No	No

Table 3. Scenarios for the 2011 Nissan leaf:

Scenario no	Driving	Dif. channels	Dif. Tx powers	Wi-Fi interference	Dif. packet size
3	No	Yes	Yes	No	No
4	Yes	Yes	Yes	No	No

5   Experimental Results and Discussion

We present the results of our measurement campaign in the following. We distinguish between results for the Hyundai and the Nissan initially, but also compare them to each other.

Signal-to-Noise Ratio (SNR): The average SNR has been used to compare the various effects of the different zones and the Wi-Fi interference at the low power wireless communication. For the calculation of the SNR value see Eq. 1.

Received Signal Strength Indicator (RSSI): The measured RSSI values contain the average RSSI level during reception of the packets and the RSSI values range is between $-100\,$dBm and $0\,$dBm.

Noise level: The noise level is measured after successful transmission or reception of the packets over a period of 384μs.

Link Quality Indicator (LQI): The LQI value is calculated by the CC2420 radio chip and based on the average correlation value on the 8 first symbols after the synchronisation header for each incoming packet. The range is between 50 and 110, where 110 represents the highest quality and 50 represents the lowest quality. The CC2420 radio chip does not use the RSSI value to calculate the LQI value because the RSSI can be increased by narrowband interference inside the channel bandwidth while the interference actually reduces the link quality.

Packet Delivery Ratio (PDR): The PDR is calculated based on all transmitted and successfully received packets from sender to individual nodes without retries.

$$SNR/\mathrm{dB} = RSSI/\mathrm{dBm} - Noiselevel/\mathrm{dBm} \tag{1}$$

5.1   Measurement Results for the 2000 Hyundai Accent GLS

The average SNR values for 0 dBm transmit power and without Wi-Fi interference are shown as point to point connections in Fig. 5 and with a colour map in Fig. 6. The colour map shows the sensor ID of the transmitter on the horizontal axis and the average SNR values of each receiver in the corresponding column. From the groups of similar average SNR values in the colour map, it can be seen that depending on the location of the wireless sensors, the channel behaviour is similar for zones inside the car, such as the boot, the passenger area and the engine section. The different zones are explained in Sect. 5.4.

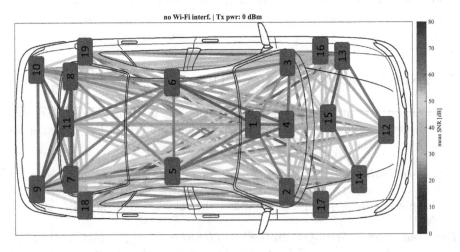

Fig. 5. Average SNR values for the different wireless sensor links for 0 dBm transmit power and without Wi-Fi interference.

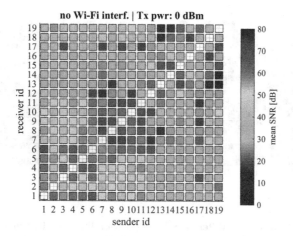

Fig. 6. Average SNR values for the different wireless sensors for 0 dBm transmit power and without Wi-Fi interference.

The effect of the Wi-Fi interference on the low power wireless communication can be seen in the Fig. 7. It shows the 0 dBm Wi-Fi interference at the Wi-Fi channel 1 which overlap the IEEE 802.15.4 channels 11 and 12. The SNR values of the IEEE 802.15.4 channels 11 and 12 is in average reduced by 8.1 dB compared to the low power wireless communication at the IEEE 802.15.4 channels 15 and 20. The PDR of the affected IEEE 802.15.4 channels 11 and 12 is also reduced because of the Wi-Fi interference (see Fig. 8). Especially for all links that originate on the outside of the passenger and boot areas, the PDR decreases on average by 15.1% compared to the PDR of the IEEE 802.15.4 channels 15 and 20.

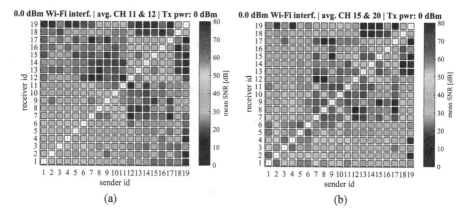

Fig. 7. Average SNR values for the different wireless sensor links for 0 dBm transmit power and with 0 dBm Wi-Fi interference level. (a) IEEE 802.15.4 channel 11 & 12 and (b) channel 15 & 20.

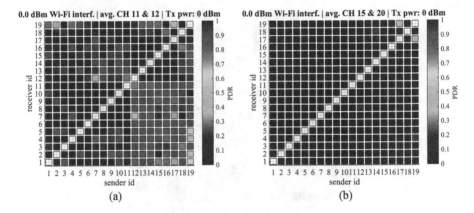

Fig. 8. PDR values for the different wireless sensor links for 0 dBm transmit power and with 0 dBm Wi-Fi interference level. (a) IEEE 802.15.4 channel 11 & 12 and (b) channel 15 & 20.

The influence of the different packet sizes on the PDR when transmitting at different power levels is shown in Fig. 9. Without Wi-Fi interference the difference between the PDR values for a payload size of 32 and 64 bytes compared to a payload of 14 bytes is less than 3.4%. At 0 dBm Wi-Fi interference, the PDR values of payload sizes of 32 and 64 bytes are close to each other with an average 5% difference. However, compared to the 14 bytes payload size, those PDR values are between 9.74% and 26.7% lower.

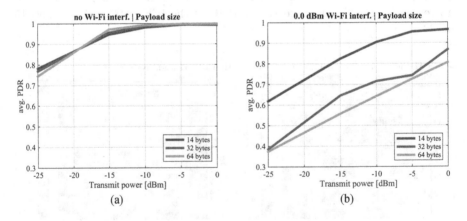

Fig. 9. Average PDR values for the different transmit powers. (a) without Wi-Fi interference and (b) with 0 dBm Wi-Fi interference level.

5.2   Measurement Results for the 2011 Nissan Leaf

The measurements taken on the inside the 2011 Nissan Leaf showed the same zone effect for low power wireless communication as was observed with the 2000 Hyundai Accent GLS, see Fig. 10. However, the distinction between the passenger area and the boot is less strict in the Nissan than for the Hyundai.

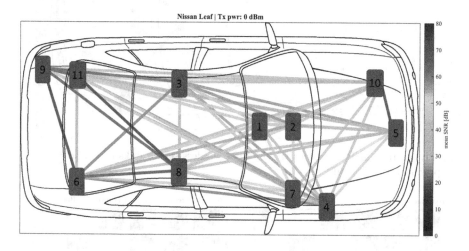

Fig. 10. Average SNR values for the different wireless sensor links for 0 dBm transmit power and without Wi-Fi interference

5.3   Measurement Results of the Engine Section

The influence of the engine (petrol or electric) on the low power wireless communication was first measured with the engine off and then with the engine on while driving.

For the petrol engine of the 2000 Hyundai Accent GLS, we did not observe significant differences in the average SNR values between driving or parking, the difference is less then 0.79%, but the PDR was reduced during driving (see Figs. 11 and 12). Mostly the communication between nodes ID 1, 2 and 3 was effected. This could possibly result from the engine noise during the driving which increases the bit error rate and packet drops. The same behaviour was also observed in [8].

However, for the 2011 Nissan Leaf, the impact on the average PDR over all IEEE 802.15.4 channels while driving was more obvious (see Fig. 13). The charging phase after the driving measurements had an effect on the average PDR for IEEE 802.15.4 channels 11 and 12. Figure 14 shows the PDR for the IEEE 802.15.4 channel 12 with the engine off and during the charging phase. The PDR of the links between the node ID 1 and node ID 3 & 4 is more than 70% reduced during the charging phase.

This noise could be produced from the battery charging unit and the high currents during the charging phase.

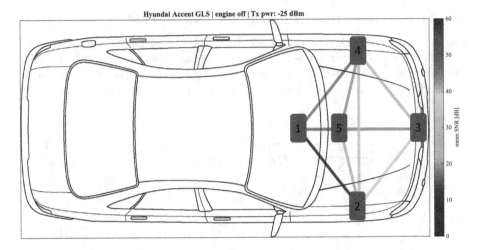

Fig. 11. Average SNR values for the different wireless sensor links for $-25\,\mathrm{dBm}$ transmit power and engine off

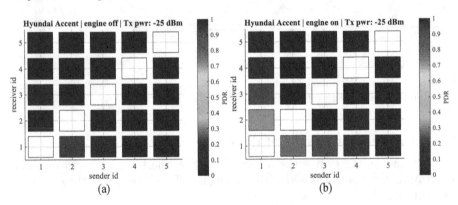

Fig. 12. Average PDR values for the different transmit powers. (a) Engine off and (b) Engine on.

5.4 Vehicle Zones

The different zones within the vehicles with similar wireless channel behaviour are shown in Fig. 15. They are the engine section, the passenger area and the boot. The two wireless sensors (Sensor ID 18 and 19) at the rear tyres show no specific link to any of the zones. The authors in [4] observed similar zones with UWB communication within the vehicle. We observed in both vehicles that the average SNR of the wireless sensor links within the zones are around 66% higher compared to other wireless sensor links.

One major advantage of splitting the vehicle into different zones is to reduce the complexity of a intra-vehicle wireless channel model. The model can take into account the zone specific influences such as an empty or heavily loaded

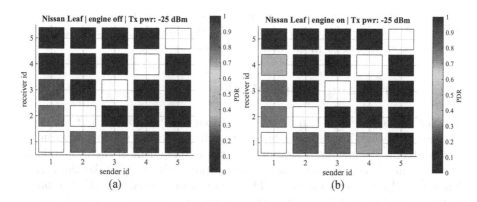

Fig. 13. PDR values for the different wireless sensor links for −25 dBm transmit power. (a) Engine off and (b) Engine on.

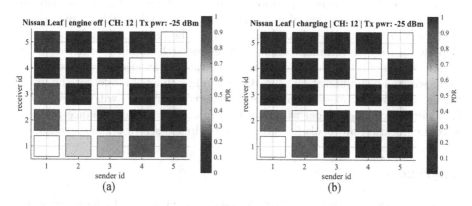

Fig. 14. PDR values for the different wireless sensor links for −25 dBm transmit power for the IEEE 802.15.4 channel 12. (a) Engine off and (b) Charging phase.

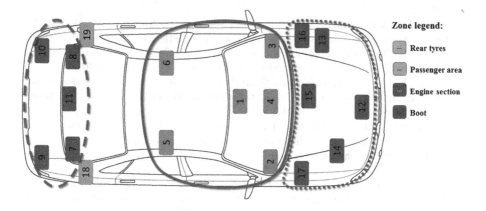

Fig. 15. The different zones inside the vehicle with similar channel behaviour.

boot, one or more passengers or different types of engine. It could also help to develop different packet routing strategies for the different zones, e.g. different priorities for each zone or more than one gateway.

6   Conclusion and Future Work

From the measurements it can be concluded that it is possible to split the wireless sensor network inside the vehicle into different zones which have similar wireless channel behaviour. This simplifies the development of the intra-vehicle wireless channel models and special routing protocols, which take the higher SNR within the zones into account. This insight can be used to further improve communication protocols for intra-vehicle low power wireless communication where so far it has generally been assumed that the channel behaviour is equal throughout the entire vehicle.

In order to judge where to position a gateway or base station for the wireless sensor network, the location of node ID 1 shows the highest PDR (avg. 97.7% PDR) in all scenarios. It is beneficial to reduce the packet size to increase the PDR for all wireless communication. Further research should be carried out to investigate the effect of the different charging rates of an electric vehicle on low power wireless communication. A realistic wireless channel model for the intra-vehicle low power wireless communication based on our study will be developed. This wireless channel model will help to support and further enhance research on communication protocols for intra-vehicle wireless sensor communication.

References

1. Lu, N., Cheng, N., Zhang, N., Shen, X., Mark, J.W.: Connected vehicles: Solutions and challenges. IEEE Internet Things J. **1**(4), 289–299 (2014)
2. Demir, U., Bas, C., Ergen, S.: Engine compartment UWB channel model for intravehicular wireless sensor networks. IEEE Trans. Veh. Technol. **63**(6), 2497–2505 (2014)
3. Tsai, H.M., Viriyasitavat, W., Tonguz, O., Saraydar, C., Talty, T., Macdonald, A.: Feasibility of in-car wireless sensor networks: A statistical evaluation. In: 2007 4th Annual IEEE Communications Society Conference on Sensor, Mesh and Ad Hoc Communications and Networks, SECON 2007, pp. 101–111, June 2007
4. Bas, C., Ergen, S.: Ultra-wideband channel model for intra-vehicular wireless sensor networks beneath the chassis: From statistical model to simulations. IEEE Trans. Veh. Technol. **62**(1), 14–25 (2013)
5. Blumenstein, J., Mikulasek, T., Marsalek, R., Prokes, A., Zemen, T., Mecklen-braeuker, C.: In-vehicle mm-wave channel model and measurement. In: 2014 IEEE 80th Vehicular Technology Conference (VTC Fall), pp. 1–5, September 2014
6. Sawada, H., Tomatsu, T., Ozaki, G., Nakase, H., Kato, S., Sato, K., Harada, H.: A sixty GHz intra-car multi-media communications system. In: 2009 IEEE 69th Vehicular Technology Conference, VTC Spring 2009, pp. 1–5, April 2009

7. Tsai, H.M., Saraydar, C., Talty, T., Ames, M., Macdonald, A., Tonguz, O.K.: ZigBee-based intra-car wireless sensor network. In: 2007 IEEE International Conference on Communications, pp. 3965–3971, June 2007
8. Tsai, H.M.: Intra-car Wireless Sensor Networks. Ph.D. thesis, Carnegie Mellon University, Pittsburgh (2010)
9. de Francisco, R., Huang, L., Dolmans, G.: Coexistence of ZigBee wireless sensor networks and Bluetooth inside a vehicle. In: IEEE 20th International Symposium on Personal, Indoor and Mobile Radio Communications, pp. 2700–2704, September 2009
10. D'Errico, R., Rudant, L., Keignart, J.: Channel characterization for intra-vehicle WSNs in the ISM bands. In: Proceedings of the Fourth European Conference on Antennas and Propagation, pp. 1–5, April 2010
11. Rao, T.R., Balachander, D., Sathish, P., Tiwari, N.: Intra-vehicular RF propagation measurements at UHF for wireless sensor networks. In: 2012 International Conference on Recent Advances in Computing and Software Systems (RACSS), pp. 214–218, April 2012
12. Aldeeb, W., Xiang, W., Richardson, P.: A study on the channel and BER-SNR performance of ultra wide band systems applied in commercial vehicles. In: 2007 IEEE Sarnoff Symposium, pp. 1–5, April 2007
13. Advanticsys: As-xm1000 sensor node. http://www.advanticsys.com/shop/asxm1000-p-24.html
14. Istomin, T., Marfievici, R., Murphy, A.L., Picco, G.P.: Trident: In-field connectivity assessment for wireless sensor networks. In: In Proceedings of the 6th Extreme Conference on Communication and Computing (ExtremeCom) (2014)
15. TinyOS Working Group: TinyOS open-source operating system designed for low-power wireless devices. http://www.tinyos.net/

Communication Requirements for Optimal Utilization of LV Power Distribution Systems

Koojana Kuladinithi[1(✉)], Helge Fielitz[2], Maciej Muehleisen[1],
Christian Becker[2], and Andreas Timm-Giel[1]

[1] Institute of Communication Networks, Hamburg University of Technology,
21071 Hamburg, Germany
{koojana.kuladinithi,maciej.muehleisen,
andreas.timm-giel}@tuhh.de
[2] Institute of Electrical Power and Energy Technology (IEET), Hamburg
University of Technology, 21071 Hamburg, Germany
{helge.fielitz,c.becker}@tuhh.de

Abstract. Decentralised electric power generation using renewable energy sources are becoming increasingly popular. As a consequence, decentralised electrical energy sources such as photovoltaic (PV) are connected to the low voltage (LV) power grids. This raises the requirement of dedicated and coordinated control of loads and power generation to realize intelligent power management in order to guarantee the full use of the available power transmission capacity. In this paper, we have analyzed the communication requirements when coupling a communication network with the LV power grid to enhance the maximum utilization of the existing physical resources. This paper identifies the exact communication requirements needed in enhancing the utilization of the LV power grid. There are, mainly two requirements: Firstly, the necessity of a fast reaction time in the range of 10 ms up to 300 ms, when the power system operates closer to its maximum utilization. Secondly, the necessity of a very low synchronisation time that should be less than 5.6 μs (required for the phasor measurements). We further discuss the usability of existing communication technologies and architectures for the discussed scenario.

Keywords: CPN · LV power grid · Latency with ultra low jitter · Reliability · Time synchronisation · Communication networks

1 Introduction

Information and communication technologies penetrate more and more into our physical world. In production technology, this is referred to as *Industry 4.0* and, in more general as Cyber Physical Systems (CPS) or Cyber Physical Networks (CPN). In CPNs, the interaction between control of physical (embedded), often distributed, systems and communication networks is becoming increasingly more important. The control loops of physical systems can typically cope with constant or no delays. Because of variable and stochastic delays and packet losses in real communication networks, reliable control cannot be guaranteed.

© ICST Institute for Computer Sciences, Social Informatics and Telecommunications Engineering 2017
R. Agüero et al. (Eds.): MONAMI 2016, LNICST 191, pp. 102–115, 2017.
DOI: 10.1007/978-3-319-52712-3_8

Following the increasing number of renewable energy generators (photovoltaics, wind power, solar power, etc.), generation of *Electrical Energy (EE)* is now much more decentralised than in traditional power grid setups. CPNs, such as *EE Networks* require a tight coupling between communication networks and physical objects, which might not be sufficiently provided by the standard TCP/IP based Internet protocol suite [1]. A number of research projects have identified different communication architectures to overcome some deficiencies in the current Internet such as dynamic service provisioning, scalability and changes in traffic patterns. Some of the prominent architectures are Information Centric Networking (ICN) [4], Netlet [2], Open Connectivity Services (OConS) [3, 5] and the Generic Path (GP) architecture [6]. These architectures, though widely discussed are primarily meant to address the requirements of human centered communications; they are not specifically made to standardize or to have any implementations for CPN applications. CPNs have a *Command-Report* [7] communication model, where the *Command* message is used to trigger a specific physical change of a certain node and the status of the change is observed in the next cycle through the *Report* message.

The main objective of this paper is to analyse the communication requirements for one of the CPN application areas in *EE networks*, viz., LV power grids, and evaluate whether IP based technology can satisfy their communication requirements or, whether future network architectures are required to enhance the utilization of the grid by coupling the power system and the communication system.

Our motivation scenario, discussed in the next section, highlights two main requirements that help to enhance the utilization of the LV power grid, namely, the *reliability and QoS of the communication channel* and the *time synchronisation in measurements*. Section 3 is devoted to highlighting the state of the art work done in power grids in general. We have done an initial investigation on how the identified requirements can be achieved with existing technologies. The results of this feasibility study will be discussed in Sect. 4. The last section concludes the paper highlighting the research challenges to achieve the optimum utilization of the LV power grid by integrating communication technologies.

2 Motivation Scenario

In this section, we discuss a CPN application scenario, which focuses on enhancing the utilization of the LV power grid. As the use of decentralized electric power generation by renewable energy sources becomes increasingly popular, the utilization of existing electrical power grids is shifting significantly from unidirectional to bidirectional power flows. This applies especially to the LV power grid to which a continuously increasing number of decentralized electrical energy sources as PV is being connected. This does not only lead to electric power flows from LV grids into overlaid medium voltage (MV) grids but also to a higher utilization of existing LV cables and lines. This is due to largely varying operating modes, which cover all possible combinations of high/low load and high/low generation. Existing LV grid infrastructures are typically designed to be very robust, allowing to transmit electrical currents occurring in maximum load scenarios. However, they are specifically dimensioned for transmission of electrical power from MV supply busbars to LV loads and not for transfers of decentrally generated electrical power. Significant increase of PV generation capacity installed in existing grids and corresponding operational scenarios may therefore lead to currents that are close to or beyond the allowed current limits of the installed lines, cables and transformers, if loads and generation units are operated without mutual coordination. Exceeding current limits of existing cables and lines leads to line trips initiated by protection devices. As shown in Fig. 1 reaction time of protection depends on current overshoot.

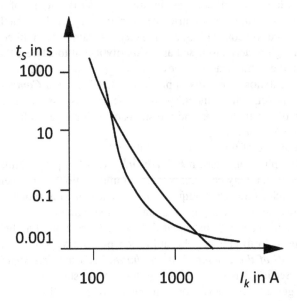

Fig. 1. Typical time-current-characteristics of line protection (t_s: reaction time in seconds, I_k": current in mA) [12]

Dedicated coordinated control of loads and power generation units in these cases would allow intelligent power management of the whole system [15]. Its task would be on the one hand to guarantee full use of available power transmission capacity and on the other hand to safely keep each transmission device of the LV power grid below its allowed current limits. This could be accomplished for instance by switching on consumers connected to the same grid section as the generating PV systems when producing large amount of power in order to prevent electric power flowing into the overlaid MV grid and overloading the transmission lines of the LV grid section resp. transformer to the MV grid. When these possibilities have been fully exploited, PV generation can be commanded off or be limited in electric power output as a further measure to be initiated during high power generation scenarios. This leads to the same effect to relieve existing cables and lines of the LV or MV transmission devices of the surrounding grid. Hence, power management in LV grids can be used as described in order to optimize and increase the utilization of existing power transmission capacity when the number of decentralized generation units increases. By this, it can be avoided to reinforce given transmission capacity of the LV grid i.e. to install new stronger lines, cables and transformers.

Reliable bidirectional communication channels are a key enabler for realization of such kind of intelligent power management systems to increase the utilization of the LV power grid. In addition, controllability of generation units and loads, and their robust access through communication interfaces are necessary prerequisites for power management purposes.

- *Reaction times of transmission line protection* in case of currents exceeding the limits is typically realized to be quite fast, i.e., in the range of a few *10 ms up to 300 ms* (see Fig. 1). Power management activities that are designed to keep currents below their allowed limits are consequently required to operate within a significantly shorter timeframe in order to guarantee realization of corrective control actions before protection devices are triggered by high currents to trip lines. Hence, power management with a distributed set of decentralized power generations and loads generally needs to operate under time-critical circumstances with reliable communication channels and short delay times.
- Due to different time-criticality requirements of control actions, it must be also ensured that the communication network is able to prioritize messages for monitoring and control of loads and generation systems. In this context it is also necessary to enable *capturing of status measurements in a time-synchronous manner* to enable control and power management instances to consistently supervise the system state.

3 State of the Art: Preliminary Work for LV Power Grid

Large interconnected electrical power systems typically operate on different voltage levels, i.e. high, medium and low voltage, depending on the distance to be bridged. High voltage level systems are used to transmit electrical power from power plants to the substations over large distances. Therefore, this part of the grid is called transmission system. Medium and low voltage levels are used to distribute electrical energy to the consumers. This network is referred to as distribution system due to its functionality [11]. Fully automated measurement and control systems are common for transmission systems. Commands for control of system components and measurement data are transferred using specifically dedicated data networks that are independent from public communication systems. A so-called state estimator is an essential part of the power system control and monitoring system [11]. It receives physical measurements of power, currents and voltages in order to statistically estimate a consistent system state from the captured measurement data.

For protection of high-voltage systems, coordinated digital protection relays are typically applied to protect generators, transformers and transmission lines against overloads and short-circuits by automatically disconnecting faulty devices [13]. Thus, transmission systems Supervisory Control And Data Acquisition (SCADA), Energy

Management Systems (EMS) as well as protection systems are widely used. Standardized communication links and protocols for control and protection of high-voltage power systems are used, off the shelf solutions are available by many manufacturers.

For distribution grids, the situation is different. Usually there are no SCADA/EMS systems continuously implemented. Consequently, grid control and switching operations need to be executed manually in many distribution systems. This especially applies to LV grids, where additionally traditional fuses are used instead of digital protection relays [13]. Furthermore, methods like state estimation are typically not used due to the fact that measurement coverage of LV distribution systems is very low.

Due to the ongoing energy transition, there is a severe change in the use of electrical power grids. Following the increasing number of renewable energy generators (photovoltaics, wind power etc.) generation of electrical energy is now much more decentralized and connected to the low and medium voltage grid. This leads to a change of traditional power flows from top-down towards a bi-directional power flow over different grid voltage levels.

As a consequence, new challenges in the control of the grid are coming up. Mainly for currently uncontrolled distribution grids there is a strong demand of research towards empowering the traditional power grid to be able to integrate many decentralized renewable energy producers without extending its given structure, but by actively controlling and coordinating generation, loads and further intelligent controllable devices like energy storages [14].

The installation of smart meters has started in several areas; a large number of publications is available on the connection of a meter to a base station for billing purposes. Focus of this contribution is not on smart metering, as the update rates of the measurement results are too slow for real-time control and state estimation of the power grids [14].

Combining a fast and reliable data transmission system with the existing low voltage power distribution grid can solve today's challenges with the integration of decentralized renewable energy generators.

Figure 2 shows a proposal to combine an existing residential power distribution grid with a fast and reliable data communication network. The black lines represent the existing uncontrolled power infrastructure. A transformer feeds the grid that can be separated into busbars and connecting cables. To prevent the cables from thermal overload, protection devices are installed on each feeder of the system. With the installation of decentralized renewable power generators, here photovoltaic and wind power, the current flows in the power grid may change. A fast data network is foreseen to collect the data measured by Phasor Measurement Units (PMU) and to transfer it to a control system that is also to be newly established. This system calculates the loading of every device in the grid and controls the generators and possibly consumers accordingly. The current flows in the lines are calculated using the phase information at each busbar. In the next section, we have conducted an initial test in a very simple setup to show the importance of accurate measurements and also to identify characteristics of the communication system.

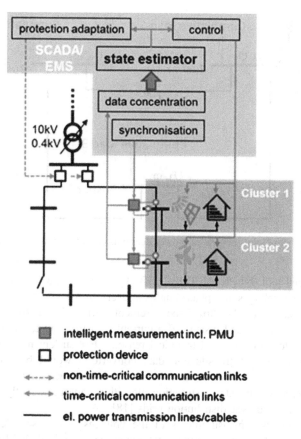

Fig. 2. Exemplary setup of a low voltage distribution system with intelligent measurement, state estimation and control, based on [15]

4   Feasibility Study

4.1   Scenario Setup

To show the effects of the communication system on the reliability of measurement data for load flow calculation of a power distribution grid, a generic power grid is created. It consists of three busbars that are interconnected to each other using cables. The cable lengths are 1 km each, the nominal voltage of the system is set to 0,4 kV, which is the normal residential voltage in most European countries [12]. Busbar 1 is fed by a static network, a so-called "infinite bus", that will not be part of the investigation in this paper. The cumulated loads at Busbars 1, 2, and 3 are set to 70 kVA each with a power factor of 0.9. These values represent a number of power consumers as typical cumulated loads for residential power distribution systems. For all connections, the cable type is the same with a thermal current limit of 165 A. Figure 3 shows the setup of the generic power grid that the simulations are based on. It can be understood as a very basic realization of a system as shown in Fig. 2.

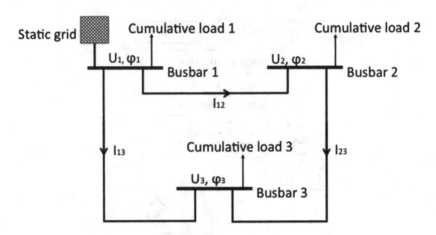

Fig. 3. Schematic of the generic power distribution grid used for the simulation

A commercial tool (NEPLAN(R) by ABB [19]) is used to calculate the currents in the cables and the voltages and phase angles at every busbar. In the further text, these results will be named as the "true" measurement results. The reason why a phasor measurement method is used instead of a current measurement to get the loading of each line is due to monetary and technical reasons: For current measurements additional equipment (current transducers, data converters) would be used. A phasor measurement can be performed by a residential smart meter. Additionally, including phasor measurements into state estimation algorithm can significantly improve state estimation results for power distribution grids [18].

For accurate phasor measurements of the voltages, a precise reference time is mandatory [16]. In the described model, the synchronous is achieved by a communication system. It is assumed that jitter in the time synchronisation is the only reason for errors in the phase measurement at every busbar.

4.2 Sensitivity Analysis of Time Synchronization and Reaction Time

In this sensitivity analysis, the effect of the time synchronisation delay on the estimated resp. calculated electrical line power flow is investigated. Inaccurate values of the voltage phasors lead to inaccurate line currents connecting the busbars which can be calculated according to Eq. (1), where $\underline{U}_i$ and $\underline{U}_j$ are voltage phasors at buses i resp. j, $\underline{Y}_{ij}$ and $\underline{Y}_{i0}$ the relevant elements of the nodal admittance matrix and $\underline{I}_{ij}$ the line current from bus i to bus j [12].

$$\underline{I}_{ij} = (\underline{U}_i - \underline{U}_j)\underline{Y}_{ij} + \underline{U}_i\underline{Y}_{i0} \tag{1}$$

The phase of the voltage at one busbar is varied in the range of 0.1° around the initial value. For a power distribution system running at 50 Hz a phase error of 0.1° corresponds to a timing jitter of 5.6 μs. Thus a very accurate time synchronisation is

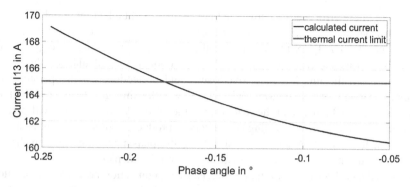

Fig. 4. Calculated current in the cable between Busbar 1 and 3 over measured phase angle φ_3 at Busbar 3

required for phasor measurements. The plots in Figs. 4 and 5 show the currents in the cables between busbars 1 and 3 resp. 2 and 3 to the corresponding phase. For Cable 13 the thermal current limit is also shown in the figure.

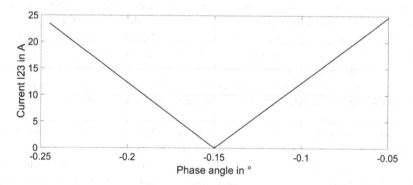

Fig. 5. Calculated current in the cable between Busbar 2 and 3 over measured phase angle φ_3 at Busbar 3

By monitoring the current flow in the power distribution grid the utilization of the lines should be increased. Today, as there is almost no information about the current values available, a large margin is used to prevent overloading of the cables. This unused power transfer capacity can be used for the connection of renewable energy. An overloading of the lines must be avoided to prevent the protection devices from tripping. Thus, a continuous reliable prediction of the line currents including information whether lines are overloaded or not is mandatory if the system is operated close to its thermal current limits.

As shown in Fig. 4, Cable 13 is operated close to its thermal limit. The true phase angle is −0.14° which corresponds to a current of 163 A. A variation by −0.1° due to timing jitter leads to a calculated current of 169 A instead. Hence, the calculation shows an overload although the true cable current is still below its thermal limit.

A small phase error leads to unwanted effects that might affect the reliability of the power distribution system: If the calculated current value is lower than the real line loading, the SCADA/EMS might increase the insertion of renewable energy into the grid leading to an increase of the line current. Although the calculated value is still below the limit, the line is in-fact overloaded and protection, which operates independently from these calculations, will disconnect the line due to overload. If the calculated value is higher than the real current, the SCADA/EMS system will perform countermeasures (e.g. disconnecting consumers or producers) although there is enough current transfer reserve. A similar sensitivity of the phasor measurement on the calculated line current of cable between Busbars 2 and 3 is depicted in Fig. 5.

This analysis shows that a reliable (precise) communication network is mandatory to enable proper and accurate state estimation including phasor measurements to facilitate the extension of current transfer capability of existing residential power distribution grids. Especially the knowledge of the delay of the communication link is mandatory. In summary, the following two requirements are the most critical for the scenario discussed in this paper.

- **Time synchronisation:** As shown in the above example sensitivity analysis, the error in the calculated line current is strongly dependent on the error of a synchronous time signal which is used for phasor measurement. To achieve an accuracy in the calculated line current of less than 4% in the shown example, a phasor measurement accuracy is needed in the range of 0,1° corresponding to a timing error of not more than 5.6 μs. Electrical power system control strategies that include processing information about existing delays in phasor measurements have already been proposed in [17]. Further research work on electrical power systems is needed to enable SCADA/EMS for LV grids including state estimation and phasor measurements [15].
- **Fast reaction time:** As already shown in Sect. 2, reaction time for closed-loop control actions is required in the range of a few 10 ms up to 300 ms, depending of time-current-characteristic of installed protection devices. Reaction time includes the time to activate further electrical consumers, re-estimate the network state, possibly a second iteration of activating consumers, re-estimate the network state and in worst case switching-off producers before the line protection fires. However, it can be expected that the overload is rather in the lower than in the higher end (see Fig. 1). This means an overall reaction time of 100 ms needs to be achieved. This includes three cycles of communication, two cycles of system state estimation, two cycles of activating consumers and one cycle to deactivate producers. If we assume 10 ms for each activation, deactivation and state estimation, we have 50 ms left for three cycles of communication. This results in around 15 ms for a complete protocol exchange.

4.3   Analysis on the Use of Existing Communication Technologies

Different kinds of communication technologies can be used to realise the communication between different components as depicted in Fig. 2. As discussed in Sects. 2 and 4.2, latency and reliability are critical factors that determine what kind of technologies

Table 1. Analysis of proposed interaction between the communication network and the LV power distribution systems (see Fig. 2)

Type of communication	Sections	Topology / number of devices	Distance/area	Target	Possible com. technologies
Time critical (fast reaction time - within 10 to 300 ms, reliable bi-directional communication)	within the cluster	star or ring topology /5–20 controlled devices	4 km^2	controlled devices	DSL, PLC, LTE, Fiber optic, WiFi Or WPAN (with multi-hop), WiMAX/LTE 450 MHz
	SCADA/EMS to cluster	direct link	2–10 km	control, data concentrator, controlled devices	DSL, PLC, LTE, Fiber optic, WiFi Or WPAN (with multi-hop), WiMAX/LTE 450 MHz
Time critical (time synchronisation accuracy of ca. 5-6 μs)	Cluster to SCADA/EMS	multi-point - 5 –20 devices (PMUs) to point (Data concentration unit)	2–10 km	intelligent measurements incl. PMU	DSL, PLC, LTE, Fiber optic, LTE 450 MHz
Non-time critical (reaction time within a couple of minutes)	SCADA/EMS to protection devices	point to multi-point (1 –10 devices)	2–6 km	triggering the protection devices	DSL, PLC, LTE, Fiber optic, WiFi Or WPAN (with multi-hop), WiMAX/LTE 450 MHz

to use, specially when the power system is running close to the maximum utilization of the power lines in order to guarantee realization of corrective control actions. Table 1 shows possible communication technologies that can be used at different sections of the proposed architecture.

4.4   Communication Architectures

As shown from Tables 1 and 2, it is feasible to use different types of technologies at different places to realize the communications between different components in the LV power grid. However, it is not enough just to use the standard way of communication to fulfill the requirements identified in Sect. 4.1. Some of the specific characteristics that should be considered for our proposed CPN scenario are:

1. **Reliable networks with low latency and ultra low jitter:** Very reliable and low latency communications are a primary requirement as shown in Table 1, especially to achieve the fast reaction time. A TCP/IP based layered architecture may introduce additional overheads due to the use of different timers and different recovery mechanisms at different layers might lead to unpredictable delays. Unpredictable

Table 2. Properties of possible communication technologies [8] proposed in Table 1

Com. technology	Data rates	Coverage	Pros/cons
DSL	ADSL2 + : 24 Mbps down and 1.4 Mbps up VDSL2: up to 200 Mpbs down/up	up to 4 km up to 1.2 km	ADSL infrastructure is already established and most commonly deployed VDSL is not deployed everywhere
Optical fibers	IEEE 802.3ah: 100 Mbps	up to 10 km	Long distance, high bandwidth, robustness against electromagnetic and radio interference High cost, difficult to upgrade
PLC	NB-PLC: up to 500 Kbps BB-PLC: up to 200 Mbps	150 km 1.5 km	Infrastructure is already established, low operational cost Multiple non-interoperable technologies, difficult to support high bit rates
WiFi	IEEE 802.11e/s up to 54 Mbps IEEE 802.11n up to 600 Mbps IEEE 802.11p	up to 300 m up to 1 km (11p)	Low cost deployment, flexible Prone to interference, not very reliable, low coverage, multi-hop connections may degrade the quality of communications
WPAN	802.15.4 WirelessHART ISA 100.11A	up to 300 m	Flexible, low data rate, low power consumption Prone to interference Improved version of 802.15.4 guaranteed reliability and security, support mesh networks Support only start topology, guaranteed reliability
LTE with 450 MHz	Max. data rate per cell, 1 Gbps down, 350 Mbps up [10]	3 times more than std LTE with 800 MHz [10]	Guaranteed QoS, better cell range and coverage, specially suitable for indoor environments Not yet widely deployed
WiMAX	IEEE 802.16 128 Mbps down and 28 Mbps up	up to 10 km	Longer distance than WiFi, more sophisticated QoS Not widely deployed in Europe, network management is complex, use of licensed spectrum

delays and jitter (delay variation) make time synchronisation difficult. The mentioned interacting control loops with retransmissions are one point, another are unknown scheduling, queueing and processing delays in the different network elements. For the exchange of these delays, future network architectures allowing cross-layer information exchange might be more suitable, than the TCP/IP architecture with clear separation of layers. The communications architectures for CPN should have flexibility, adaptability and configurability in order to achieve the requirements of high reliability, low latency with almost zero jitter.

2. **Distributed functions:** In order to achieve the low latency and ultra low jitter (for example, the communication of synchronization signaling among PMUs), some of the areas need to function in a distributed manner. It is very important to have local optimisations while trading off other aspects. For example, low latency is typically more important than having higher throughput in the whole network. The flexibility in deploying different networking functions at different nodes that are able to operate independently may be suitable for this scenario to achieve the low latency with almost zero jitter.

3. **Resilient of the communications network:** As a result of the tight coupling required in communications and power systems, recovery from failures becomes an important aspect. For example, in case of a failure in the communication links, the power system should be functioning for a certain time and should also be capable of setting up communication links satisfying the minimum requirements. This is also valid in case of a failure of the power system.

In general, some of the future internet architectures such as OConS [3], GP [6] and Netlets [2] allow to orchestrate the protocol stack depending on the requirements. These architectures also cater for the deployment of distributed functions. However, further investigations should be done first to analyse how to optimise the protocol stack to achieve the identified requirements. This depends on many factors such as communication technology used, optimisation of parameters (e.g., retransmission time-outs), micro analysis of delays and jitter in different nodes and different components.

5 Conclusion

This paper shows how to enhance the utilization of the LV power grid by coupling the power system and the communication system. One of the CPN application areas in *EE networks*, viz., LV power grids was selected due to the following reasons:

- Decentralized electric power generation using renewable energy sources becomes increasingly popular. As a consequence, electric power flows of existing electrical power grids are shifting significantly from unidirectional to bidirectional mode. This applies especially to the LV power grids to which a continuously increasing number of decentralized electrical energy sources such as photovoltaic is connected.
- Especially, existing LV cables and lines need to be utilized to a much larger extent and often need to be operated close to their thermal current limits.
- Dedicated coordinated control of loads and power generation is foreseen to realize intelligent power management in order to guarantee full use of available power transmission capacity and on the other hand to safely keep each transmission device of the LV power grid below its allowed current limits.

The realization of coupling the power system and the communication system is to be done by SCADA/EMS. This requires the use of state estimation to continuously capture the state of the system from a given set of measurements. The implementation of SCADA/EMS requires reliable bidirectional communication channels that enable execution times of 15 ms for iterative closed-loop control cycles. Additionally, time-synchronization of PMUs shall be realized to increase measurement coverage of LV power grids. Sufficiently accurate distributed phasor measurements require an error of the synchronizing time that is less than 5.6 µs. Based on the analysis of Sect. 4, these requirements need to be realized by the use of appropriate communication media and the communication architectures and protocol stacks.

5.1   Outlook

As discussed in Sect. 4.4, there are so many factors which influence the realization of our scenario. Therefore, as next steps, further investigations should be done to see the following aspects.

- *Optimization of the protocol stack for reliable and low latency communications:* In our scenario, this is not always required, but it is very important to have a reliable and low latency communication channel, when the power system operates closer to its maximum utilization.
- *Low latencies with ultra low jitter for time synchronisation:* This could be achieved by enabling distributed functions and reconfigurations of the protocol stack.

We plan to use a co-simulation platform for our future work. When simulating either the power system or the communication system separately, it is very difficult to capture the correct and exact behaviour. The research in the area of integrating event-driven network simulators with time based simulators for power systems is very challenging [9].

References

1. Ahlgren, B., Dannewitz, C., Imbrenda, C., Kutscher, D., Ohlman, B.: A survey of information-centric networking. In: Information-Centric Networking, number 10492 in Dagstuhl Seminar Proceedings. Schloss Dagstuhl - Leibniz- Zentrum fuer Informatik, Germany (2011)
2. Dannewitz, C.: Netinf: An information-centric design for the future internet. In: Proceedings of the 3rd GI/ITG KuVS Workshop on the Future, May 2009
3. Udugama, A., Goerg, C., Timm-Giel, A.: Prototype: OConS multi-path content delivery with netinfn Mobile Networks and Management, vol. 58, pp. 323–327. Springer, Heidelberg (2013)
4. Jacobson, V., Smetters, D., Thornton, J., Plass, M., Briggs, N., Braynard, R.: Networking named content. In: Proceedings of the 5th International Conference on Emerging Networking Experiments and Technologies, pp. 1–12 (2009)
5. Zhao, L., Zaki, Y., Udugama, A., Toseef, U., Goerg, C., Timm-Giel, A.: Open connectivity services for future networks. In: CEWIT 2011, November 2011

6. Singh, A., Nass, C., Timm-Giel, A., Schefczik, P., Roessler, H., Scharf, M.: Generic connectivity architecture for mobility and multipath flow management in the future internet. In: Pentikousis, K., Agüero, R., García-Arranz, M., Papavassiliou, S. (eds.) MONAMI 2010. LNICSSITE, vol. 68, pp. 1–13. Springer, Heidelberg (2011). doi:10.1007/978-3-642-21444-8_1

7. Abad, F.A.T., Caccamo, M., Robbins, B.: A fault resilient architecture for distributed cyber-physical systems. In: IEEE International Conference on Embedded and Real-Time Computing Systems and Applications, 19–12 August 2012

8. Ancillotti, E., Bruno, R., Conti, M.: The role of communication systems in smart grids: Architectures, technical solutions and research challenges. Comput. Commun. J. 36(17–18), 1665–1697 (2013). Elsevier

9. Li, W., Zhang, X., Li, H.: Co-simulation platforms for co-design of networked control systems: An overview. Control Eng. Pract. 23, 44–56 (2014). Elsevier

10. Hägerling, C., Ide, C., Wietfeld, C.: Coverage and capacity analysis of wireless M2M technologies for smart distribution grid services. In: IEEE SmartGridComm, Venice, Italy, November 2014

11. Wood, A.J., Wollenberg, B.F.: Power Generation, Operation, and Control, 3rd edn. Wiley Inc., Hoboken (2014)

12. Heuck, K., Dettmann, K.-D., Schulz, D.: Elektrische Energieversorgung. 9. Auflage. 2013, Springer Vieweg, Wiesbaden, Deutschland

13. The Institution of Electrical Engineers: Power System Protection, Volume 1: Principles and Components, Electricity Association Services Ltd., London, UK (1995)

14. Marger, D.: VDE-Positionspapier – Kommunikationsnetz für das Smart Grid. VDE, Frankfurt, Deutschland (2015)

15. Huang, Y., Werner, S., Huang, J., Kashyap, N., Gupta, V.: State Estimation in Electric Power Grids. IEEE Signal Processing Magazine, September 2012

16. Lixia, M., Muscas, C., Sulis, S.: On the accuracy specifications of phasor measurement units. In: Instrumentation and Measurement Technology Conference (I2MTC). IEEE, Austin, Texas (2010)

17. Soudbakhsh, D., Chakrabortty, A., Alvarez, F., Anaaswamy, A.: A delay-aware cyber-physical architecture for wide-area control of power systems. In: Proceedings of IEEE (2015)

18. Zhou, M., Centeno, V.A., Thorp, J.S., Phadke, A.G.: An alternative for including phasor measurements in state estimators. IEEE Trans. Power Syst. 21(4), 1930–1937 (2006)

19. Neplan (R) - Planning and Optimization for electrical, gas, water, and district heating networks, ABB AG, Mannheim, Germany. www.abb.com

Techniques and Algorithms for Cellular Networks

Proposing a New Solution to Reduce the International Roaming Call Cost

D.R. Ranasinghearachchi(✉), A.K.S.T. Chaminda,
W.M.D.H. Wanasinghe, and T.L. Weerawardane

Department of Electrical, Electrical and Telecommunication,
Faculty of Engineering, General Sir John Kotelawala Defence University,
Ratmalana, Sri Lanka
dumindurr@gmail.com, thilina.chaminda@gmail.com,
tlwkdu@gmail.com, wdilantha@ymail.com

Abstract. The cost of an international roaming call is high for majority of the countries. As a remedy for this, free VoIP services can be utilized, but both originating and terminating parties need to have suitable internet connectivity. Though, this issue is already addressed by certain VoIP services, by terminating the calls via lines owned by them, the call charges are still relatively high. This research paper is directed towards implementation of a cost effective solution for international roaming, where only the international roaming party requires internet connectivity and the local terminating party does not need internet connectivity. This roaming solution is assisted by the Public Switched Telephone Network (PSTN) line of a local fixed operator. The service architecture includes two components. The Customer Network (CN), which consists of a Customer Premises Equipment (CPE), VoIP Gateway (GW), Internet connectivity (preferably ADSL line) and PSTN phone line. The Provider Network (PN) which consists mainly of a Roaming Connectivity Server (RCS) and Call Accounting Server (CAS). Through this proposed system, the cost of originating a call when roaming can be reduced nearly to a local call charge. This solution will have marginal initial cost but still economical from customer point of view.

Keywords: Roaming · CN · PN · CPE · RCS

1 Introduction

International roaming is the primary option which is used by the roaming users while travelling to other regions. But in this method the calling cost is very high. So the subscribers are searching for a low cost voice call connection when roaming abroad, especially for official work, to talk to relatives, friends and other persons in the home country.

The roaming charges vary from operator to operator and country to country. Generally, these costs are predefined by the relevant operators (home network and visited network) according to business agreements between the two operator. These agreements depend on many aspects such as profit, taxes, cost of setting up connectivity between the two networks etc. If a roaming party latches on to a visited network whom with which the home network does not have an agreement with, the charges will be even higher.

© ICST Institute for Computer Sciences, Social Informatics and Telecommunications Engineering 2017
R. Agüero et al. (Eds.): MONAMI 2016, LNICST 191, pp. 119–130, 2017.
DOI: 10.1007/978-3-319-52712-3_9

In international roaming, the customer has the option to make a considerable high deposit to the operator before roaming. The charges are deducted from this deposit until it is depleted. If the customer does not make the deposit, the charges are added until the customer's credit limit is reached, thereafter he/she will be barred from service.

The charges for originating and terminating calls when roaming, generally range from 5–20 times that of normal local call charges. But is some extreme cases these charges are 30–400 times higher than the local call charges.

As a solution for this issue, VoIP Services such as Skype and Viber can be utilized. But in this case, to generate a free call using these services both parties have to be connected to a stable internet connection to complete the call successfully. However, with the increase of data traffic and online applications, mobile network coverage might not be eligible to provide customers sufficiently. The above mentioned services also have the option to terminate calls using lines (PSTN/PLMN) owned by them for a certain charge. Yet these charges are relatively high compared to the proposed system in this paper.

Recently, the roaming costs between the European countries have been reduced drastically due to the EU roaming rules. But in the rest of the world, the costs are still too much high. A majority of these effected countries are developing countries. The proposed system is a solution mainly targeted towards the roaming subscribers of these countries.

Therefore, in this paper, we address the main problems which are high cost of roaming and the need of an internet connectivity for both parties. Through this concept, this solution will terminate the roaming call for any subscriber connected to the system at nearly the same cost of local outgoing call charges. This is beneficial for both single users as well as large scale organizations.

This system is an Over-The-Top (OTT) solution to reduce charges for internationally roaming users. It was developed solely with the roaming user's best interests in mind. Even though, it is targeted towards internationally roaming PLMN subscribers, this system negates the need of a PLMN home operator when roaming and relies on stable internet connectivity only on the roaming party's end.

In this paper, we'll be discussing how the node of this system are deployed. Section 2 will focus on the Conceptual Architecture. Section 3 will concentrate on the Customer Network (CN) portion of the system. Section 4 will discuss about the Provider Network (PN) portion of the system. Section 5 will elaborate on connectivity between the major nodes of the system. Section 6 discusses about the codecs used in the system. Section 7 talks about the deployment and testing to the system. Section 8 discusses result of the analysis. And finally Sect. 9 talks about the future work regarding this solution.

2   Conceptual Architecture

In this design, the system can be divided into two main networks. The Customer Network (CN) and the Provider Network (PN). Both of these networks are connected to one another other internet via Inter-Asterisk eXchange (IAX) Trunks.

Each consists of components crucial for the deployment of the service. There can be more than one Customer Network, but only one Provider Network. This setup is used to provide seamless connectivity for the Customer Roaming Entity (CRE), device/softphone used to connect to the PN, to the relevant CN. Each CRE can only connect to the CN that it is registered to CREs cannot connect to other CNs. This is done to maintain security and privacy between the separate CNs.

3 Customer Network (CN)

The Customer Network is the network on the customer's side of the system. In order for this part of the network to function the customer must have existing internet connection, preferably ADSL internet connection, and a PSTN telephone line connection. This PSTN connection will be used to terminate the user's roaming call to the destination number. In the CN there are two main components that need to be introduced to the network to provide the connectivity between the Provider Network and the PSTN connection of the customer. The two main components are the Voice over IP (VoIP) Gateway and the Customer Premises Equipment (CPE) (Fig. 1).

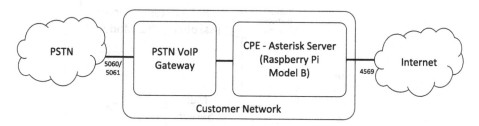

Fig. 1. Customer network components

3.1 Customer Premises Equipment (CPE)

The CPE is a low powered, low cost server running FreePBX. FreePBX is a Graphical User Interface (GUI) with Asterisk PBX server. This serves as a VoIP server within the CN which provide VoIP serves. And this also the main entity that provides IAX connectivity to the RCS for the CN. Additionally, this serves as a routing point which is used to connect to the VoIP Gateway of the CN.

3.2 VoIP Gateway

The VoIP Gateway is used to provide an interface between the internal VoIP network and the external PSTN network. It basically converts the VoIP Real-Time Protocol (RTP) packet data to analog signals and sends them through the PSTN interface and vice versa. This also performs the function of dialing the number in Dual Tone – Multi Frequency (DTMF) tone when taking a call to the PSTN network and signaling the VoIP server for an incoming call.

A SIP Trunk is setup between the CPE and the VoIP Gateway. All the calls that are terminated to the PSTN line from the CPE are sent on this trunk.

4   Provider Network (PN)

The Provider Network is the network of nodes in the provider's side of the system. This is used to provide connectivity between the Customer Network and the Customer Roaming Entity (CRE), customer device/equipment used to connect to the system. This connects the relevant customer entities to its relevant Customer Network via an IAX trunk which is established between the two networks. The Provider Network consists of several main components. This includes the Remote Connectivity Server (RCS), the Call Accounting Server (CAS) and a Mail Server. Of which the CAS and the Mail Server performing value added supporting roles such as generating Call Detail Records (CDR) and sending the said CDR to the relevant user (Fig. 2).

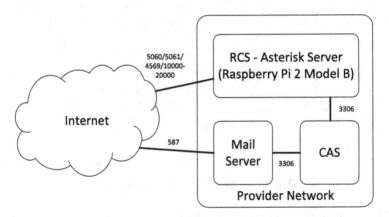

Fig. 2. Provider network components

4.1   Roaming Connectivity Server (RCS)

The RCS is the main entity that provides the connectivity between the Customer Network and the Customer Roaming Entity (CRE). It does this by establishing an IAX trunk between the CPE of the Customer Network and the RCS. This trunk will use only the 4569 port on both the CPE and the RCS.

The RCS runs Asterisk IP PBX server. Asterisk is a back-to-back user agent (B2BUA). It can function as a server on one end and a client on the other to control all aspects of a VoIP call [1].

5 Connectivity

5.1 Connectivity Between the CN and PN

In order to fulfill the primary function of this solution, both the Customer Network and the Provider Network must be connected together through internet. This connection is established between the CPE and the RCS of the respective networks. The connection is established to route VoIP data from one network to the other and vice versa. This is done through the use of an IAX trunk.

IAX trunks has some advantages over SIP Trunks. (i) IAX uses less bandwidth than SIP. This is because the header size of the IAX packets are comparatively smaller than the SIP packet headers. (ii) In SIP the RTP packets are sometimes dropped during call sessions due to NAT issues. IAX was specifically designed to overcome issues caused by NAT by sending the RTP packets and the signaling together on the same channel. (iii) In SIP, the signaling is done on port 5060/5061 and the RTP packets are sent through any two random port numbers between 10,000 and 20,000. Whereas in IAX, the signaling and RTP packets are sent through the same port, port 4569. Due to these reasons the IAX trunk is used connect the CPE and the RCS.

Taemoor Abbasi et al. [7], compared SIP and IAX signalling, structure, media transfer, signalling efficiency, and NAT issue. In this study, it was observed that, performance with packet loss of IAX is 24.70% higher than that of SIP. Also, performance with packet delay was 7.16% higher in IAX than that of SIP performance with packet reordering was 7.27% higher in IAX than that of SIP. Therefore, in general, IAX is better compared to SIP.

Just like the SIP Trunk configured in Customer Network the IAX Trunk must be setup between the CPE and the RCE. This IAX trunk is encrypted, therefore the security is considerably higher compared to SIP Trunk. Another reason for use IAX trunk over SIP trunk was that, SIP exposes 10,000 ports to the internet. That is, these ports would be port forwarded from the user's home router to CPE server. This exposes the CPE to the internet and open for hackers to encroach the system. Therefore, when only one port is exposed to the internet, the number of paths a hacker can use to enter the system are significantly less. Additionally, When the PN is exposed to the internet rather than the CN, the PN serves as a first line of defense for the network and protects the CN.

Additionally, the trunk is encrypted using AES-128 encryption standard. This helps to protect the trunks even from eavesdropping attacks by hackers. Also, MD5 algorithm is used to check the authentication details at the initiation of each call session [2, 6].

Another reason for connecting to the VoIP gateway via the CPE rather than connecting directly, is due to the fact that VoIP gateways that support IAX connectivity are rather expensive. Due to this, a low cost SIP VoIP Gateway is used.

5.2 Connectivity Between the RCS and the User

In this system, when a user is roaming in a foreign country, the user simply needs to use a connection with suitable QoS and connect to the RCS server via softphone or mobile device (with SIP compatibility). Once the user is connected to the system, calls can be originated to the home country via the system as long at the CPE is in operational state. The user simply needs to initiate the call to the desired terminating number and the call session will begin. The call will be terminated via the PSTN line at the customer premises, that is owned by the user.

The call is routed through multiple nodes before it is terminated to the intended terminating parting. Signals are exchanged through both SIP and IAX protocols between the relevant nodes. Figure 3 illustrates the signaling flow between each node during a call.

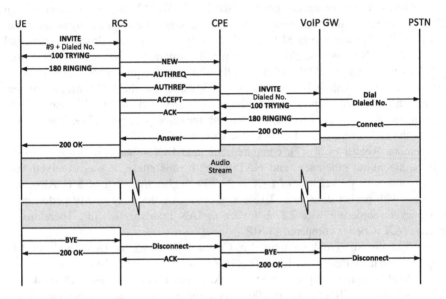

Fig. 3. Roaming user call initiation call flow

6 Codecs

During deployment, the default audio codec used was G.722 wideband codec. This codec has a bit rate of 64kbps. Due to its wideband property, this codec is used for high definition audio streaming between the nodes. The IAX Trunk between the RCS and the CPE, and the SIP connectivity between the RCS and the UE are configured to utilize the G.722 codec by default. The UE can use this codec only if it supports it. If the UE does not support G.722, the next alternative, G.711 will be used.

The VoIP Gateway used during testing (Cisco SPA3102) only supported G.711 narrowband audio codec. Therefore, all calls that were terminated within the CN and PN network had high definition audio support. Whereas all calls terminated to PSTN/PLMN subscribers were all subjected to the G.711 narrow band audio codec. Due to this the audio experienced when termination out via the VoIP Gateway was of narrow band audio quality.

7   Deploying the System and Testing

This system was deployed and tested in relatively controlled environment. The CN and PN were deployed in two geographically separate locations within Sri Lanka. Both of which had stable internet connectivity.

The primary goal was to reduce the roaming cost. Therefore, we wanted to keep the cost of the CN to a minimum. Due to this, the CPE was deployed on a "Raspberry Pi Model B". The single core CPU of the Raspberry Pi Model B is generally clocked to 700 MHz. This was overclocked to 800 MHz to provide better performs without effecting the Raspberry Pi. This version of Raspberry Pi can run Linux in a stable manner. The Raspbian is the most stable and function of all the Operating Systems supported by Raspberry Pi. It is a version of Debian Linux modified to run on the Raspberry Pi platform. [5].

The VoIP Gateway that was used in this system was the Cisco SPA3102 VoIP Gateway. This VoIP gateway has the option to connect to the PSTN line at the user's home.

For testing purposes, the RCS was deployed on a "Raspberry Pi 2 Model B". The CPU of the Raspberry 2 is a Quad-Core ARM Cortex-A7 CPU clocked are 900 MHz We did not over clock this as we felt that this clock rate on a quad core CPU was sufficient enough to sever the function of the RCS.

When setting up the CN (CPE and VoIP Gateway), the user merely needs to connect it to the home network. Further configuration can be done via the CPE and VoIP Gateway web interface or by the PN via the internet.

For Android devices the native internet calling settings can be configured. Further for IOS and Windows phones, a softphone application can be used to setup the user account in the mobile device. For desktop/laptops, running Windows/Mac OS/Linux, softphone applications can be used to connect to the RCS.

Finally, when the system was setup the operational architecture illustrated by Fig. 4.

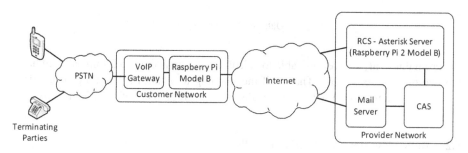

Fig. 4.   Operational architecture

During the testing phase, the system was tested thoroughly. Data for call setup delays, bandwidth usage etc. where gathered. Moreover, the system was tested for relatively high loads. The RCS, with it Raspberry Pi 2 Model B was easily able to support 5–6 call simultaneously within its network without any sign of delay or packet loss.

Furthermore, the exposure of the ports of the PN to the internet caused many security issues. On three separate occasions, the system was encroached by hackers from outside the network. This was a serious issue as in all these occasions, the RCS became inoperable. The RCS was manually rebooted in order to get it back to a useable state.

8 Analysis

The data flow in system was analysed by obtaining traces from RCS and CPE. From these traces we were able obtain the average data usage between the respective nodes. Additionally, we compared the call setup time and the average call costs on the proposed system and existing solutions such as Viber and Skype.

8.1 Data Usage of Roaming User

The data flow between the RCS and the CRE flows entirely in SIP and RTP. From the trace obtained from the RCS, we were able to analyse the data flow between the two nodes. The graphical interpretation on the data flow of a call of 2 min duration can be seen in Fig. 5.

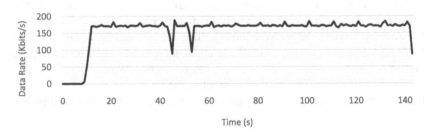

Fig. 5. Data usage of roaming user

From this analysis, we were able to calculate that, on average a 2-min call will have a usage of 2.7 MB of data. That is, if the roaming user takes a 10-min call, the data usage on average is 13.5 MB. This results in an average data rate of 23.04 kbps.

8.2 Data Flow Between RCS and CPE

The data flow between the RCS and CPE flows entirely on the IAX trunk. From the trace obtained from the CPE, we were able to analyse the data flow between the two nodes. The graphical interpretation of the data flow of a call of 2 min duration can be seen in Fig. 6.

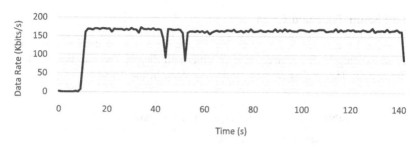

Fig. 6. Data usage of CPE

From this analysis we were able to calculate that on average a 2-min call will have a usage of 2.6 MB of data. That is, if the call session is 10 min long, the data usage at the CN is 13 MB. This results in an average data rate of 28.19 kbps.

From the analysis of the traces we were able to calculate that, the data usage of the IAX trunk is 4% less than that of the SIP data flow. This is due to the smaller header size of the IAX packets compared to the SIP packets. Additional statistical data obtained from three different 2-min long calls can be seen in Table 1.

Table 1. Data rates and usages of 2-min long calls

Call #	Node	Usage (MB)	Average (Kbits/s)	% Diff
1	CPE	2.59	149.68	3.28%
	User	2.70	154.66	
2	CPE	2.65	150.74	4.32%
	User	2.73	157.40	
3	CPE	2.55	150.42	4.60%
	User	2.69	157.50	

If a user made calls with the total duration of 1 h per day, the average total amount of data usage at the CN end is 78 MB and the usage for the roaming user is 81 MB.

The difference in the data rates is mostly due to the fact that the RTP and IAX media have different header sizes. i.e., RTP media has a header size of 12 bytes and IAX media has a header size of 4 bytes. This can be clearly be observed in Figs. 5 and 6.

In the initial stages of the call session, we observed that the delay is due to signalling between nodes. This delay ranges from 3–8 s when initiating the call from WLAN or 4G connection. Generally, the time taken by the signalling within the CN and PN to setup the call is around 1–2 s. It is usually due to the signalling and setting up of security parameters between the nodes of the system [3, 4]. The addition delay is due to the in-band DTMF dialling of the VoIP Gateway and call setup time at the PSTN end.

8.3   Call Setup Time and Costs

The call setup times were analyzed during testing by initiating calls in the proposed system and existing VoIP services such as Viber and Skype. The out dialing functions were also tested. The results of these test are shown in the Table 2.

Table 2. Call setup time compared with existing services

		Call Setup Time (Seconds)							
		Sample 1	Sample 2	Sample 3	Sample 4	Sample 5	Sample 6	Sample 7	Average
Proposed System	VoIP	2.64	2.10	1.74	5.12	7.12	1.83	3.40	**3.42**
	Out	9.16	8.84	8.26	9.00	11.75	9.62	6.96	**9.08**
Viber	Normal	4.17	3.74	4.58	4.05	4.13	10.19	9.94	**5.83**
	Out	8.39	17.90	9.10	7.80	7.34	13.30	12.43	**10.89**
Skype	Normal	3.34	4.21	3.67	3.98	4.23	4.42	4.32	**4.02**
	Out	9.82	8.76	9.24	9.54	8.43	9.23	9.14	**9.17**

The call cost during the test were recorded for comparison purposes. The following table illustrates the calling charge induced by the proposed system and by existing VoIP services such as Viber Out and Skype Out.[1] (Table 3)

Table 3. The call charges of proposed system compared with existing systems

		Call Charges (Per Minute)	
		USD	LKR
Proposed System	Out	$0.03	LKR 3.64
Viber	Out	$0.23	LKR 33.50
Skype	Out	$0.41	LKR 59.71

9   Future Work

There are several areas in which the system can be improved. Some are in areas of security of the system and others in the efficiency of the system.

When referring to the security aspects of the system, solutions need to be found for external threats such as brute force attacks and SIP vicious attacks. These attacks render the SIP servers unusable.

To avoid security threats similar to that which was experienced during testing, VPN (Virtual Private Network) can be implemented between the RCS and the CPE, and an

---

[1] These result were obtained by tests done in Sri Lanka. These values were obtained during the month on September, 2016, and may be subject to change.

advanced firewall can be implemented to protect the RCS from threats from the internet. This will reduce the risk of the RCS being vulnerable to hacks and threats.

Further, The RCS can be deployed in cloud environment to coup with expanding customer base. The cloud environment will let the RCS virtual machine expand with load. This will also enable higher efficiency, availability and resource sharing.

Additionally, the delay experienced at the beginning of the call needs to be reduced. This need to be reduced to improve the system and VoIP Gateway efficiency.

As an additional functionality, the ability to show the roaming user's Caller Line Identification to the terminating party needs to be integrated to the system.

In commercial deployment of this service, we can preferably come to an agreement with a fixed operator such that the generated revenue will be profitable to the utilized network operator.

10 Conclusion

This paper proposes a solution to reduce the roaming charges solely with the roaming user's best interests in mind. This concept reduces the call costs of the user when roaming nearly to the cost of local call charges. This is achieved through the support of the PSTN line owned by the user in the home country.

The roaming user merely need to use a SIP compatible device/softphone to connect to the RCS server via SIP protocol. After connection is established, the user can initiate call where they will be terminated out through the user's PSTN line in the home country.

Furthermore, the results show that this system is relatively cost effective compared to the existing systems.

References

1. Zhuang, W., Tang, Y., Hu, Y.: Design and implementation of SIP B2BUA server. In: International Conference on Anti-Counterfeiting, Security and Identification (ASID), pp. 1–5 (2013)
2. Gallo, P., Levický, D., Bugár, G.: Authentication threats in PSTN-VoIP architecture using multi-service gateways, ELMAR, pp. 153–156 (2012)
3. Subramanian, S.V., Dutta, R.: Measurements and analysis of M/M/1 and M/M/c queuing models of the SIP proxy server. In: International Conference on Computer Communication and Networks (ICCCN), pp. 1–7 (2009)
4. Subramanian, S.V., Dutta, R.: Comparative study of secure vs non-secure transport protocols on the SIP proxy server performance, an experimental approach. In: Conference on Advances in Recent Technologies in Communication and Computing (ARTCom), pp. 301–305 (2010)
5. Alexander, A., Wijesinha, A.L., Karne, R.: A study of bare PC SIP server performance. In: Fifth International Conference on System and Networks Communication, An Experimental Approach, Conference on Advances in Recent Technologies in Communication and Computing, pp. 392–397 (2010)

6. Dakur, A., Dakar, S.: Eavesdropping and interception security hole and its solution over VoIP Service. In: An Experimental Approach, IEEE Global Conference on Wireless Computing and Networking (GCWCN), pp. 6–10 (2014)
7. Abbasi, T., Prasad, S., Seddigh, N., Lambadaris, I.: A comparative study of the sip and iax voip protocols. In: Canadian Conference on Electrical and Computer Engineering (2014)

Generic Wireless Network System Modeler:
Fostering the Analysis of Complex LTE Deployments

Luis Diez$^{(\boxtimes)}$, Sergio Izuel, and Ramón Agüero

University of Cantabria, Santander, Spain
{ldiez,ramon}@tlmat.unican.es,
sergio.izuel@alumnos.unican.es

Abstract. Despite the huge research effort in the field of LTE networks, there is not a widely accepted methodology to conduct the corresponding analysis. Various approaches and tools are used, each of them having several advantages, but showing some drawbacks as well. One of the most limiting aspects is that they are not usually able to cope with network deployments having a large number of elements, as it would be in dense Heterogeneous Networks (HetNets). In other cases, they do not usually pay too much attention to the requirements that different types of services might have, overusing the so-called *full-buffer* approach. In this paper we introduce the Generic Wireless Network System Modeler (GWNSyM), a flexible framework that allows the deployment of rather complex networks, which can be exploited to analyze a wide range of resource management techniques, solutions and, even, novel architectural approaches. The tool is validated over a high-dense network deployment, embracing different types of cells, users and services. Over such scenario, we assess the performance of CoMP techniques and we leverage the Network Virtualization Function paradigm.

Keywords: Network modeling · Simulation · LTE/LTE-A

1 Introduction and Motivation

Current forecasts expect a remarkable increase on the traffic demand for mobile wireless systems [1]. One of the main reasons behind this unseen growth is the consolidation of novel services, such as video streaming, gaming applications, etc., which would need to share the corresponding resources with more traditional data services, such as web browsing or file download.

Although we have not yet seen the consolidation of the 4G technology, several works and research initiatives are already anticipating the arrival of 5G. However, it is believed that both technologies will coexist and seamlessly deployed and used. For instance, it is expected a prominent role of the so-called small-cell densification strategy [2], since it will yield a remarkable capacity increase. Other elements that have been recently included in the corresponding 3GPP specifications are the cooperation between access elements (Cooperative Multi-Point

© ICST Institute for Computer Sciences, Social Informatics and Telecommunications Engineering 2017
R. Agüero et al. (Eds.): MONAMI 2016, LNICST 191, pp. 131–145, 2017.
DOI: 10.1007/978-3-319-52712-3_10

(CoMP) techniques) or the decoupling of downlink and uplink connections [3], among others.

On top of that, there is another key ingredient of the forthcoming wireless communications landscape, which is the exploitation of virtualization techniques and Software Defined Networks (SDN) elements for this type of network deployments [4], leading to the Network Function Virtualization (NFV) paradigm [5]. This would, for instance, facilitate cooperation strategies between base stations, if some of their core functions are moved to the cloud.

Despite the clear advantages of all the previous aspects, it goes without saying that new challenges will certainly arise. In this sense, the scientific community is working on this dynamic and complex playground, advocating new techniques and solutions, assessing their performance for certain scenarios and use cases.

One of the first issues that need to be addressed is the tool, or set of tools, which can be used in order to carry out an accurate analysis at different abstraction levels. We can basically distinguish three possibilities, each of them with their own advantages and disadvantages: (1) utilization of link-level simulators, (2) use a system-level approach, or (3) exploit a network simulation platform to carry out a more detailed analysis. The first approach focuses on the last hop of the communication and allows the investigation of link related topics such as channel estimation, Multiple-Input Multiple-Output (MIMO) techniques or Adaptive Modulation and Coding (AMC) solutions; Vienna LTE simulator [6] appears as one of the most widely accepted solution. The second alternative usually gives a larger degree of flexibility, although some assumptions or simplifications are usually required; furthermore, there are works that are based on proprietary developments (in this case the use of Matlab is quite popular), while others use some of the few tools that have been made available, highlighting again the Vienna LTE Simulators [6]. On the third group, the choice that has gathered more attention is the `ns-3` platform [7], and the LTE-EPC Network Simulator (LENA) extension [8], which is in almost constant evolution. In this case, the most stringent limitation is the long simulation times, which are caused by the high level of detail that is added in the corresponding models. Table 1 provides a detailed analysis of some important characteristics to be considered. One of the limitations of the existing approaches is that they are not usually able to support relatively large and complex scenarios and if they were anyway used, the required simulation time would be unacceptable. Besides, existing solutions do not generally allow studying services evolution, nor the impact that different network techniques and solutions have on them.

Hence, the question is: what should a researcher do if he/she is interested in assessing the performance of a novel technique over a high-dense network deployment, comprising hundreds of access elements and users? According to our best knowledge there is not an answer to such question, and it is unlikely to find a one-fits-all solution. The Vienna LTE Simulator [6] is implemented in Matlab and it is rather focused on the lower layers, so it cannot appropriately model different service types (saturation or full-buffer scenarios are usually assumed) and the simulation is rather time-consuming, so the analysis do not usually

Table 1. Coverage of different parameters by analysis alternatives for wireless networks (LTE). A subjective ranking is established per parameter, filled circles mean good fitness while empty circles represent poor fitness

Parameter	Link level simulation	System level simulation	Network simulation
Description of the simulation characteristic that needs to be supported	*Detailed modeling of the lower layers, making it difficult to analyze solutions involving more than one source/destination pair*	*Most of the related literature use Matlab to carry out the analysis. Vienna LTE Simulator is one of the most relevant examples*	*ns-3, along with the LENA extension is one of the most relevant alternatives*
SCENARIO CHARACTERISTICS			
Scenario complexity: # of users and base stations	◑ Due to the great level of detail within this type of tools, the number of elements is usually low; typically one access element and a number of users [9]	◑ Some simplifications are usually considered, so that the number of elements that can be included in the experiments is usually larger	◔ Simulation time required to analyze large network deployments is usually unacceptable [10], without the use of parallelization techniques [11]
Time dimension: time that can be simulated, and possibility to keep track of services evolution	◑ Due to the computational load [12],simulated time is usually rather short, no need to keep track of services history	◔ The use of heavy development environments (Matlab) usually prevents from long simulated times	◔ Service evolution is usually considered; however, rather large computational time is required for long experiments
Accuracy: degree of precision of the models that are used in the different experiments	● The detailed modeling of the lower layer mechanisms is the main goal of link level simulators, which ensures a rather accurate outcome	◑ Some simplifications are usually taken, although existing works follow the recommendations of the 3GPP	◑ Although some simplifications are assumed, precise implementation of the protocols is used

(Continued)

Table 1. (*Continued*)

	Parameter	Link level simulation	System level simulation	Network simulation
TECHNOLOGICAL LANDSCAPE	*Architecture shift: possibility to add support to new networking paradigms: SDN and NFV*	As link-level solutions, they do not usually consider architectural issues, focusing on lower layers mechanisms and techniques	Some of the possibilities brought by novel networking functionalities (tighter cooperation schemes) can be usually modeled	Although it would require a large implementation effort, the integration of novel architectural approaches is usually possible
	Support for different technologies and solutions/techniques	They are rather limited to the functionalities that were included from the beginning. The integration of different technologies is quite complex	They usually have the flexibility to incorporate novel techniques and solutions due to some simplifications in the modeling of the physical layer	Broad network simulation platforms, such as ns-3, are rather flexible, and allow the integration of different technologies and novel techniques and solutions
	Services modeling. Saturation conditions and/or constant load is assumed	Very little attention is paid to the services modeling; the solutions usually focus on how the packets arrive at the lower layers	Basic services characteristics can be included, although it is more frequent to see constant load and/or full-buffer [13]	In network simulators real applications and services can be even used to generate the corresponding traffic
ADDITIONAL ISSUES	*Specific Vs. Generic purpose and learning curve*	Since their scope is usually very focused, link-level frameworks require a shorter learning curve	They are much more focused than network simulators, but not all its components might always be relevant	They are usually rather heavy frameworks, and it takes a long time before being able to analyze the required scenarios
	Use of complementary methodologies. Use of optimization techniques?	The usual goal is to analyze the performance of particular techniques, and the do not usually seek optimum performances	Although this is not within the objectives of this type of tools, optimization techniques could be integrated	The simulator architecture can be exploited to get an overall vision from which global optimization strategies might be executed

cover long time periods. The consequence is thus that several researches develop their own tools. This has some drawbacks, since most of the time put into the development is worthless from the point of view of the analysis that needs to be done and in addition, being quite ad-hoc solutions, the obtained results are not easily reproducible and integrated in other solutions.

In order to provide a better answer for such question, in this paper we introduce Generic Wireless Network System Modeler (GWNSyM), a flexible platform that allows easy-configuration and easy-analysis of rather large and complex system deployments, and that is specially focused on the evaluation of service performance when applying different network techniques. It has been designed and built with the main goal of being easily extended, with either new functionalities or strategies. We discuss its main design guidelines and some of its most relevant implementation features and we assess its feasibility, by carrying out an analysis comprising a highly dense access network and a large number of users.

The rest of this paper is structured as follows: Sect. 2 describes the main functionality of the developed tool, highlighting its most relevant implementation aspects. Then, Sect. 3 presents the overarching view of the scenario to be evaluated and the implemented network models; afterwards, the assessment of the proposed scenario will be discussed in Sect. 4. Finally Sect. 5 concludes the paper, providing and outlook of the future research lines we will pursue, exploiting the possibilities brought by the platform presented herewith.

2 Simulation Methodology

This section depicts the main principles of the methodology used by GWN-SyM, which, in short, carries out the scenario assessment in a step-wise manner. It evaluates consecutive snapshots (i.e., discrete time moments), by applying the models implemented over the corresponding network elements, so that the outcome of one snapshot feeds the following one. This allows capturing the system memory, which is specially relevant for analyzing the quality of services. We start by describing the overall simulation work-flow, to afterwards depict the implementation principles that have been added to the tool to facilitate its extensibility.

2.1 General Approach

The overall methodology can be seen as a single experiment, which represents the analysis of a particular scenario according to some specific settings. An experiment comprises two main loops: (1) the outer one iterates over a number of snapshots, in each of them the network state is updated, considering, among other aspects, the outcome of the previous snapshot; (2) the inner loop deals with enforcing the adequate network behavior, according to the implemented models.

This methodology is generic enough and it is therefore not constrained by a particular technology or access policy. To this end, the following two concepts have been introduced to ensure this abstraction level.

- Type: it establishes an archetype of the elements in the network. A *Type* defines a particular network element, ranging from operators to user devices, as well as its particular configuration. The instantiation of elements belonging to the same *Type*, according to the current configuration, defines the set of elements of such *Type* for the experiment. A *Type* can be configured to aggregate other *Types*, and all of them together are treated as an independent set. For instance, we can define a *Type* for an LTE cell, C, which is then aggregated to macro (M) or pico (P) eNodeBs. This would result in two sets of C type: the first one comprising macro eNodeBs cells, $M \leftarrow C$, and the second one having the cells aggregated to pico eNodeBs, $P \leftarrow C$.
- Action: it represents a particular model to be used over the scenario; they range from propagation models of a specific technology to operator access policies. Each action takes one or more sets of elements and they are sequentially executed during the evaluation of every snapshot. On the other hand, there might be actions that do not need to be applied at every snapshot, but they are only meaningful at the beginning/end of the experiment. We have thus defined two specific action categories: *Pre-Action* and *Post-Action*.

Algorithm 1. Overall work-flow

1: *Types* definition
2: Configuration load
3: Elements instantiation and aggregation
4: $T \leftarrow$ *All set types*
5: $A_{pre} \leftarrow$ *Pre-Actions*
6: $A \leftarrow$ *Actions*
7: $A_{post} \leftarrow$ *Post-Actions*
8: $i = 0$
9: $n \leftarrow$ *# Snapshots*
10: **for** $b \in A_{pre}$ **do**
11:     Apply pre-action $b(M_b \subseteq T)$
12: **end for**
13: **while** $i < n$ **do**
14:     **for** $a \in A$ **do**
15:         Apply action $s(M_s \subseteq T)$
16:     **end for**
17: **end while**
18: **for** $e \in A_{post}$ **do**
19:     Apply post-action $e(M_e \subseteq T)$
20: **end for**

Algorithm 1 illustrates the overall methodology. First, we define and instantiate the corresponding types, according to the current configuration. As was discussed before, the configuration may define the aggregation of some types, resulting in sets that are independently treated within the scenario. Once all the network elements have been instantiated, the *Pre-actions* are applied over the corresponding type; this is particular useful for network deployments, since they are just performed at the beginning of the experiment. Afterwards, the main loop, line 13, iterates over the sequence of snapshots, and the inner loop, line 14, sequentially applies the appropriate actions. Finally, the experiment finalizes by executing the post-actions over the corresponding types, for instance, to generate experiment traces and statistics. It is worth highlighting that actions are assumed to be stateless and, hence, the network state is kept within the network elements.

2.2 Implementation Principles

Once the overall methodology has been introduced, we discuss some implementation details, by illustrating the definition of a scenario. The framework implementation comprises a set of C++ libraries, leveraging generic and template-meta-programing (TMP) techniques, which have proved fundamental to provide the required abstraction level.

```
gnsm::System net_;
...
net_.AddType<User, UserConf>("USER");
net_.AddType<LteUe, LteUeConf>("LTE_UE", {Params});

net_.AddType<LteCell, LteCellConf>("CELL", {Params});
net_.AddType<LteEnb, LteEnbConf>("MACRO", {Params});
...
```

(a) Types definition

```
UserConf::ReadInnerConf(void) const
{
    return{{"LTE_UE", 1}}; // read from configuration
}
```

(b) Aggregation

Fig. 1. Example of element instantiations

The first step during the scenario description is the definition of *Types*. Figure 1 shows how different *Types* are defined and aggregated in an illustrative example. As can be seen in Fig. 1a, a name is given to a type, which is then defined with the C++ classes that implement the network element functionality and its configuration. Furthermore, we can pass a number of arguments to the configuration class, for example, the path to where the configuration file is located. Finally, the libraries also allow the aggregation of types, as defined by the current configuration. In the example shown in Fig. 1b, the *USER* type will keep one element belonging to the *LTE_UE* type.

Once the types are defined, the different actions that establish the network behavior are registered, identifying the elements that have to be passed around during the execution; Fig. 2 shows different ways of using the actions. It is worth noting that aggregated elements can be also passed around, by indicating the

```
net_.PreAction<MacroDeploymentr>({"MACRO"}, {Params.});
...
net_.Action<LteScan>({"USER", "MACRO"}, {Params.});
...
net_.PostAction<MacroLoad>({"MACRO::*::CELL"}, {Params.});
...
net_.Run();
```

Fig. 2. Example of action registrations

set where they have been inserted; for instance, MACRO::*::CELL would indicate that cells belonging to all macro base stations set will be passed to the MacroLoad action.

Besides the aforementioned details, the tool libraries have been implemented with the idea of fostering their re-usability. To this end, two main decision were taken: first, the tool libraries do not impose any inheritance constraint to the C++ classes for both types and actions, but minimal interface checking is performed at compilation time; on the other hand, a wrapping functionality has been added, enabling that some types can be passed to specific classes with a customized interface. These two aspects facilitate reusing legacy code of network models, in particular the implementation of actions.

3   Scenario of Interest

This section describes the main characteristics of the scenario that will be used to assess the feasibility of GWNSyM, as well as the different modules that have been implemented to appropriately model it.

The evaluation comprises a large dense urban LTE environment, where both macro and small cells are deployed, and different types of end users generate the corresponding traffic demand. The analysis that will be discussed in the Sect. 4 focuses on the downlink.

In order to show the capabilities of the GWNSyM framework, we have incorporated two different aspects, affecting both the system architecture and the access selection procedure, over the corresponding access network.

– **Cell clustering.** This feature is related to the use of NFV techniques in the so-called Cloud Radio Access Network (C-RAN) concept, where the eNodeB functionalities are moved to the cloud, to leverage a more centralized management of the corresponding resources.
– **CoMP - Joint Transmission.** We assume that access elements can exploit cooperation capabilities, so that a group of cells can use the same resources for a particular user. Note that the two aspects are related, since the NFV approach would facilitate these cooperation techniques.

In order to include the aforementioned functionalities, we can exploit the aggregation capabilities of the proposed framework. In this sense, access elements are grouped in clusters, so that each of them comprises one macro eNodeB and a configurable number of small cells. Furthermore, we assume that each cluster is managed by one Baseband Unit (BBU), and we impose computational constraints, so that we effectively limit the number of bearers each cluster is able to manage.

Concerning traffic, the service model does not assume saturation (full-buffer) conditions, and resources just need to be granted when a user has an active service, according to the defined access policy; both aspects are detailed below.

3.1 Services Modeling

As was already said, and for a particular time (snapshot), users just require connectivity if they have an active service. During a single experiment, a user can initiate a number of sessions of a service; if any of them are rejected (or dropped), we assume that it is not recovered. Hence, if a service is not satisfied at a particular snapshot, such particular service session is not considered until a new one is started; this feature, which allows keeping the history of the simulation, can be exploited to reproduce the very same traffic patterns in different experiments. In order to model this behavior, we have implemented a state-machine with the states described below.

- **Idle**: this is the initial state of a service, corresponding to a situation in which connectivity is not required.
- **Active**: the service has an ongoing active session and it is connected.
- **Rejected**: the service reaches this state when the network cannot allocate resources to satisfy its demand when it is initially started. This state will be kept throughout the session (its duration is known a-priori), to move to *Idle* state afterwards (until a new session is started again).
- **Dropped**: a service is considered as *Dropped* once it has already started but it cannot finish successfully. As in the previous case, this state is maintained until the current session finishes.

It is worth noting that *Dropped* and *Rejected* states, despite modeling similar circumstances, have a different impact on the perceived Quality of Experience (QoE), since it is usually considered that dropping a service has a much more negative impact on the QoE.

3.2 Access Selection and Resource Allocation

When a user has a specific traffic demand for a particular service, the access selection action is executed to satisfy such demand. In the scenario that we have assumed for this work, we are analyzing the benefits of CoMP techniques, and therefore a set of different cells are selected to provide connectivity for a particular user/service request.

The process basically works as follows: we sort the cells according to the received power, Reference Signal Received Power (RSRP), which is established using the propagation model that was previously configured (we are exploiting the ones established by the 3GPP specifications). Afterwards, according to the number of cells a user is able to connect to (configuration parameter of the CoMP functionality), those with the highest RSRP are selected, and the number of required resources is calculated. If one of the previously selected cells is not able to allocate such number of resources, it is discarded, and the next in the list is then selected.

Access elements manage a number of resources, corresponding to the system bandwidth that is configured during the scenario setup, following the characteristics of the LTE-OFDMA scheme. In this sense, assuming that user i selects a set of cells $\mathcal{J}$ for a given demand D_i, the number of resource blocks that need to be allocated is given by: $N_{\text{RB}i|\mathcal{J}} = \frac{D_i}{b_{\text{RB}} \cdot S_{i|\mathcal{J}}}$; where b_{RB} corresponds to the bandwidth of each resource block, and $S_{i|\mathcal{J}}$ represents the link spectral efficiency, which is calculated as shown in Eq. 1 where both b_{eff} and SINR_{eff} are system parameters, as indicated in [14]. Finally, the Signal to Interference plus Noise Ratio (SINR) is calculated with Eq. 2, where γ_{mk} is the power received by user m from cell k.

$$S_{i|\mathcal{J}} = b_{\text{eff}}\eta \log_2\left[1 + \frac{\text{SINR}_{i|\mathcal{J}}}{\text{SINR}_{\text{eff}}}\right] \tag{1}$$

$$SINR_{i|\mathcal{J}} = \frac{\sum\limits_{j \in \mathcal{J}} \gamma_{ij}}{N_0 + \sum\limits_{k \notin \mathcal{J}} \gamma_{ik}} \tag{2}$$

4 Scenario Assessment

Once the general components and functionalities of the scenario have been presented, this section discusses the results that were obtained with GWNSyM, paying special attention to network load and Quality of Service (QoS) levels.

The scenario consists of a two-tier LTE network. The first layer corresponds to tri-sector macro eNodeBs, deployed following an hexagonal pattern, while the second layer comprises small eNodeBs, characterized by a lower transmission power. The main scenario settings can be found in Table 2. Besides, from an architectural point of view, we assume that a BBU manages one cluster, which contains one macro and a number of small cells. We furthermore consider that the front-haul connection (from the LTE cells to the BBU) has un-limited capacity (i.e. fiber connection) but processing capacity constraints are imposed in the BBU, so that only a number of cells can be processed at the same time. Concerning propagation models and antenna patterns, we have implemented those defined by the 3GPP for urban areas and different cell sizes [15,16]. As shown in Table 2 the scenario considers the possibility of having non-line-of-sight between the users and the corresponding cells.

Users are running two different types of services: a light one, which could resemble an application such as web browsing; and a heavier one, which requires 1 Mbps, that would mimic a video service. Both types of services follow an

Table 2. Simulation setting

LTE layout FDD 2x20MHz @2.1 GHz	
Macro layer	ISD 500 m, 7 tri-sector sites
	Max. tx. power 46 dBm
	Antenna GAin 15dBi, 15 down-tilt
Pico layer	Random Location
	Max. tx. power 37 dBm
	Omni-antenna
UE	DL NF 7 dB
	Rx. Gain 7 dB
LTE layer	L (dB) as a function of the distance $d[m]$
Macro$_{\mathbf{NLOS}}$	$139.1033 + 39.0864 * (log_{10}(d) - 3)$
Macro$_{\mathbf{LOS}}$	$36.2995 + 22 * log_{10}(d)$ if $d < 328.42$
	$40 * log_{10}(d) - 10.7953$ if $d > 328.42$
Small$_{\mathbf{NLOS}}$	$145.48 + 37.5 * (log_{10}(d) - 3)$
Small$_{\mathbf{LOS}}$	$103.8 + 20.9 * (log_{10}(d) - 3)$
	LOS probability as a function of the distance d $[m]$
Macro	$P_{LOS} = \min(\frac{18}{d}, 1) \cdot (1 - e^{\frac{-d}{36}}) + e^{\frac{-d}{36}}$
Small	$P_{LOS} = 0.5 - \min(0.5, 5 \cdot e^{\frac{-156}{d}}) + \min(0.5, 5 \cdot e^{(\frac{-d}{30})})$

Service	Traffic (Kbps)	ON/OFF (s)	% users
Heavy	1000	300/600	60
Light	128	120/60	40

ON-OFF model whose parameters are indicated in Table 2. Furthermore, 500 users are deployed, and they follow random way-point mobility pattern, with a speed that is randomly selected within $(1, 3)$ $\frac{m}{s}$; hence, the position in one snapshot is not independent from the previous ones. It is worth noting that in order to ease the evaluation, we have restricted it to those cells within the central cluster, while the rest of cells in the scenario are considered as interfering ones. It is worth noting that, although the scenario includes two different services, only one of them is active at each user, according to the statistics shown in Table 2.

In the following, we will discuss a number of illustrative results that can be obtained with GWNSyM, for different configurations, in terms of network load and service performance. In order to ensure the statistical validity of the results, 10 independent runs have been executed per configuration, each of them lasting one hour (3600 s.), with a step of 10 s. Hence, 360 snapshots are evaluated in each experiment.

First, we study the impact that different CoMP configurations (i.e. maximum number of cells a user can be simultaneously connected to) have over the cells

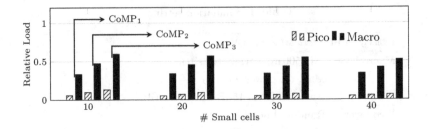

Fig. 3. Cell load for different number of deployed pico-cells

load, increasing as well the small cell density; in all cases, we assume that the BBU has unlimited processing capacities. In the different figures, the CoMP configuration is indicated by a sub-index, so that $CoMP_n$ would actually mean that users connect to n cells.

Figure 1 shows the average relative load of the cells for the two base station types. As can be seen, most of the traffic is carried by the macro layer. On the other hand, we can observe that the deployment of more small-cells does not yield a strong impact, since we do not see a remarkable difference when either 10 or 40 small-cells are deployed.

In order to assess the influence that CoMP configurations and network density have on the service QoS, Fig. 4 shows the probability of a service to be successful, dropped or rejected. If we compare the results for both types of service, we can conclude that light connections (with less stringent capacity requirements) are more likely to finish successfully, in particular for smaller network densities. Furthermore, we can also see that it is more likely for a service to be dropped than rejected; this would correspond to a situation in which the service started with a pico-cell and then, if the user moved out of its coverage, there were not available resources at the macro base station to keep the service active. Finally, if we look at the influence of CoMP configurations, the results show that they does not have a relevant impact on the service performance.

In our last result, we are interested in assessing the impact of having limited processing capabilities on the BBU. For that, we start from the scenario with the highest density (40 small cells) and Fig. 5 shows the QoS when some of those small cells are switched off. In particular, we incorporate a smart switching-off policy, discarding those with the lowest accumulated RSRP (values measured at the end-users). This rule is applied for every snapshot during the experiment. If we compare the performance obtained when switching off those cells with the one achieved earlier (that would actually mimic the case where the cells to be switched off are randomly selected), we can observe that the service performance is improved, more notably for the heavy services. For instance, if we compare the values when switching-off 10 small-cells (30 are still available) with the ones that were previously see for 30 cells, we can see a gain of around 5%.

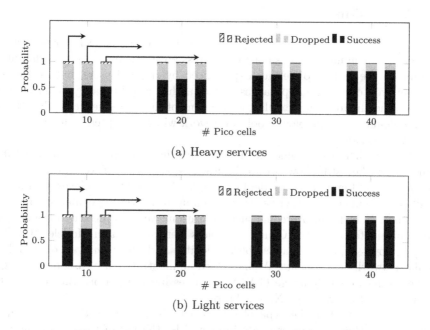

(a) Heavy services

(b) Light services

Fig. 4. Service performance vs. number of small cells

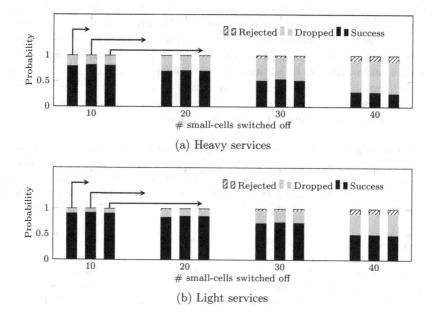

(a) Heavy services

(b) Light services

Fig. 5. Service performance vs. number of switched-off small cells, when 40 small-cells are initially deployed

5   Conclusion

The advent of the 5G is broadening the research landscape of cellular networks. The scientific community does not just address novel technologies, or techniques to improve the quality of service experienced by the end users, but new axis, such as novel topological approaches and/or architectural paradigms, have been added to the already complex playground. One of the consequences is that there is not a *de-facto* methodology/tool/framework widely accepted to analyze such complex scenarios.

Although there exist some alternatives that have reached more momentum than others, they still show several limitations, especially if we aim at analyzing complex and large network deployments and/or we want to leverage a more detailed modeling of the services, as was seen in the survey-type analysis that we carried out. In order to overcome such limitations we have presented the design and implementation of the Generic Wireless Network System Modeler (GWN-SyM), a novel approach that enables a flexible and quick analysis of complex cellular network deployments. We have used an illustrative use case, over a large HetNet scenario, to challenge GWNSyM, assessing the performance of CoMP techniques and leveraging a NFV solution.

We have seen that the type of service clearly influences the performance results, while they are not strongly impacted by the use of CoMP techniques. Furthermore, we also assessed that a selective cell switching-off technique would actually be beneficial from the point of view of the performance.

The GWNSyM framework opens a broad range of possibilities and we are planning to exploit it in our near-term research. We are in particular interested in fostering the use of optimization techniques to set a reference level to compare the performance of different access selection policies, and resource management techniques and solutions. In addition, we are also planning to make the whole framework available to the scientific community as open source. The idea is to allow other researchers to use GWNSyM and, at the same time, benefit from their feedback to continuously improve and broaden it.

Acknowledgements. This work has been supported by the Spanish Government (Ministerio de Economía y Competitividad, Fondo Europeo de Desarrollo Regional, FEDER) by means of the projects COSAIF, Connectivity as a Service: Access for the Internet of the Future (TEC2012-38754-C02-01), and ADVICE, Dynamic provisioning of connectivity in high density 5G wireless scenarios (TEC2015- 71329-C2-1-R)).

References

1. C. and/or its affiliates, Cisco visual networking index: global mobile data traffic forecast update, 20152020 white paper, Feb 2016. http://www.cisco.com/c/en/us/solutions/collateral/service-provider/visual-networking-index-vni/mobile-white-paper-c11-520862.html
2. Bhushan, N., Li, J., Malladi, D., Gilmore, R., Brenner, D., Damnjanovic, A., Sukhavasi, R., Patel, C., Geirhofer, S.: Network densification: the dominant theme for wireless evolution into 5g. IEEE Commun. Mag. **52**(2), 82–89 (2014)

3. Boccardi, F., Heath, R.W., Lozano, A., Marzetta, T.L., Popovski, P.: Five disruptive technology directions for 5g. IEEE Commun. Mag. **52**(2), 74–80 (2014)
4. Agiwal, M., Roy, A., Saxena, N.: Next generation 5g wireless networks: a comprehensive survey. IEEE Commun. Surv. Tutor. **PP**(99), 1–1 (2016)
5. Peng, M., Li, Y., Zhao, Z., Wang, C.: System architecture and key technologies for 5g heterogeneous cloud radio access networks. IEEE Netw. **29**(2), 6–14 (2015)
6. Mehlführer, C., Ikuno, J.C., Šimko, M., Schwarz, S., Wrulich, M., Rupp, M.: The vienna lte simulators - enabling reproducibility in wireless communications research. EURASIP J. Adv. Signal Process. **2011**(1), 1–14 (2011). http://dx.doi.org/10.1186/1687-6180-2011-29
7. The ns-3 network simulator. http://www.nsnam.org/
8. Piro, G., Baldo, N., Miozzo, M.: An lte module for the ns-3 network simulator. In: Proceedings of the 4th International ICST Conference on Simulation Tools and Techniques, ser. SIMUTools 2011. ICST, Brussels, Belgium, Belgium: ICST (Institute for Computer Sciences, Social-Informatics and Telecommunications Engineering), pp. 415–422 (2011). http://dl.acm.org/citation.cfm?id=2151054.2151129
9. Schneider, C., Thom, R.S.: Evaluation of LTE link-level performance with closed loop spatial multiplexing in a realistic urban macro environment. In: 2012 6th European Conference on Antennas and Propagation (EUCAP), pp. 2725–2729, March 2012
10. Fujimoto, R.M., Perumalla, K., Park, A., Wu, H., Ammar, M.H., Riley, G.F.: Large-scale network simulation: how big? how fast? In: 11th IEEE/ACM International Symposium on Modeling, Analysis and Simulation of Computer Telecommunications Systems, MASCOTS 2003, pp. 116–123, October 2003
11. Pelkey, J., Riley, G.: Distributed simulation with mpi in ns-3. In: Proceedings of the 4th International ICST Conference on Simulation Tools and Techniques, ser. SIMUTools 2011. ICST, Brussels, Belgium, Belgium: ICST (Institute for Computer Sciences, Social-Informatics and Telecommunications Engineering), pp. 410–414 (2011). http://dl.acm.org/citation.cfm?id=2151054.2151128
12. Ikuno, J.C.: LTE Link- and System-Level Simulation. Wiley, New York (2011). http://dx.doi.org/10.1002/9781119954705.ch11
13. Taranetz, M., Blazek, T., Kropfreiter, T., Mller, M.K., Schwarz, S., Rupp, M.: Runtime precoding: enabling multipoint transmission in lte-advanced system-level simulations. IEEE Access **3**, 725–736 (2015)
14. Mogensen, P., Na, W., Kovacs, I., Frederiksen, F., Pokhariyal, A., Pedersen, K., Kolding, T., Hugl, K., Kuusela, M.: Lte capacity compared to the shannon bound. In: IEEE 65th conference on Vehicular Technology Conference, VTC 2007 Spring, pp. 1234–1238, April 2007
15. 3GPP, Technical specification group radio access network; further advancements for e-utra, 3rd Generation Partnership Project (3GPP), TR 36.814. http://www.3gpp.org/dynareport/36814.htm
16. 3GPP, Technical specification group radio access network; evolved universal terrestrial radio access (e-utra); radio frequency (rf) system scenarios, 3rd Generation Partnership Project (3GPP), TR 36.942. http://www.3gpp.org/dynareport/36942.htm

Distributed Computing of Management Data in a Telecommunications Network

Ville Kojola[1(✉)], Shubham Kapoor[2], and Kimmo Hätönen[3]

[1] Center for Ubiquitous Computing, University of Oulu, Oulu, Finland
ville.kojola@student.oulu.fi
[2] Department of Computer Science, University of Helsinki, Helsinki, Finland
shubham.kapoor@helsinki.fi
[3] Nokia Bell Labs, Espoo, Finland
kimmo.hatonen@nokia-bell-labs.com

Abstract. In this paper, we propose a concept for distributed Management Plane data computation and its delivery in the cellular networks. Architecture for proposed concept is described. Calculation of Key Performance Indicators is distributed to the cellular network edge, close to the managed network elements which reduces the volume of the Management Plane traffic. In this concept, further aggregation and refinement of data is done in the nodes located in the operator's cloud, close to consumers of Management Plane data. Distribution of calculation to the network edge reduces load at the network operator's central database. This paper presents an analysis to the benefits of the proposed concept. Efficient on-demand type streaming data delivery model allows network management functions to be plugged in to receive Management Plane data directly without database access. A demonstrator system has been implemented. The feasibility of the implementation is evaluated in terms of resource consumption and latency.

Keywords: Cellular network · Key performance indicator · Network management

1 Introduction

Cellular network elements provide a wide array of performance metrics called performance counters. The performance counters and the Key Performance Indicators (KPIs) calculated from them are essential in Performance Management (PM) of a cellular network. Network management systems collect data to the operation centers, where it is monitored and analysed to detect any defects or suboptimal states in performance or service quality [12,17].

With the usage growth and development in technology, the number of network elements in cellular networks is growing. The recent developments in Fourth Generation (4G) cellular network has been towards flat Radio Access Network (RAN) hierarchies which simplifies network but also removes hierarchical processing of PM data which was there in earlier cellular generations [15].

© ICST Institute for Computer Sciences, Social Informatics and Telecommunications Engineering 2017
R. Agüero et al. (Eds.): MONAMI 2016, LNICST 191, pp. 146–159, 2017.
DOI: 10.1007/978-3-319-52712-3_11

A centralized processing of this PM data is thus required for monitoring network, which makes centralized models a popular choice for monitoring PM data [7].

For effective performance management and emerging concepts such as Self Organizing Networks (SON) [3] there is a need for higher frequency performance reporting by network elements. In a centrally operated cellular network these factors contribute to a large Management Plane (M-Plane) data volumes and high computational complexity. In past, semantic compression and local processing have been proposed as means to distribute computation in network management and to reduce network management traffic [7].

The motivation of this paper is to demonstrate the concepts of local processing and streaming of data in a telecommunication environment and to show how these concepts could help to solve the problem for processing high volumes of management plane data that is about to arise in cellular networks due to its evolution. This paper presents a demonstrator system, which implements local processing and refinement of cellular network performance reports in near-real-time. The refined or aggregated performance reports are directly and instantly transferred to network management functions in on-demand streams.

Section 2 of this paper presents the concept of our proposed solution. Section 3 presents the architecture of the demonstrator system. In Sect. 4 we discuss about experiments conducted on our system. In Sect. 5 we discuss about achievements of our implemented system with respect to current systems and discuss future direction of our research. Finally, we conclude our paper in Sect. 6.

2   Concept

The objective of proposed concept is twofold: to minimize the amount of transferred data and to maximize the relative amount of up-to date information in it. We propose two major changes to telecommunications networks management systems to achieve this: do the needed computation close to the place where the data is generated and let the data flow directly to applications analyzing it in real time. These changes are inline with recent development in Mobile Edge Computing (MEC) paradigm [2].

To do the distributed processing and to transfer its results to management system applications, we introduce three types of components that are embedded in the network: Data Fetchers next to data sources, Data Switches in the operator's core cloud and Data Hubs next to the Consumers of M-Plane data, i.e., OSS applications (see Fig. 1). This set-up corresponds to a publish-subscribe system [10], where Data Fetchers are data publishers and Data Hubs are subscribers.

A Data Fetcher is a component that does the processing of the data next to the place where it is being generated. In Fig. 1 that is shown to be next to each Base Station. Data Fetcher publishes the computation results to Data Switches that act as data brokers in this publish-subscribe architecture.

Data Switch is responsible for routing data coming from Data Fetchers to those Data Hubs that are serving applications that have requested the data. Data Switch does this so that data flows are not unnecessarily duplicated in

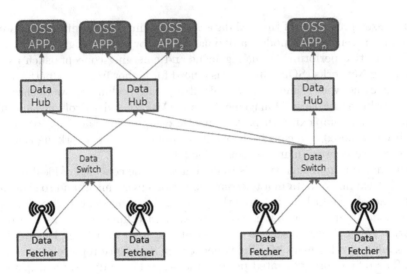

Fig. 1. Elements of the proposed concept. The novel elements of the concept are the Data Fetcher, the Data Switch and the Data Hub.

the network and the content is published only once by a Data Fetcher. In Fig. 1 there are two Data Switches, of which the left one is routing data from two Data Fetchers towards OSS applications 1, 2 and 3, and the right one transfers the data flows from two Data Fetchers to the same applications but also mirrors those flows to OSS application n in upper right corner.

Data Hub serves applications that make requests for data. In Fig. 1 three Data Hubs are shown serving four OSS applications. A Data Hub has an interface, to which an application can send a subscription, in which it specifies what content, from where and how often it wants to receive from the network. The Data Hub sets up the corresponding data collection and processing in appropriate Data Fetchers or, if the similar request has been placed already by someone else, mirroring of the data flow to Data Hub where the request was made. When the Data Hub receives the data, it delivers that to applications via specified interface.

2.1 Streams

The system aims to optimize data collection and delivery from a managed device, such as base stations, by implementing a streaming pattern, where consumers only needs to subscribe to a stream to start receiving data. Inspiration is drawn from the publish/subscribe communication pattern [10] and Information-centric networking [18], which abstract away from the traditional point-to-point connectivity. Publish/subscribe pattern reduces interaction required in collecting the data by removing the need for repeated data queries [9]. Publish/subscribe allows publisher and subscriber to be fully decoupled in time, space and synchronization, which leads to increased scalability [10]. Information-centric networking trades host centric view into a one where network mediates named content based on the interests advertised by the nodes [18].

Two methods are used to optimize data collection, assuming that data needs to be collected repeatedly and that multiple consumers require the data. Firstly, request interaction is minimized with the subscription pattern. A stream of some specific data is created when a consumer makes a subscription for the data. This request starts data processing and delivery in a Data Fetcher, which will publish stream content either sporadically or periodically, depending on the type of the request. No further requests or queries are required and the Data Fetcher continues publishing stream content on its own without the need for further interaction.

Secondly, multiple consumers may subscribe to the same stream, which minimizes the need to send duplicate queries to a Data Fetcher. Therefore, the Data Fetcher needs to send the same data only once using its limited bandwidth resources. Further replication of the data is done in the Data Switch in operator cloud where abundant network resources are expected. A Data Fetcher can publish the data with minimal delay, because it is in control of the publishing and does not depend on polling from other elements. Consumers are decoupled from Data Fetchers and each other, but they can still receive the subscribed data with low latency.

Ideas are lent from the publish/subscribe pattern, which can also be part of the implementation. However some changes are made. Decouplings provided by publish/subscribe system are limited to some extent: Data Fetchers will publish only after a stream has been created (no full decoupling in time) and streams may be tied to some specific Data Fetchers (no full decoupling in space). Subscription model used is based on the idea from information-centric networking of named content which can be requested on demand.

Delivery mechanism to consumers is also simplified. Instead of consumers needing to poll for updates and a database struggling to fulfil those requests, a Data Hub can immediately forward each new data record it receives to subscribed consumers. Subscribing, streaming and data replication are depicted in Fig. 2. First, in quadrant (a) in upper left corner, an OSS application places an order for some data coming from all three Data Fetchers in the figure. In quadrant (b) in upper right corner, the system sets up streams of data flowing from all Data Fetchers to the application that subscribed for it. Later another OSS application makes the same request as is depicted in lower left quadrant (c). This makes Data Switch in the middle to mirror established flows to the Data Hub serving that OSS application. This is depicted in lower right quadrant (d) of Fig. 2.

2.2 Distributed Computing

As mentioned earlier, the system aims to reduce the management traffic and the need for centralized computation of the management data in telecommunications network. These two goals are considered in regards to two points of interest, which are identified as potential bottlenecks. Firstly, management traffic is mainly of concern in the link between the network element and the operator

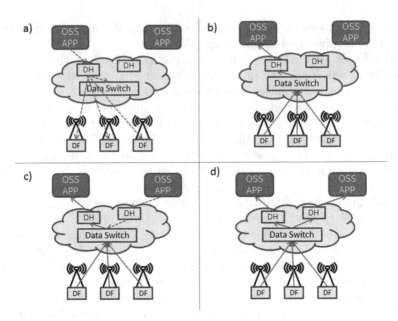

Fig. 2. Stream initialization and delivery. In stream subscription a Data Hub forwards stream initialization request to Data Fetchers. Stream contents are delivered through Data Switch. Pre-existing streams can be replicated to other Data Hubs from Data Switch.

cloud, because of the assumption of a limited bandwidth. Secondly, computational concerns relate to the centralized OSS applications, which may need to process large volumes of data. By moving computation from a central OSS application to Data Fetchers at the edges of the network, the data can be refined already at the source [16].

There are various kinds of data that the network operator collects from a network element. [12,17] Distributed computing of that data close to the source could be leveraged in many ways. One example is raw counter data that is measured by the network element. The network element measures thousands of counters, which need to be collected periodically and then KPIs are calculated from the counters. This calculation is done in the central server before inserting KPIs to the central database. From there, the KPI data can be used to manage the network element using the closed-loop principle [5,13].

KPIs are calculated from the counter values by using simple formulas where one or more counter values are summed, subtracted, multiplied by a constant or divided. By computing all the needed KPIs in the Data Fetcher, the data to be transferred can be reduced in volume. The reduction depends on the complexity of KPI formulas used. Some may consist of only one counter while others may consist of a dozen. A KPI consisting of 6 counters roughly reduces the data volume needed to transfer to a sixth. Equations 1 and 2 shows equation for a typical KPI calculation from raw counter values [4].

$$InitialEPSBEstabSR = \times \frac{\sum_{cause} RRC.SuccConnEstab.[cause]}{\sum_{cause} RRC.AttConnEstab.[cause]}$$

$$\times \frac{\sum RRC.SuccConnEstab}{\sum SuccConnAtt}$$

$$\times \frac{\sum_{QCI} SAEB : NbrSuccEstabInit.[QCI]}{\sum_{QCI} SAEB.NbrAttEstabInit.[QCI]} \times 100$$

$$(1)$$

$$MobilitySuccessRate_{QCI=x} = \frac{HO.ExeSucc}{HO.ExeAtt}$$

$$\times \frac{HO.PrepSucc.QCI_{QCI=x}}{HO.PrepAtt.QCI_{QCI=x}} \times 100[\%]$$

$$(2)$$

3   Implementation

The system implements a middleware between the OSS applications and the base stations. As described earlier, the main components of the system are: Data Fetchers, Data Switches and Data Hubs. For controlling the system, there are also Global Repositories, that help in coordinating subscriptions in the system. The system architecture is depicted in Fig. 3. The Data Hubs communicate directly with data consumers, i.e., OSS applications. They receive requests from the applications and forward resulting data to those. Each Data Fetcher is paired with a base station and communicates directly with the base station. Communication streams, such as performance data streams or log streams, are relayed through a Data Switch layer from Data Fetchers to Data Hubs. Data Switch layer is a network of Data Switches, publisher/subscriber brokers, which temporarily caches data and delivers it efficiently.

We chose to use Apache Kafka [6,11] as the Data Switch layer. It includes many features and functions that are needed in our system. We interfaced it with base stations and OSS applications by Data Fetcher and Data Hub layers. We do management of data streams and book keeping of their subscribers by using a combination of Apache Zookeeper [6] and our Global Repositories.

3.1   Data Fetcher

Data Fetcher is the element that resides at the network edge close to a network element. The computing environment of Data Fetcher is characterized by limited CPU, RAM, bandwidth and disk resources. Data Fetcher can be in one-to-one relation or one-to-many relation to managed network elements. Close proximity to network elements reduces network latency and allows Data Fetcher to minimize the network load resulting from the transfer of data. Data Fetcher consist of Fetcher and Sender. Fetcher receives requests for streams and fetches data

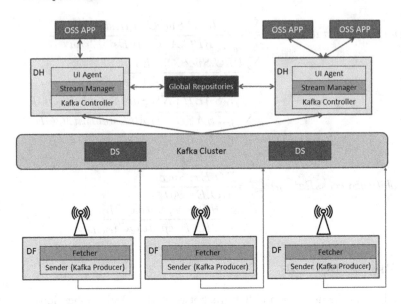

Fig. 3. System architecture. Data Switches are implemented as Apache Kafka cluster. Data Fetcher and Data Hub consist of subcomponents. Sender and Kafka controller contain Apache Kafka producer and consumer clients.

from managed network element it is connected to. Fetcher fetches raw counter data. Sender is a Kafka producer client which publishes stream contents to Kafka broker.

Based on the consumer requests Data Fetcher receives stream requests from Data Hubs. Requests can, for example, initiate collecting and processing of data or cancel it. Start request contains list of names of KPIs that need to be collected. For each KPI name a script is started which consumes counters and produces a KPI value. When the Data Fetcher collects a new set of counters it forwards the relevant counters to KPI scripts which then calculate the KPI values. KPI values for a topic are then grouped together and published to Kafka. Cancel request stops all processes involved in producing a particular stream.

Data Fetcher acts as an interface to this network element data so that no OSS application needs to directly request the data from the network element, but all the data that is needed in the process of network operation is fetched by the Data Fetcher. The data that has been fetched is rapidly forwarded by the Data Fetcher to Data Switch, so that the data does not need to be stored for long on Data Fetcher and is fresh when it reaches OSS applications.

Before the data is sent, it can be processed in the Data Fetcher. Volume of the data can be reduced by refining it to a format that better fits OSS application or operator needs, such as calculating key performance indicator from the raw counter data. Refining the data at the Data Fetcher reduces the amount of calculation needed at the center of the operator cloud.

3.2   Data Hub

Data Hub resides in the network operator cloud. The computing environment of Data Hub is characterized by sufficient hardware and network resource. Data Hub consists of UI Agent, Stream Manager and Kafka Controller. Kafka Controller manages creation and deletion of Kafka topics. Kafka Controller communicates with Global Repositories to synchronize subscription counts by Data Hubs to topics. Kafka Controller also embeds Kafka consumer. Stream Manager corresponds to Fetcher in DF and can be used to further aggregate data, for example by geography. UI Agent is the consumer side interface of DH, which serves requests by consumers and delivers stream contents to the consumers. Redundancy of Data Hub instances is possible. Data Hub receives and serves requests made by consumers by doing book keeping in Global Repositories and forwarding requests to appropriate Data Fetchers.

Requests can be either of stream subscription type or of one-off request-response type. Traditional request-response model can be used to pull data from Data Fetchers on-demand. Stream subscription subscribes a consumer to regular or irregular stream of packets from one or more Data Fetchers which the Data Hub delivers to the consumer.

Data delivery in the streaming model is optimized by reducing the amount of communication required between the Data Hub and Data Fetcher. A stream is started when a Data Hub issues a start command to one or more Data Fetchers. When the stream is started the stream delivery continues Data Hub and Data Fetchers decoupled. Multiple consumers can receive the same streamed data through the same Data Hub. Multiple Data Hubs can also receive same data from the same Data Fetchers, yet Data Fetcher only needs to send the data once.

3.3   Data Switch

Data Switch is a publish/subscribe broker residing in the operator cloud. In our implementation it is a Kafka broker and we implement our data streams with Kafka topics. Task of broker is to deliver stream contents from a Data Fetcher to one or more Data Hubs. Data published by Data Fetcher to a Data Switch is available to Data Hubs and consumers from Data Switches so that direct requests to the Data Fetcher can be limited.

3.4   Coordination

Information about Data Fetchers, Data Hubs and running streams is stored in Global Repositories. Global Repositories contains the global view of the components running in the system and is used to coordinate the different requests. When a consumer requests a stream the involved Data Hub will communicate with Global Repositories to decide whether a request needs to be sent to a Data Fetcher or the stream already exists and can be subscribed to in the Data Switches.

4   Experiments

The feasibility of the proposed system is measured in an experimental setup. In the experimental configuration 12 Data Fetcher instances are run in separate virtual machines of a cloud environment. Each virtual machine has 1 GB of RAM and a 2400 MHz dual core processor. In the experiment the virtual machines are not communicating with actual network elements, but are replaying recorded M-Plane data of real LTE Cells which are the part of live LTE network hosted by Nokia for research and development purposes. ZooKeeper and Kafka broker are deployed on a separate virtual machine. Data Hubs receive data from the Data Fetchers through the Kafka broker. Data Fetchers produce two streams of data. One to measure the resource consumption of the Data Fetcher and the other to emulate management data computing and collection. The usage of network, CPU and memory resources by Data Fetchers are monitored to evaluate the feasibility of the Data Fetcher and distributed management data computation concepts.

Data Fetchers were set to produce different numbers of KPIs. Resource utilization in each case was recorded. Mean, median and maximum values for each resource statistic were calculated for each Data Fetcher instance. By analyzing the results the resource requirements to produce KPIs can be estimated.

Data Hub was installed on a separate virtual machine with 4GB of RAM and 2400 MHz dual core processor. KPIs from base stations could be requested by operator/consumer in which he is interested. Based on the request Data Hubs subscribe to Kafka topics. Current network Performance data which we had was sufficient to calculate 220 KPIs.

We thus created one consumer which subscribed to different number of KPIs for different Data Fetchers. The number of KPIs requested for different Data Fetchers increased linearly from 20 KPIs to 220 KPIs. This consumer also subscribed for resource metrics of each Data Fetchers. Resource metrics were reported on each Data Fetchers using Linux utility Collectl [1]. Once these Resource consumption metrics were generated on Data Fetcher, they were streamed to the consumer using our system. Hence we got Resource consumption metrics of each Data Fetchers at a single place to analyze Data Fetcher performance.

Raw real network performance data were replayed in each Data Fetcher for 24 h, while each Data Fetcher was calculating different number of KPIs from this data. Resource metrics of all Data Fetchers were analyzed for this period and statistical data was extracted from it.

This experiment gave us interesting performance insights of our concept. We analyzed Resource metrics of Data Fetchers such as CPU utilization, Memory Utilization and network stats for all Data Fetchers. CPU consumption increased almost linearly with number of KPIs subscribed. We got mean and median CPU usage figure of about 22% and 21.0046% respectively for Data Fetcher with all 220 KPIs subscribed.

There was relatively higher CPU consumption at all Data Fetchers when streaming was started but that could be regarded as a startup overhead as CPU utilization settled back from that peak value. Free, Buffered and Cached memory for each Data Fetchers were analyzed and provided similar findings that free memory was decreasing with amount of KPIs subscribed. Plots in Fig. 4 shows variation of CPU Utilization and Free Memory with number of KPIs subscribed.

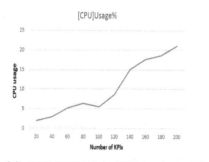
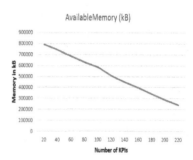

(a) CPU Utilization VS Number of KPIs

(b) Available Memory VS Number of single KPI subscription topics

Fig. 4. CPU utilization and free memory distribution of a Data Fetcher with the number of single KPI subscription topics.

High frequency performance reporting is necessary in optimizing the future mobile networks. Low end-to-end delay was considered a vital part of the implementation.

We calculated latency of our proposed solution and studied its variation with the number of Kafka topics. We wanted to find out what kind of topic set-up would be optimal to implement a data stream. For measuring latency we installed Data Hub on same machine in which Data Fetcher was installed. This was done in order to get precise latency figures. Topics subscriptions to same machine's Data Fetcher were made. Time difference between publishing of data at Data Fetchers and receiving of this data which has traversed entire network was measured. Single topics which subscribed for multiple KPIs and individual topic per individual KPI were created. Latency figures for each topics were then measured separately.

We noticed that when a stream is started the initial latency will be high and is an outlier, but it then settles down to a "steady state" where latency figures mostly stays in the same range. Since these performance management data streams would be long lived, we are more interested in these steady state latency figures. Hence we removed initial reading, which was an outlier, from our latency records. Latency was higher with one KPI per topic scenarios. Largest recorded steady state latency in the experiment was with scenario when 200 KPIs were subscribed, with each KPI having a separate topic. In this case latency at 99.99 percentile was 2.8274 s while the median latency was 0.932 s. Average Round Trip Time (RTT) between Data Switch and Data Fetcher using ping was measured at 3.665 ms. Figure 5 shows percentile graph for variation of latency figures with different topics in the steady state.

Overall the end-to-end delay of the implementation appeared low and suitable for near-real time reporting.

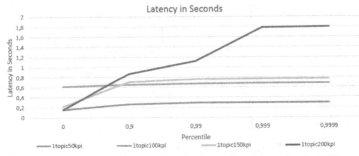

(a) Latency distribution for single topic with multiple KPIs

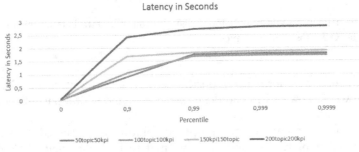

(b) Latency distribution for one KPI per topic

Fig. 5. Latency distribution with different number of topics. In the single topic case, all calculated KPI values are sent in the same stream. In the KPI per topic case multiple separate streams are used.

5   Discussion and Future Directions

In this section we will discuss briefly the related work and existing models in the telecommunication management systems and achievements of our implemented system against them. We also discuss about some future directions for our work.

In their paper [16] Simões et al. compared five different telecommunication management system models ranging from mobile agents model to static centralized model based on SNMP [8]. This paper explored benefits of mobility, locality and distribution in different models. Models which were explored were the Static Centralized Model, the Migratory Model, the Master/Worker Model, the Static Delegated Model and the Migratory Delegated Model. The performance of these models were estimated and measured as the time needed to complete an operation. Tests were carried out with different network condition parameters. Network traffic was also measured. The steady state behavior and setup cost are compared separately. Simões et al. [16] concluded that for performance, as measured by time it takes to perform the management operation, distribution provides better results than locality when bandwidth is abundant. The gains of locality became more apparent when bandwidth was limited.

Current LTE architecture have already incorporated concepts of indoor small cells, HeNB, etc. [14] which have scaled up complexities for a cellular operator as they need to monitor performance of these exponentially multiplying network elements. Providing abundant bandwidth for North Bound (NB) interface or management interface for such new base stations would be an expensive task. So Operators would rather prefer limited bandwidth for NB interface. This means gains of locality would be considerable in that scenario as discussed in [16].

Network traffic can be reduced in uplink direction by processing and extracting out information needed from raw performance data. We did an analysis of this compression due to extraction of information at edge. Let's consider a single OSS application interested in performance management data of a base station, the data required to send in uplink from that base station can be given by expression

$$T_c = h + C \times i \tag{3}$$

where h is the overhead introduced by the communication protocol, such as headers, C is the number of raw counters needed to be transferred at once and i is the size of a counter value. For the proposed system this case could be expressed as

$$T_d = h + K \times i \tag{4}$$

where K refers to the number of computed KPI values. It can be assumed that $K \leq C$, because a KPI is a extracted from one or more counters. This is the semantic compression provided by the system. Reduction in traffic volume depends on the complexity of the requested KPIs. A KPI can be a singular counter value so it does not compress in that case, while more complex KPIs can consist of dozens of counters and then the volume that needs to be transferred may be reduced to a tenth of the original size.

Network traffic is reduced in the downlink direction by the use of publish/subscribe pattern which omits the periodical requests of polling pattern and thus saves bandwidth in long run. The initial stream start request can be larger in size than a simple SNMP request, but it needs to be issued only once for a particular type of stream. For the centralized system the traffic generated would be for a one application

$$T_c = \sum (h + C \times i) \tag{5}$$

where C is the number of counters fetched, and i is the size needed to represent a request of a counter. Summation represents that the request needs to be sent before each response. Expression

$$T_d = (h + K \times i) \tag{6}$$

gives the required bandwidth in the decentralized case. Here K $\times$ i represents the size needed to request K KPIs of size i. The size i depends on the methods selected for storing and/or transferring KPI formulas. In case multiple applications are assumed, if they request same data, overlapping topics provide further gains for the publish/subscribe model.

Integration of the proposed concept into a real networks managements system is an interesting future research topic, which may propose needs for additional open standards. One promising future standard seems to be the Mobile Edge Computing standard. With Mobile Edge Computing (MEC) [2] being standardized we believe our Data Fetchers could be installed on MEC platforms connected to the base stations. This computation of information would not be computationally heavy for MEC platform as demonstrated in Sect. 5. The proposed approach could help operator to save precious bandwidth resources. Moreover reducing performance traffic at network edge by computing out and sending only information required would also decrease complexities which could otherwise arise in a centralized system which would then have to handle enormous volumes of raw performance data of entire network and then extract information required by any OSS application.

There are various other future directions to evaluate performance of proposed solution and tune it up according to telecommunication guidelines. For example, we are planning to evaluate our system performance with up to thousands of scattered Data Fetchers to find out its problems and limitations.

6   Conclusion

Ongoing digital evolution demands for scaling up of cellular network infrastructure with new network devices and technologies. This will complicate existing centralized monitoring of network performance due to increase in volume of M-Plane data. In this paper we discussed and evaluated a solution based upon local processing of required information from raw performance data at the network edge, near base stations. This information is then streamed on demand using publish-subscribe scheme across the network through our solution. Proposed solution helps in reducing M-Plane traffic both in uplink and downlink directions and reduces complexities of centralized processing of data. Current Evaluation of proposed solution gave encouraging results for its performance and reduction of M-Plane data.

References

1. Collectl. http://collectl.sourceforge.net/
2. ETSI-Mobile Edge Computing. http://www.etsi.org/technologies-clusters/technologies/mobile-edge-computing
3. NGMN use cases related to self organising network. https://www.ngmn.org/uploads/media/NGMN_Use_Cases_related_to_Self_Organising_Network_Overall_Description.pdf
4. 3GPP. Telecommunication management; Key Performance Indicators (KPI) for Evolved Universal Terrestrial Radio Access Network (E-UTRAN): Definitions. TS 32.450, 3rd Generation Partnership Project (3GPP), August 2008
5. 3GPP. Telecommunication management; Self-Organizing Networks (SON) Policy Network Resource Model (NRM) Integration Reference Point (IRP); Requirements (3Gpp. TS 32.521 version 9.0.0 Release 9). TS 32.521, 3rd Generation Partnership Project (3GPP), April 2010
6. Kafka, A. June 2016. http://kafka.apache.org/documentation.html,
7. Baldi, M., Picco., G.P.: Evaluating the tradeoffs of mobile code design paradigms in network management applications. In: Proceedings of the International Conference on Software Engineering, pp. 146–155. IEEE (1998)
8. Case, J., Fedor, M., Schoffstall, M., Davin, J.: RFC 1157: Simple network management protocol (SNMP) (1990)
9. Clemm, A., Wolter, R.: Network-Embedded Management and Applications: Understanding Programmable Networking Infrastructure. Springer, Heidelberg (2013)
10. Eugster, P.T., Felber, P.A., Guerraoui, R., Kermarrec, A.M.: The many faces of publish/subscribe. ACM Comput. Surv. (CSUR) $35(2)$, 114–131 (2003)
11. Goodhope, K., Koshy, J., Kreps, J., Narkhede, N., Park, R., Rao, J., Ye, V.Y.: Building linkedin's real-time activity data pipeline. IEEE Data Eng. Bull. $35(2)$, 33–45 (2012)
12. Hertel, G.: Operation and maintenance. In: Hillebrand, F. (ed.) GSM and UMTS The Creation of Global Mobile Communication, pp. 445–456. Wiley, Chichester (2002)
13. Hämäläinen, S., Sanneck, H.: LTE Self-Organising Networks (SON): Network Management Automation for Operational Efficiency. Wiley, New York (2011)
14. Nossenson, R.: Long-term evolution network architecture. In: IEEE International Conference on Microwaves, Communications, Antennas and Electronics Systems, COMCAS, pp. 1–4. IEEE (2009)
15. Olsson, M., Mulligan, C.: EPC and 4G Packet Networks: Driving the Mobile Broadband Revolution. Academic Press, Amsterdam (2012)
16. Simões, P., Rodrigues, J., Silva, L., Boavida, F.: Distributed retrieval of management information: is it about mobility, locality or distribution? In: Network Operations and Management Symposium, NOMS. IEEE/IFIP, pp. 79–94. IEEE (2002)
17. TeleManagement Forum. Telecom operations map. Approved version 2.1. GB910. TeleManagement Forum, March 2000
18. Trossen, D., Reed, M.J., Riihijärvi, J., Georgiades, M., Fotiou, N., Xylomenos, G.: IP over ICN-the better IP? In: European Conference on Networks and Communications (EuCNC), pp. 413–417. IEEE (2015)

Coding Schemes for Heterogeneous Communication Links Using Channel Bundling

Vanessa Eichhorn[✉], Maciej Mühleisen, and Andreas Timm-Giel

Institute of Communication Networks (ComNets),
Hamburg University of Technology, Hamburg, Germany
{vanessa.eichhorn,maciej.muehleisen,timm-giel}@tuhh.de

Abstract. Communication over geostationary satellite links is improved by introducing end-to-end Forward Error Correction (FEC) and simultaneous transmissions over two links (channel bundling). The main objective of this work is to investigate to which degree the goodput and the reliability can be enhanced using the mentioned techniques. The performances of the two FEC schemes Reed-Solomon Codes and Random Linear Network Coding are compared. Uncorrelated and correlated packet errors are considered, the latter with a Gilbert-Elliot channel model. Experiments are conducted in a testbed consisting of a single PC with virtual network interfaces to determine the influence of various parameter settings on performance. Results are compared against a scenario with one link offering the same capacity as the two links together. It is concluded that using two heterogeneous links is beneficial for the goodput and losses for generation sizes larger than 20 for three correlated lost packets on average.

Keywords: Forward Error Correction · Random Linear Network Coding · Reed-Solomon codes · Gilbert-Elliot channel model · Satellite communication

1 Introduction

Reliable communication is a major goal for many applications in today's networks. A common approach to achieve reliable per hop and end-to-end transmission is the use of Automatic Repeat reQuest (ARQ), which is a Backward Error Correction (BEC) scheme. Here, retransmissions generate extra delays and therefore significantly decrease the performance in high delay scenarios such as satellite communications. ARQ also requires resources on the backchannel and is not feasible for multicast. Forward Error Correction (FEC) can be an alternative or complement to ARQ. It is a common approach to gain reliability in lower layers through introduction of channel coding on point-to-point links. Redundancy is added at the sender allowing reconstruction of the original packet even with some bit errors. Coding schemes can also be introduced in higher layers across several hops. There redundancy is added by packet-level FEC schemes generating extra packets to recover lost ones. A trade-off must be found between added

© ICST Institute for Computer Sciences, Social Informatics and Telecommunications Engineering 2017
R. Agüero et al. (Eds.): MONAMI 2016, LNICST 191, pp. 160–173, 2017.
DOI: 10.1007/978-3-319-52712-3_12

additional packets and the gain to be expected in reduced data loss and increased goodput. Coding results in en- and decoding delays as well as additional bandwidth usage. Furthermore, channel bundling can increase the throughput and also adds diversity. This is in particular beneficial, if the channels show a burst error behavior. If the different channels are uncorrelated to each other, substantial improvement can be expected. During bad channel conditions in one link, the other link still is expected to show good performance.

This paper is organized as follows: In Sect. 2 an overview of related work is given, with an introduction to two types of linear codes used in this work. Afterwards, the evaluated scenario is presented in Sect. 3 and the results are given in Sect. 4. Finally, conclusions are drawn and future work is described in Sect. 5.

2   Overview of Coding Schemes and Related Work

In the following, the basic concept of linear codes and their applications is presented. The use of these codes in previous work is also discussed. Finally, the Gilbert-Elliot model is explained to address how to model a transmission channel with correlated errors.

2.1   Coding Schemes

Two coding schemes will be evaluated in this paper: Packet-level Reed-Solomon (RS) codes and Random Linear Network Coding (RLNC). Both schemes are Linear Codes. This codes use the properties of linear algebra [1]. A (n, k)-linear block code is specified most of all by the choice of the so-called generator matrix G. The code can be written as $Y = X \times G$. X denotes a (m, k)-matrix with packet length m and number of original packets k. G is the (k, n)-generator matrix, where n is the number of coded packets. Y represents the (m, n)-matrix of n coded packets with length m.

The decoder solves a linear equation system $\hat{X} = \hat{Y} \times \hat{G}^{-1}$ for any k received linearly independent packets. In this case, $\hat{G}$ describes a (k, k)-invertible matrix. The received packets are placed in the matrix $\hat{Y}$. The generator matrix coefficients must be known to the decoder.

Computations are performed in a finite (or Galois) field GF. A field is closed under addition and multiplication, so the result still is part of the field. A finite field has a finite number of elements meaning that the results only needs as much bits for representation as the original data [1]. Usually a finite prime field $GF(q = p^r)$ is used with p prime and r being a positive integer. Using packet erasure channels, p equals 2.

For encoding, every packet is split into smaller chunks of length r. These are separately multiplied with the coding coefficients in the generator matrix which results in encoding delay.

There are some sources for additional decoding delay. First, there is the processing delay at the receiver, as Gaussian elimination algorithm for matrix inversion and costly multiplications have to be done. A second source is the fact that a generation can only be decoded after receiving enough packets.

Reed-Solomon Codes. Using a (n, k)-Reed-Solomon code, k source packets defined over a finite field $GF(q = 2^r)$ are encoded to n coded packets. The number of different coded packets n is upper bounded by $q - 1$. The generator matrix is built from a Vandermonde matrix $V_{k,n}$ [2]. The matrix consists of $v_{i,j} = \alpha^{i \cdot j}$, where $0 \le i \le k - 1$ and $0 \le j \le n - 1$. α is a fixed root of the primitive polynomial of degree r [2]. This matrix is transformed to a systematic matrix. The code rate is fixed and defined as k/n. The decoder does not need to receive the coding coefficients from the sender, as the generator matrix is fixed for different r. Nevertheless, the decoder needs the index of the generator matrix used for encoding. Protocols can either use a single matrix or define a set of matrices and point at the used one on session establishment.

RS codes are Maximum Distance Separable (MDS) codes. Therefore, there exists no other FEC coding scheme that is able to recover lost packets from fewer received coded packets [3]. The computational complexity increases with the use of larger finite fields, so e.g. [4] focuses on $GF(2^8)$ only. The field size of $GF(2)$ cannot be chosen in RS as the number of different coded packets per generation would be upper bounded by 1. The minimum field size is $GF(2^2)$.

The minimum number of redundant packets h should be chosen depending on the measured or estimated loss rate of the channel. Thus, $h = (k \cdot p)/(1-p) = p \cdot n$ with $0 \le p \le 1$ and $n = k + h$. The generator matrix can be computed with complexity $\mathcal{O}((n - k) \cdot k \cdot (log(k))^2)$ [2]. Then for encoding, k additional operations per vector-matrix multiplication are needed. For decoding using Gaussian elimination algorithm, the matrix inversion takes $\mathcal{O}(k^3)$ operations and the vector-matrix multiplication requires $O(k^2)$ operations.

Random Linear Network Codes. In RLNC k original packets are encoded into n coded packets. The parameter k is denoted as generation size. The field size q describes the size of the Galois field from which the coding coefficients are chosen. The case $q = 2$ is possible in RLNC and is called binary coding. In binary coding, either a packet is chosen to be mixed or not, thus a coded packet formed of original packets A, B and C is, e.g., $1A \oplus 0B \oplus 1C$. In the case of $q = 2^8$ the coefficients are chosen between 0 and 255. Thus, a packet like $255A \oplus 3B \oplus 145C$ is possible.

As soon as the decoder receives k linearly independent packets, decoding can be performed. For decoding to be possible, the receiver must know the coding coefficients used to create the coded packet. Therefore, a coding vector in the header is necessary. In [5], it was shown that choosing the coding coefficients independently and uniformly at random from elements of a finite field is sufficient. The size of the coefficients in the header is $k \, log_2(q)$ bits in total. It does not matter exactly which coded packets are received, as long as there are enough linearly independent packets for decoding. So the system is stateless.

There is a trade-off between the computational complexity of encoding and decoding, introduced overheads and the residual error probability. On the one hand, coding information (the random generator matrix coefficients) must be known to the receiver and are therefore added to the header of each packet. On the other hand, overhead is introduced due to linearly dependent packets resulting from unfortunate random number constellations and not adding any information for decoding. Thus, packets can be linearly dependent because of the randomness of the code.

In network coding each node in a network can generate new coded packets and forward them, instead of only storing and forwarding packets. *Recoding* at intermediate nodes means mixing different coded packets without decoding them first [6]. If no recoding option at nodes in the network is needed, there is the possibility to exchange once a seed at the beginning of the transmission. Then the random coefficients do not have to be sent over the network in every packet. Thus, the overhead is reduced. Using this method, the number of unique coding vectors is reduced to the size of the seed [6].

Comparison. The field size q defines the number of unique field elements. In RLNC, a large field size has the advantage that the packets are linearly independent with a high probability. Therefore, the number of additional redundant packets can be reduced compared to using small field sizes. Apart from that, a high field size in RLNC results in a large coding vector added to the header of each packet with a size of $k \ log_2(q)$ bits in total. In RS the field size upper bounds the number of different packets per generation. Furthermore, the computational complexity grows with the field size. Addition in $GF(q = 2^r)$ can be implemented with complexity $\mathcal{O}(r)$, whereas multiplication requires $\mathcal{O}(r^2)$ operations [7]. Multiplication runtime can be improved by using look-up tables. The generation size k defines the maximal number of packets that can be mixed to generate a coded packet. In case a high generation size is chosen, it is possible to mix many packets into the coded packet. This leads to a large decoding delay, because at least k coded packets must be received before decoding can be performed. From this perspective, high generation sizes can be chosen for a file download, whereas for streaming live events a small generation size is preferable to reduce delay [8]. Decoding is performed by Gaussian elimination algorithm. The computational complexity increases with $\mathcal{O}(k^3)$ [9].

In RLNC and RS, the number of additional packets h should be chosen at least according to the packet loss probability of the link. In RLNC it can be adapted flexible to the link conditions if feedback is available. Then it is possible to increase the number of additional packets h according to the new estimated error probability of the link. Systematic coding means that the original packets are part of the coded packets. This option is possible in both RLNC and RS. In case systematic coding is used, the encoding process can be speeded up because for the first k packets no encoding is needed. This is especially beneficial if there are only a few losses and the number of required coded packets is small.

For RLNC, there are multiple variants which have to be evaluated depending on the scenario, e.g. also sparse codes. Using sparse codes a lot of coding coefficients are set to zero and therefore reduces computational complexity. This means that in a coded packet only a few packets of the generation are mixed.

2.2   Related Work

In [9], a channel bundling scenario was analyzed over multiple wireless interfaces with half-duplex constraints. In a testbed a file transfer was implemented between two Android smartphones using Bluetooth, WiFi and cellular networks. Instead of sending data through a single interface at a time, splitting the data across interfaces or repeating the same data over multiple links, the data was coded at packet-level using RLNC. The throughput was increased by channel bundling and by making transmissions more robust.

In [10], an example was discussed with a RS code considered at packet-level within the DVB-H standard. Gaussian elimination algorithm was compared to Berlekamp-Massey algorithm for decoding. It was shown that the complexity of both algorithms is similar for small packets considered in the standard.

In [3], RS codes were used for reliable multisource video streaming. This work uses an extended Gilbert-Elliot model. The system dynamically choose one of four different FEC schemes to adapt to the network conditions. Besides pure RS, an unequally interleaved FEC for correlated packet losses was considered. Here, RS codes were extended by a specific uneven FEC interleaving scheme, which needs feedback through the backchannel. In [11], Reed-Solomon codes were analyzed analytically using a Gilbert-Elliot channel model and interleaving.

In [4], the behavior of packet-level RS code was analyzed in a real-time video streaming application. It was found that using RS results in high CPU loads. The real-time performance constraints were not met in scenarios with high losses.

Compared to the previous work, the contribution of this paper is to investigate the use of pure FEC schemes without feedback and using channel bundling for links with correlated and uncorrelated losses.

2.3   Transmission Channel Models

Two kinds of packet erasure channels are investigated in this paper. First, a channel with uncorrelated errors is considered. Second, a channel with correlated errors is evaluated. Either the whole packet without error is received or the packet is lost in packet erasure channels.

The Gilbert-Elliot channel model is used to describe correlated burst errors in the wireless channel. In [12], it is validated that the two-state Gilbert-Elliot model is suitable for satellite channels. This model is also used in, e.g., [13,14]. Here, a two-state continuous time Markov model consisting of states $\Omega = \{Good, Bad\}$ is used, where ϵ_{Good} defines the error rate in the $Good$ state. In the Bad state, the error rate ϵ_{Bad} is much higher than in the $Good$ state. In Fig. 1, λ_{Good} and λ_{Bad} are the transition probabilities between the states. The state sojourn time can be

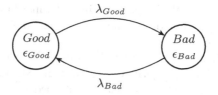

Fig. 1. The continuous time Gilbert-Elliot model

approximated by an exponential distribution. Thus, the sojourn time in the *Good* state is exponentially distributed with rate $\lambda_{Good} = 1/\mu_{Good}$, where μ_{Good} denotes the mean of the exponential distribution [15]. The sojourn time in the *Bad* state is exponentially distributed with rate $\lambda_{Bad} = 1/\mu_{Bad}$.

In Fig. 2, the received packets over a time of 10 s are shown in the emulator. The Gilbert-Elliot model is implemented with the parameters $\epsilon_{Bad} = 1$, $\epsilon_{Good} = 0$ and μ_{Bad} being at least three times the packet sending interval. This results in approximately three consecutive packet losses on average. μ_{Good} is chosen in such a proportion to μ_{Bad} so the overall error probability of the model equals the intended loss rate, e.g.: $P(Bad) = 0.1 \stackrel{!}{=} \frac{\mu_{Bad}}{\mu_{Good}+\mu_{Bad}}$.

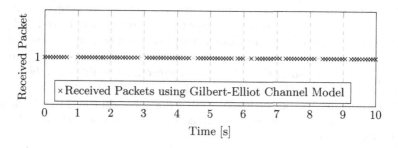

Fig. 2. Gilbert-Elliot channel with 10% loss, $\mu_{Bad} = 0.125$ s and $\mu_{Good} = 1.125$ s

3 Problem Description

A single link scenario will be compared to a two link channel bundling scenario with a lossy and a lossless link. While using uncorrelated error models, this should not make a difference. These errors can be compensated relatively well with FEC. In a correlated error model, the lossless link might help to reduce the losses in a row depending on the burst duration. This is due to still receiving parts of the data through the lossless link. Gains are expected although this is not a proper interleaving behavior. Losing only a few packets in a generation is important for coding, because as soon as more packets per generation are lost than redundancy is added, no decoding is possible and the entire generation is lost. Similar benefits should be possible in a channel bundling scenario with two independent correlated error channels, as the channels are lossy with a low probability at the same time.

Different FEC schemes are compared, namely RS codes and RLNC. It is expected that RS performs slightly better than RLNC in terms of goodput, because in RS the coding vector overhead is not needed.

3.1 Scenario

Presenting the channel bundling scenario with two links, the network can be represented as a directed graph with four nodes. The source, e.g. a ship or an air-craft, located at a vertex of the graph sends the information to a single receiver. The edges from the sender to the two different ground stations correspond to packet erasure channels, the different satellite links. The ground stations are connected to the receiver via wired links. The losses and delays on these links are neglected, because they are small compared to the ones of the satellite links. The throughput of the wired links is sufficient.

A satellite link is characterized by the following parameters. An available and guaranteed throughput of 96 kbit/s per link on layer 2 is assumed in the two link scenario. Using one link, a throughput of 192 kbit/s is assumed. Those values correspond to typical ones offered by the Inmarsat BGAN service [16]. A latency of 0.25 s is chosen for all modeled links corresponding to the propagation delay from the sender to a geostationary satellite to a ground station. Correlated losses are typical for satellite links [13]. Correlated losses happen in case the antenna of the sender is not oriented correctly, e.g. due to heavy waves in maritime communication. For a short time there is no connection possible until the antenna is again aligned. In Ku-Band high losses also occur during heavy rain.

The communication on the lossless link is done, e.g., in the L-Band, the lossy one in the Ku-Band. In general, Ku-Band communication is cheaper but less reliable than L-Band communication.

The goodput and packet loss ratio of the link, being important performance metrics, are evaluated.

3.2 Testbed Set-Up

The multipath scenario is emulated using one PC (see Fig. 3). This brings the advantage of easy and exact time measurements. Two virtual loopback interfaces (see Fig. 4) are created. This is done by assigning two IPv4 address to the local interface. The Linux based Network Emulator NetEm [17] and Traffic Control are used to modify the static loss rate and the delay of the virtual links. The functionalities of NetEm were studied in [18]. The Gilbert-Elliot channel is imple-mented by adjusting the packet loss through NetEm on state transition. The Steinwurf Kodo C++ library [19] is used for implementation of Reed-Solomon and Random Linear Network Coding. The coding in done above the transport layer. The coded packets are sent via UDP.

Same Machine

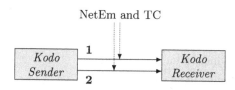

1 Satellite Link 1: Delay = 0.25 s, Throughput = 96 kbit/s, Loss = 0 %

2 Satellite Link 2: Delay = 0.25 s, Throughput = 96 kbit/s, Loss variable

Fig. 3. Testbed scenario with two links

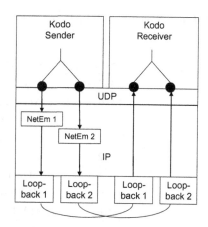

Fig. 4. Loopback interfaces OSI-Layer

In the following, the set-up for the emulator is described based on the criteria defined in Sect. 2.1. In the presented scenario two links with 96 kbit/s of throughput and a delay of 0.25 s are assumed. The links are used simultaneously with a 50%/50% scheduling. The total packet size is chosen to be 960 bytes in all tests, so the maximum possible throughput of the link is achieved at 40 ms fixed interarrival time. A data packet is sent every 40 ms on one of the two links. Thus, every 80 ms a packet is put on the lossy and every 80 ms a packet is put on the lossless link. This means that 25 packets per second are sent in the ideal case. For comparison, an identical scenario with regard to packet loss rate and total throughput with just one link is evaluated. Here, the throughput is set to 192 kbit/s and 960 bytes packets are sent every 40 ms. UDP, IP and MAC headers as well as network coding headers are subtracted from the total packet size to determine the payload size. For RLNC, the size of the network coding header changes with the field size and generation size.

For all tests a field size of $GF(q = 2^8)$ is chosen as in [9]. For RLNC, the packets should be linearly independent with a high probability. For RS, the number of different packets per generation is upper bounded by 255.

Depending on the test, the generation size is either fixed or varied. A specific amount of redundancy h is added. The redundancy must be added in the form of whole additional packets. Therefore, generation sizes of, e.g., $k = 2$ are not that useful. In case generation size $k = 2$ is chosen, 3 packets (50% redundancy) have to be sent also in a case where only 10% redundancy should be added. Therefore, comparison would be unfair and this is excluded. Very large generation sizes are not investigated. For example, a coding vector of 128 bytes has to be added using generation size $k = 128$ and field size $GF(256)$ in RLNC. This results in around 19% of total overhead for the 960 bytes long packets and is therefore not further analyzed. Decoding delay is not important in the scenario, as a file transfer scenario is emulated. That is why also larger generations of up to 80 are

Table 1. Content of a single network coded packet with a generation size of 16 packets and the field size $GF(q = 2^8)$ on layer 2

Size in bytes	Content
893	Payload
16	Network coding vector
1	Network coding meta data
2	Network coding sequence number
2	Network coding generation number
8	UDP header
20	IP header
18	MAC header
960	Total packet size

taken into account. Choosing large generation sizes and a low field size might be a considerable option for RLNC, but is not considered in this work.

It is expected that depending on the redundancy still high losses are possible. This is because of generations being lost entirely when they cannot be decoded. Therefore, even more data might be lost as without using any coding scheme. In this case, a backward error correction scheme might improve the performance.

For comparison, the parameters for RS are the same as for RLNC. This means, that the code rate is chosen at least according to the loss rate of the channel. The field size is set to $GF(q = 2^8)$, which is the default setting in [2] and is used, e.g., in [4]. A RLNC packet with generation size 16 has the structure displayed in Table 1. RS packets require no coding vector but instead an additional symbol index increasing their payload size to 908 bytes.

4   Results

At first, it will be investigated how much redundancy should be added to a packet erasure link given that the goodput should be maximized while the losses are preferably low. For the objective to nearly eliminate losses, the redundancy should be as high as possible. This contradicts with the aim to have an appropriate goodput. Therefore, a test with one packet erasure link with a throughput of 192 kbit/s is performed. The behavior of the system with correlated errors is compared to the system with uncorrelated errors in terms of measured average goodput and the loss rate. An uncorrelated loss rate of 5% is configured. For correlated errors, a mean sojourn time of 0.125 s in the *Bad* state and 2.375 s in the *Good* state of the Gilbert-Elliot model is chosen. The generation size is fixed to $k = 32$, as previous tests showed that this is a reasonable size. It is expected that RS will perform slightly better in terms of goodput due to its lower header overhead. Nevertheless, the loss rates should be the same.

The behavior of RLNC is displayed in Fig. 5 and the one of RS in Fig. 6. The average goodput is shown with a 95% confidence interval of multiple runs. As only full-packets can be added, sending an amount of 34 to 42 coded packets is observed, corresponding to around 6% to 31% redundancy. In each run data with a size of 91 MB is transmitted, so every run lasts around 10 min.

The theoretical maximum goodput for no losses is displayed as well. This threshold decreases as more redundancy is added and therefore the transmission takes longer. Assuming that k is the generation size, r is the redundancy to be added in percentage terms, g_p represents the goodput per packet in bit, and the number of send packets per second is p_s, then the maximum goodput g_s in bit/s is calculated as:

$$g_s = \frac{k}{(k + \lceil r \cdot k \rceil)} \cdot g_p \cdot p_s \tag{1}$$

Observing uncorrelated losses, an amount of extra four to five packets, thus a redundancy of 12.5% or 15.625%, should be chosen in terms of the observed goodput. Choosing a redundancy of 18.75% nearly no losses can be observed. This is noticeable, since the loss on the link is 5%. Therefore, a lot more redundancy must be added than there are losses. This shows a major disadvantage of coding with pure FEC: In case more losses occur than redundancy was added, the entire generation is lost as it cannot be decoded.

Using a correlated burst error model, even with an added redundancy of over 30% still errors of around 5% occur. This is not satisfactory. In terms of goodput, an added redundancy of 18.75% gives the best results. All in all, correlated losses affect the goodput far more than uncorrelated ones. Observing uncorrelated losses, nearly no losses can be achieved with less redundancy.

Comparing RLNC to RS, using RS results in a higher goodput in both cases of correlated and uncorrelated losses. The losses show nearly identical behaviors. To achieve almost zero losses using RS and an uncorrelated error model, a redundancy of 18.75% should be chosen as well.

For the next tests, a fixed redundancy is chosen and the generations sizes are varied. The channel bundling scenario with two heterogeneous links (see Fig. 3) will be compared to the scenario with one link, whereas the single link has 5% loss and the lossy channel in the two link scenario has a loss of 10%. The tests are restricted to RLNC, as it is assumed that RS has a similar behavior with the difference that RS has more goodput available due to the lower coding header size. The redundancy is set to 18.75% in all tests. This is not feasible in the correlated case for a real scenario, since then high losses are accepted. However, a comparison of the goodput between correlated and uncorrelated errors is possible this way.

The usage of two heterogeneous links should perform equal or better compared to one link in a scenario with correlated errors. In a scenario with two links with equal end-to-end delay and 50%/50% scheduling, packets are received alternating from one link and the other one. The observed phenomenon of losing an entire generation is reduced, because packets still arrive on the lossless link. This is especially useful in case the correlated errors occur close to the end of

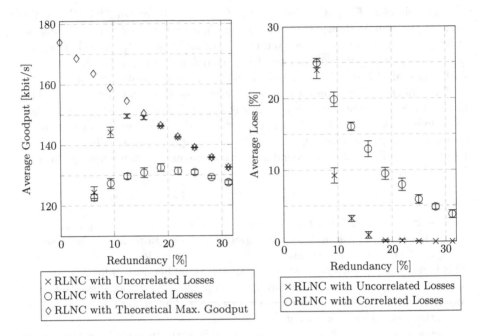

Fig. 5. Results for RLNC using one link with 192 kbit/s and 5% loss

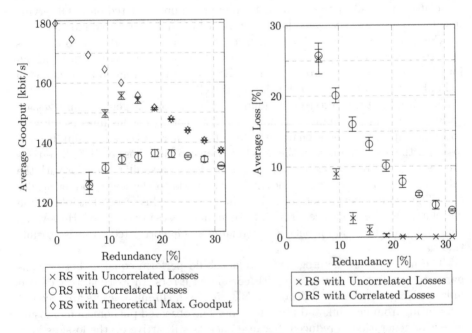

Fig. 6. Results for RS using one link with 192 kbit/s and 5% loss

a generation. Imagine a generation on the single link is lost. In the two link scenario however, the generation is not lost necessarily with conditions being equal. It is not lost in case two generations are affected by the errors and the first generation loses data at the end, the second one at the beginning. Both receive enough packets to be decoded. As an example, it is assumed that eight packets and two redundant packets are transmitted. In case three packets are lost, also the remaining seven packets are useless. If the seventh to ninth packet out of ten are lost on a single link due to correlated errors, the generation is useless. The following generation is not affected. Having two links in the same constellation, due to the scheduling the seventh and ninth packet of the first generation and the first packet of following generation are lost by a burst duration of three packets. Therefore, both generations can be decoded. This advantage is linked to the ratio of burst duration to the number of send packets or rather the generation size.

The impacts on losses and goodput is investigated for different generation sizes and a fixed burst duration of three packets on average. A performance improvement in terms of goodput should be visible, as less generations are expected to be lost. To achieve confident results, the transmitted data is increased and more runs are considered. For correlated errors of two links, a mean sojourn time of 0.250 s in the *Bad* state and 2.25 s in the *Good* state in

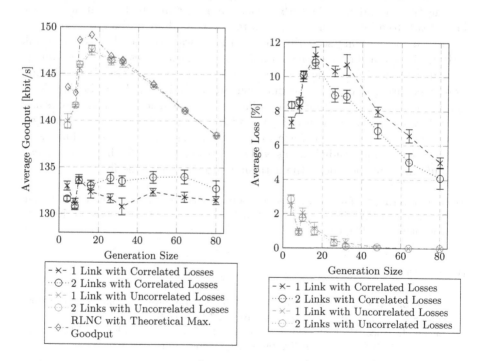

Fig. 7. Comparison of 1 and 2 links for different generation sizes using RLNC and 18.75% redundancy. 5% loss on 1 link equals 10% loss/0% loss on 2 links.

the Gilbert-Elliot model is chosen, which corresponds to three lost packets on average and a 10% loss rate. In Fig. 7 the goodput using at least 18.75% redundancy is displayed for different generation sizes. For generation sizes $k = 4$ and $k = 8$, 25% redundancy is assumed as only whole packets can be added. Nevertheless, it is possible to compare the one link scenario to the two link scenario.

As a conclusion, it is estimated that using two links is beneficial for higher generation sizes. Here, the number of sent packets is large compared to the burst duration. For generation size $k = 4$ using one link performs better. This is related to the fact that the average burst duration nearly equals the generation size. For uncorrelated losses it makes no difference whether one link or two links are considered, as expected.

5   Conclusion and Outlook

The tests showed that the amount of redundancy determines the performance of FEC. Choosing the redundancy too low or too high results in low average goodput. For redundancies of at least 18.75% on a channel with 5% uncorrelated errors, packet losses can be nearly eliminated. Pure FEC coding in the presented way suffers from losing entire generations. Therefore, the coding parameters have to be chosen carefully. RLNC and RS show a similar behavior of losses when varying the redundancy. The RS payload is larger due to lower header sizes, which leads to a better performance in terms of goodput in the given scenario.

A channel bundling scenario with two links was compared to a single link with the determined redundancy for different generation sizes and a fixed average burst duration. Here, a benefit while using two links was observed for generation sizes much larger than the burst duration. An analytic model is to be developed to predict the losses and goodput for different redundancies, generation sizes and burst durations. The model is to be extended to adaptively react to link changes. It is planned to enhance the scenario with, e.g., highly heterogeneous links with different delays and bandwidths as well as additional links. Furthermore, instead of emulating a file download the data should be coded on-the-fly.

Acknowledgment. This work was partially funded by the German Federal Ministry for Economic Affairs and Energy (BMWi) as part of the *RekoTrans* project with reference number 20Y1504B.

References

1. Rizzo, L.: Effective Erasure Codes for Reliable Computer Communication Protocols. SIGCOMM Comput. Commun. Rev. **27**(2), 24–36 (1997)
2. Lacan, J., Roca, V., Peltotalo, J., Peltotalo, S.: Reed-Solomon Forward Error Correction (FEC) Schemes, April 2009. https://tools.ietf.org/html/rfc5510
3. Lamoriniere, C., Nafaa, A., Murphy, L.: Dynamic switching between adaptive FEC protocols for reliable multi-source streaming. In: Global Telecommunications Conference, GLOBECOM 2009, pp. 1–6. IEEE, November 2009

4. Matsuzono, K., Detchart, J., Cunche, M., Roca, V., Asaeda, H.: Performance analysis of a high-performance real-time application with several AL-FEC schemes. In: 2010 IEEE 35th Conference on Local Computer Networks (LCN), pp. 1–7, October 2010

5. Ho, T., Medard, M., Shi, J., Effros, M., Karger, D.R.: On randomized network coding. In: Proceedings of 41st Annual Allerton Conference on Communication, Control, and Computing (2003)

6. Heide, J., Pedersen, M.V., Fitzek, F.H.P., Medard, M.: On code parameters and coding vector representation for practical RLNC. In 2011 IEEE International Conference on Communications (ICC), pp. 1–5, June 2011

7. Langberg, M., Sprintson, A.: Recent results on the algorithmic complexity of network coding. In: Tutorial appearing in Proceedings of Workshop on Network Coding, Theory, and Applications (NetCod) (2009)

8. Pedersen, M.V., Lucani, D.E., Fitzek, F.H.P., Sorensen, C.W., Badr, A.S.: Network coding designs suited for the real world: what works, what doesn't, what's promising. In: 2013 IEEE Information Theory Workshop (ITW), pp. 1–5. IEEE, September 2013

9. Moreira, A., Lucani, D.E.: Coded schemes for asymmetric wireless interfaces: theory and practice. IEEE J. Sel. Areas Commun. **33**(2), 171–184 (2015)

10. Garrammone, G.: On decoding complexity of Reed-Solomon codes on the packet erasure channel. IEEE Commun. Lett. **17**(4), 773–776 (2013)

11. Celandroni, N., Gotta, A.: Performance analysis of systematic upper layer FEC codes and interleaving in land mobile satellite channels. IEEE Trans. Veh. Technol. **60**(4), 1887–1894 (2011)

12. Lutz, E., Cygan, D., Dippold, M., Dolainsky, F., Papke, W.: The land mobile satellite communication channel-recording, statistics, and channel model. IEEE Trans. Veh. Technol. **40**(2), 375–386 (1991)

13. Shang, Y., Hadjitheodosiou, M.: TCP splitting protocol for broadband aeronautical satellite network. In: The 23rd Digital Avionics Systems Conference, DASC 2004, vol. 2, pp. 11.C.3–11.1-9, October 2004

14. Casone, L., Ciccarese, G., De Blasi, M., Patrono, L., Tomasicchio, G.: An efficient ARQ protocol for a mobile geo-stationary satellite channel. In: Global Telecommunications Conference, GLOBECOM 2001, vol. 4, pp. 2692–2697. IEEE (2001)

15. Zhang, Y., Hu, H., Fujise, M.: Resource, Mobility, and Security Management in Wireless Networks and Mobile Communications. Wireless Networks and Mobile Communications. CRC Press, Boca Raton (2006)

16. Colledge, G., Hiesler, R., Febvre, P., Platt, P., Sharma, A., Maiolla, V., Schuster Bruce, A., Huggins, G.: SwiftBroadband capabilities to support aeronautical safety services WP1: technical description and application to ATS, June 2006

17. Linux Foundation. NetEm - Network Emulator (2016). http://www.linuxfoundation.org/collaborate/workgroups/networking/netem. Accessed 10 May 2016

18. Jurgelionis, A., Laulajainen, J.P., Hirvonen, M., Wang, A.I.: An empirical study of NetEm network emulation functionalities. In: 2011 Proceedings of 20th International Conference on Computer Communications and Networks (ICCCN), pp. 1–6, July 2011

19. Pedersen, M.V., Heide, J., Fitzek, F.H.P.: Kodo: an open and research oriented network coding library. In: Casares-Giner, V., Manzoni, P., Pont, A. (eds.) NETWORKING 2011. LNCS, vol. 6827, pp. 145–152. Springer, Heidelberg (2011). doi:10.1007/978-3-642-23041-7_15

Security and Self-organizing Networks

Security in Mobile Computing: Attack Vectors, Solutions, and Challenges

Sara Alwahedi, Mariam Al Ali, Fatimah Ishowo-Oloko, Wei Lee Woon,
and Zeyar Aung$^{(\boxtimes)}$

Department of Electrical Engineering and Computer Science,
Masdar Institute of Science and Technology, Abu Dhabi, UAE
{salwahedi,maralali,fishowooloko,wwoon,zaung}@masdar.ac.ae

Abstract. With the growth of the mobile industry, a smart phone has
the ability to store large amounts of valuable data such as personal and
bank information, the users' location, call logs and more. Thus, the security of data in the mobile world has become an important issue. The main
objective of this survey paper is to review the state-of-the-art technologies for the security of mobile computing. It covers the modern mobile
operating systems that are being widely used today. It also identifies
the various types of attack vectors particularly designed to infect mobile
devices and highlights the available security solution to counter each
type of attack. Finally, it briefly discusses the outstanding limitations
and challenges in the mobile computing world.

Keywords: Mobile computing · Smart phone · Security · Attack vectors

1 Introduction

Mobile Computing is an emerging technology that serves users at anytime and
anywhere, it is a combination of mobile and wireless communication services. The
increasing demand for mobility along with the features of wireless networks, which
differ from those of traditional networks, makes mobile computing more susceptible to challenges and threats. For that reason, providing security for mobile computing technology is important and critical for developing safe applications.

Mobile Computing includes three main parts: the hardware which consists of
the physical components like the processor chip, the software that facilitates the
computing process which is the operating system (OS) and the infrastructure
such as protocols, services, bandwidth etc. [4]. Most attacks in mobile computing
affects the OS and so we start by reviewing the popular OS for mobiles.

1.1 Contributions

The main contributions of this survey paper are as follow:

1. Describing different platforms of mobile computing and comparing between
   the two most widely-used ones, namely, Google's Android and Apple's iOS.

© ICST Institute for Computer Sciences, Social Informatics and Telecommunications Engineering 2017
R. Agüero et al. (Eds.): MONAMI 2016, LNICST 191, pp. 177–191, 2017.
DOI: 10.1007/978-3-319-52712-3_13

2. Exploring common security issues in mobile computing, such as confidentiality and integrity, and exploring different attack vectors on those issues.
3. Analyzing existing solutions to these attack vectors.
4. Identifying limitations in challenges for mobile security solutions.

2 Mobile Computing Platforms

The common mobile OS are Google's Android, Apple's iOS, Nokia's Symbian, RIM's BlackBerry OS, Samsung's Bada and Microsoft's Windows Phone [15]. Given that Android and iOS have the largest share of the market population, this survey focuses on these two operating systems and in this section, we review the architecture, advantages and disadvantages of the two of them.

Apple's iOS developed by Apple Inc. was first announced in 2007 and was developed only for Apple products. The operating system is coded in Objective-C and is known for being user-friendly. It is however very tightly guarded. iOS acts as an intermediary between the underlying hardware and the apps. Apps do not talk to the underlying hardware directly. Instead, they communicate with the hardware through a set of well-defined system interfaces. The iOS SDK allows developers to make applications for the iPhone and test them in an "iPhone simulator". Apple approves apps by signing with encryption keys after which, such an app can be downloaded from the App store. This is to ensure that only apps satisfying Apple's security policy can be distributed to iPhones [8].

Currently, the most popular OS is Android owned by Open Handset Alliance. Android applications are open-source, written in Java and compiled by the Android SDK tools along with any data and resource files into an Android package (APK) file. Each Android application runs in its own space called a sandbox and can't access data from other applications without user permission [7]. This helps to ensure a certain level of security in Android phones. On the other hand, this feature is also detrimental as it prevents antivirus applications from accessing other applications too in order to scan them or update its virus database.

2.1 iOS vs. Andriod

Apple iOS has a major advantage over Android in terms of security due to the closed nature of the Apple store whereby all apps are vetted by Apple before release. This helps to reduce the number of malware apps found in the store. This is an advantage over Android that runs an open market and thus allowing a proliferation of malicious apps in its market. Yajin et al. collected over 1,200 malware samples of existing Android malware families within a period of 14 months [31].

However, once an app has been installed on to the phone, Android has the advantage with the sandbox system which confines each app to its directory alone. It is thus separated not only from every other app but from the main OS's files and folders [7]. This is unlike iOS applications that can access many system resources by default.

The openness of the Android market does offer a significant advantage over iOS which is the ease of development. The fact that Android is open sourced and development is done in Java and supports cross platform has led to a lot of apps being developed for the Android market which in turn has led to its growing popularity. In terms of similarities, both iOS and Android offer a public marketplace, however android users also have the option of downloading non-market apps.

Given the differences in their architecture, it's not surprising that there are differences in the vulnerabilities of each OS. Some attacks are more frequent and successful on the Android platform than on the iOS platform. Having introduced the common OS in mobile computing, the rest of the survey is organized as follows: Sect. 3 discusses in detail the security issues in mobile computing, this section is divided into a number of sub sections each focused on a specific kind of attack along with the existing solutions in the literature. Sometimes an attack might cut across more than one security issue. Then, Sect. 4 mentions the limitations in the solutions. Finally, we conclude our survey with a discussion in Sect. 5.

3   Security in Mobile Computing

Security issues in mobile computing are generally divided into three main categories, Confidentiality, Integrity, and Availability (CIA). An attack usually targets one or more of these categories and can render great damage to a system. CIA can be defined briefly as follows:

1. Confidentiality: It is the prevention of unauthorized access to the file or system by attackers. It deals with the privacy of the data [4].
2. Integrity: It prevents editing the data in any way, by modifying, creating or deleting data within the system or file [11].
3. Availability: It ensures that the data is accessible to the authorized user [20].

Other important categories that are related to mobile computing and that may be targets of attacks are:

1. Authentication: It has to do with verifying and validating the systems. Authentication seeks to make sure that the user is indeed who he says he is by proving his identity using certain means and credentials that the system requests for. This also is related to confidentiality since it helps in preventing unauthorized access [11].
2. Authorization: It verifies that the user is only viewing the data that he has the right to access. It has to do with availability and confidentiality in which it makes sure the appropriate user is authorized to access the data and whether or not he is able to [4].
3. Accountability: The user is held responsible for the actions he may take. This is arranged such that the link between both systems and users cannot be denied, as in the user is accountable for what he or she does, it can also be called non-repudiation [20].

Figure 1 shows the taxonomy of attack vector types specifically applicable to the mobile computing platform.

Although most of these attacks have solutions, the solutions also have some limitations. In the following sections, we explore different attacks on specific areas of security. Each attack is immediately followed by its solutions. General weaknesses and limitations to these solutions are discussed in a later session.

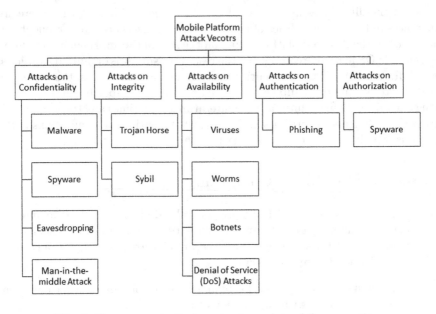

Fig. 1. Taxonomy of attack vector types in mobile computing.

3.1 Attacks on Confidentiality

A breach in confidentiality takes place when an attacker is able to read the data stored on the mobile phone. This is a very common form of attack because of the value of the information stored on the phones. One way in which this attack is usually carried out is by the use of malware.

Malware: Malware or malicious software is a piece of software that is used to attack the operating system of a victim to perform a series of harmful operations. These includes disrupting the system's operations, deleting or altering data, gathering sensitive data and information, gaining unauthorized access into the computer system, or clandestinely controlling the system to carry out illegal operations. Malware tends to target all the three categories of CIA depending on the type of malware used. There are different types which include viruses, worms, Trojans, and spyware. The type of malware that is typically used to breach confidentiality is called spyware.

Solutions: Malware detection programs can be used to detect and remove types of malware from a device including Trojans, viruses and worms which will be discussed in the upcoming sections. Android has several anti-virus applications available in its play store which are recommended to install on one's device. Early detection is the most important thing to mitigate the harmful effects of malware. Throughout the years, a number of malware detection methods have been proposed. These can be broadly categorized into: Signature-based, Change-based, and Anomaly-based methods.

- Signature-based methods: A signature based intrusion method detects a malware based on its signature. First, it gathers data and analyzes it, then any program or file with a similar signature to an already existing malware (compares to a database) is detected. This method is often used for detecting popular malware signatures, but it can be quite slow since it would have to compare the signatures to a large database, meaning it cannot be instant [28]. Data mining techniques are used in these applications for malware classification and it has been proven to be very effective. These include: Rain Forest Neural network, decision tree, Bayesian, Naive Bayes, Classification-based Multiple Association Rule (CMAR) [1].
- Change-based methods: Change based detection is a method that identifies when changes occurs in the system. It relies on probability distribution to detect the changes. These techniques include online and offline change detection techniques.
- Anomaly-based methods: Anomaly based systems look for abnormal behavior in the system tagged as anomalies. These anomalies are detected by first estimating or modeling the normal behavior of the system. Then, any changes or deviations from the estimated normal behavior (usually above a pre-defined threshold) are flagged as possible attacks [9,28].

While malware attacks can be prevented by installing anti-malware software on the mobile devices, one may consider using personal firewall software to restrict access. Since all types of data from and into the device passes through the firewall, the system is able deny access to unwanted intruders [15]. Although this solution seems appropriate, it has two main weaknesses. First, such software tends to consume a lot of power when installed in mobile devices. As a result, most users find themselves uninstalling them in order to conserve power. Alternatively, users are forced to purchase very expensive batteries in order to achieve the desired battery life [14]. Second, they also interfere with website links, access to certain internet updates, and other applications.

Spyware: Spyware is a type of malware that collects data from the system it infects, more accurately it spies on the mobile system. These days, smartphones can store huge amounts of data on the device, most users store important information on their devices such as bank account information. In regards to security issues, spyware is viewed to be a great threat to the confidentiality of the system though it can also affect authorization [10]. A phone infected by spyware can have the user's location, messages, emails and calls tracked, spied on as well as recorded. An example of android spyware is Android Tapsnake which is a game software that actually steals user's information. Though, most spyware on android require the device to be rooted in order to successfully infect it, some of them can access information using standard permissions in an unrooted android device [3]. Similarly, jailbroken iOS devices are more prone to malware and spyware attacks.

Solutions: The defense methods for spyware are the same as those for malware as discussed above.

Eavesdropping: Another attack on mobile computing is eavesdropping (also known as disclosure attacks), which is considered to be the most known form of attack that affect data privacy. In this type of attack, the attacker will try however possible to access confidential information by observing and analyzing messages which go through the network [18]. Those information are transmitted through communication and could include passwords, location, private keys, etc., which should be secured and protected from any unauthorized access. This is where data is usually intercepted by an attacker who tends to observe communication that is being transmitted from a mobile device or being sent to it. The messages need to be protected and secured by using cryptographic mechanisms. The eavesdropping attack is divided into two parts:

- Passive Eavesdropping: The attacker will monitor and listen to the transmitted messages via network to detect useful information.
- Active Eavesdropping: It includes detecting information by appearing to the transmitters as friendly and known nodes.

Solutions: There are several measures that can be taken to address the above threats. However, such measures are sometimes inadequate since they also have their own weaknesses. One of such measures by which eavesdropping can be avoided is securing the communication channel. Here, the messages being sent are encrypted once they leave the source and are only decrypted after they are received by the intended recipient [5]. Since the message is usually in a coded form during the transit, even if the attacker intercepts it, it might not make much sense to him. Encryption also offers a solution to the message modification attack. However, encryption is not foolproof. This is because depending on the attacker's sophistication level; the message can be decrypted while in transit. To lower chances of such an eventuality, the encryption should be as strong as possible.

Man-in-the-middle Attack: Smart phones are prone to man-in-the-middle (MitM) attacks. This is when "an adversarial computer comes between two computers pretending to one to be the other" [17]. Here, the attacker positions himself between the receiver and the sender. He then sniffs information that is being transmitted between the two nodes. Such an attack renders the confidentiality of mobile computing useless. MitM attack can be used to gain access to a smart phone and perform a financial malware attack (FMA). An FMA is an attack whose main objective is to steal important data from the user, such as the user's credentials, through the mobile device [10].

An FMA attacker can attack a phone by impersonating a bank or the attacker can use the MitM attack for banking transactions in which he will be able to steal the user's information. Android.Sniffer is a program that was used to steal bank information by using the MitM [3]. MitM attacks are also achieved by the setting up a fake Wi-Fi hotspot via a wireless router. The mobile phone will automatically detect the signal and request access, thus allowing the attacker to access all of the user's information through the router. Both Android phones and iPhones are prone to this attack [2].

Solutions: The certificates for verification and validation that a device has embedded in it or the applications it uses can help in preventing or mitigating MitM attacks. Often times, these are disabled by rooting or jailbreaking the smart phone, making it less secure. Additionally, certificate authority private keys should be used and are also pre-installed in the device. Android for example has over 100 of them [26].

3.2   Attacks on Integrity

Encryption is a common way of protecting the integrity of data as mentioned in the previous section. Thus, to attack the integrity of the data, attacks can attack the encryption system itself. Once, the encryption system is corrupted, then the integrity of the data is easily compromised. This kind of attack is usually disguised as a utility, essential third-party software application, or a game. Once it attacks a mobile device, it launches several attacks on the system as it continues to spread to any other devices sharing common connection [5].

Trojan Horse: A Trojan horse is a type of malware that "claims" to be legitimate. It often presents itself as a form of software update. It then sabotages the system by providing a backdoor for other illegitimate activities. It is different from viruses and worms because it does not replicate itself. An example of a Trojan horse for iPhones is iPhone firmware 1.1.3 prep that presented itself to users as an important software upgrade. Upon installation however, it corrupted other tools on the phone e.g. OpenSSH that were essential for data encryption [12].

Zeus Trojan horse is another malware that has infected personal computers using Windows OS, it is used to collect data while posing as an online banking service. Recently, a Trojan horse called Zitmo (Zeus in the mobile) collaborates with Zeus in order to hijack a user's android device by prompting the user (using Zeus) to install a security application on the mobile through an HTTP link. The application is Zitmo posing as "Trusteer Rapport" to fool the user and infect the android device thus gaining access to the user's data [26]. Since, Trojans

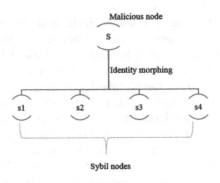

Fig. 2. Sybil attack.

such as Zitmo are able to access user information they are also an attack on confidentiality and authorization.

Solutions: The solution to the Trojan horse attack are the same as those explained in detail for preventing malware attacks.

Sybil: Another attack on the integrity of a system is Sybil attack (Fig. 2). This attack targets mobile networks and it affects the integrity of the data by introducing large amounts of false data into the network. In this attack, one malicious entity presents many fake identities to dominate an essential portion of the system [24]. This is a serious and severe challenge in many areas. For instance, an attacker can rig internet polls by submitting many votes through using many IP addresses [22]. In Sybil attack each node imitates multiple several other linked nodes and try as possible to create confidence by using different malicious methods [22]. The main effects of Sybil attacks in mobile computing include: data aggregation, fair resource allocation and routing [26].

- Fair Resource Allocation: Sybil attack can affect this scheme by giving a malicious node benefit from any network resource allocated to a node by presenting many different identities to that node.
- Data Aggregation: The Sybil attacker can change the result of data gathering or data aggregation by participating in the aggregation with multiple spoofed and fake identities.
- Routing: The performance and function of routing protocol on a path from initial node to destination node can be affected by Sybil attack. By presenting multiple, fake and spoofed identities for each malicious node, the routing process will be disrupted as a result of evolving into multiple paths. When the legitimate node wants to send message to a malicious node, the message will be sent to different paths because many nodes will have the same identity, while it is actually sent to one malicious node.

Solutions: There are existing solutions to prevent the effects of Sybil attack. One of these solutions of this attack is by stopping Sybil attacker from creating fake identities [21]. This can be done by adopting additional infrastructures that build relationship between identities and cryptographic keys. Some examples of these infrastructures include admission control and public key servers. The problem or weakness with this solution is that implementing these infrastructures in any network is very expensive and not easy.

Another solution is by the installation of SybilGuard [30], which is disclosure technique that focus on peer-to-peer users' social media. This mechanism works by identifying Sybils by exchanging keys between a user and limited number of his trusted friends. By combining these social networks, the user or observer can see that Sybil attackers have a small number of friends, so it will be easy to identify him. The problem with SybilGuard is that it suffers from high misclassifications or false negatives. For example, in some cases honest users are unfairly classified as Sybil attackers.

3.3   Attacks on Availability

Viruses: Viruses are a type of malware that were commonly used until recently. They are known to self-replicate by means of another system or person in order to circulate. There are many types of computer viruses, categorized according to the objects they infect.

– File infectors: which are divided into two subparts, direct infectors and memory-resident viruses. Direct infectors are viruses that are usually in an executable (.exe) file format and they instantly infect the system as soon as they are executed, and from there, they start to infect other files. Memory-resident viruses, as their name implies waits in the memory of the device for a host to execute it. WinCE.Duts.A is a virus that infected mobile devices that run Windows OS in 2004. The user receives a message prompting him to download a software, which turns out to be a virus. Then, the virus proceeds to infect the system [13].
– Boot-sector viruses: These types of viruses reside in the boot of the system and try to gain control of the system before the operating system. Dust also affected Windows devices, it resides in the kernel of the device and its main purpose is deleting all the data on the phone and resetting it to its factory settings [19].
– Multipartite viruses: are a combination of both file infectors and boot-sector viruses in which they have the abilities of both. It can be said that Dust can be an example of a multipartite virus since it also infects files.

Solutions: Several commercial and free-ware anti-virus software for mobile platform are available nowadays. The internal working of those software are similar to those of anti-malware, which is explained in detail in the above Sect. 3.1 on preventing malware attacks.

Worms: Worms are almost identical to viruses except for one major difference, they do not require "outside assistance", meaning they self-replicate within the network and do not require the interference of a user [25]. The first mobile worm to have been created is the Cabir Worm, it is a cross-platform worm meaning it can infect a number of OSs, these include Motorola, Nokia, Panasonic, and Sony Ericsson that support the Nokia-licensed Symbian Series 60 platform [13].

Both viruses and worms are a threat to mobile systems since they can spread very easily. They therefore threaten the availability of the mobile phone because of their replication property and thus denying the legitimate owner access to the functionality of his/her phone. Also, an expected increase in worm attacks is predicted with the "network function virtualization" that is expected to be released for new generation mobile networks [10]. Network function virtualization is a method involving running "multiple concurrent virtual networks over a common physical network infrastructure". It uses Bluetooth and other wireless technologies to infect the devices [6].

Solutions: Like other malware threats, virus and worm infections in mobile phones can be prevented or at least limited by installing anti-malware, mentioned previously, and firewalls.

Botnets: A botnet is a network of machines which are under the control of a botmaster who uses them to conduct malicious attacks [25]. A computer or system being controlled by a botmaster is called a bot or zombie. Smart phones are prone to being turned into bots, and the device can be greatly affected by this issue. The signs of being infected include:

- Slowing down of the system, the phone will be much slower than usual and have lags more often, in other words the performance of the system will be lower.
- The device will freeze from time to time and may reboot by itself.
- The smart phone will send and receive data regularly even when there are no applications that would require it to do so.
- Strange behavior of the system.

Solutions: Botnets are quite dangerous and detecting them is obviously important, recent research for detection include behavioral detection approach, which checks the messages of the phone and detects which messages have been sent by or include malware by identifying the signature.

Denial of Service (DoS) Attacks: In addition, another type of attack is the denial of service attack. It occurs when the attacker attempts to render a system or device inaccessible by flooding it with data which will force the device to use its resources and make it unavailable [11]. In this case, the attacker ensures that the users of certain services are not able to use them. This kind of an attack is usually worse in the wireless networks. It enables the attacker to remain anonymous when launching his attacks.

Normally, the attacker floods the access point or the communication server with many requests in a manner that keeps the server busy trying to respond to these requests instead of connecting what the legitimate user wants [11].

Solutions: In order to deal with this kind of attack, the user deploys highly dedicated DoS mitigation systems. These systems are essential in filtering any malicious traffic. Normally, they are installed in front of the routers and the servers. Alternatively, one can use cloud computing mitigation providers, who are usually experts in DoS mitigation [29].

3.4   Attacks on Authentication

Authentication seeks to make sure that the user is indeed who he says he is by proving his identity using certain means and credentials that the system requests for. To defeat the system, hackers steel the identifying information and then use it to carry out unauthorized tasks.

Phishing: An typical attack on authentication is phishing. This is where criminals and fraudsters trick the mobile users in a manner that makes them share highly personal information with certain illegitimate websites. This usually occurs when mobile users are online and a pop-up appears. By clicking on such pop-ups, the criminals are able to obtain the information they want about the individual. They then use this information to commit fraud or other criminal offenses. Some of these frauds end up risking an individual's good name and good standing with his clients or other organizations that he deals with [27].

Solutions: There are many ways of dealing with phishing. The first solution to phishing is to try and avoid it at all costs. In order to do so, one must be careful to ensure they guard against all spams. In doing so, one should be careful when dealing with emails that seem to come from unrecognized senders. One should also be very suspicious with any email that ask for confirmation on their financial information or personal information. Such requests are usually made in urgency and sometimes they can appear when one is connected to internet doing something that may or may not be connected to the kind of information the email is requesting [27]. In some cases, such mails even tend to threaten the users with any frightening information in order to compel them to act swiftly.

Secondly, one should only ensure that they communicate personal information only when their mobile devices are secure. In doing so, they should also ensure they are also using secure websites. One of the best ways to distinguish between a secure website and an insecure website is by confirming that the website's URL begins with "https" and not simply "http". The URLs that have "s" tend to be more secure as the "s" stands for secure. Besides this, users can also avoid phishing by ensuring that they do not end up divulging personal information whenever they receive phone calls from numbers they have not saved in their mobile devices. This should be the case especially where the user is not the one who has initiated the call [27].

3.5   Attacks on Authorization

Authorization is similar to authentication in terms of granting access to users. It however differs from authentication as it has to do with the levels of rights and privileges given to each legal user [25]. In mobile computing, when a user downloads an app, he is usually asked to grant certain permissions that the app needs for its operation. This permissions determine the level of authorization or access control given to that particular app. For example, Android apps can query the APIs for user information like IMEI, location, contacts or call history and download history. A popular attack on authorization is whereby an app makes use of a covert channel to send out information to hackers.

Spyware: As mentioned previously, spyware is a type of malware that collects data from the infected system. A recent example of a spyware that exploits an app's privileges is Zitmo [10]. This spyware intercepts confirmation SMS sent by banks and thus it gains access to the user's confidential banking information like password, biodata. This information is then passed to the hacker for carrying out fraudulent activities.

Another example of a spyware that sends out users' information covertly is JackeeyWallpaper [23]. The collected data such as phone history, IMEI can then be sold to other illegal parties like scammers and phishers.

Solutions: The solutions are as discussed above in Sect. 3.1.

4   Limitations and Challenges

There exists challenges to security in mobile computing some of which have been addressed by the solutions in the previous section. These challenges exist due to the limitations in the mobile computing infrastructure itself and due to lack of compliance on the part of the users.

Lack of centralized management in mobile networks remains one of the challenges facing mobile computing security along with inadequate security standard [15]. Also, power constraints limit the ability to use and the effectiveness of anti-malware solutions in mobile devices. Often times, such anti-malware need to search through huge databases which deplete the power of the devices making them unattractive to the users.

On the part of the users, most users are incentivized to un-root their phones in other to have more control and to increase the functionalities of their devices. This however makes the devices easily susceptible to attacks. Another limitation is due to human error. Even with all the information, people tend to forget or genuinely make mistakes and they end up being affected by attacks. Therefore all mobile computing users are encouraged to ensure their devices are protected with an anti-virus, spam filters, anti-spyware software, and a secure firewall [27].

User education for security and privacy plays an essential role when it comes to mobile phone usage in personal as well as in business settings. Users' security education requires a holistic approach encompassing four aspects [16]:

- **Legal and Reputation:** Safeguarding, health and safety, data protection, intellectual property rights and copyright.
- **Organizational:** Learner recruitment, learner and employer relationship management, financial risk management, and staff development.
- **Technical and Operational:** Device management, network management, data management, and content management.
- **Teaching, Learning, and Assessment:** Materials and activities authoring, behavior management assessment, exams and marking, and candidate identity authentication, and plagiarism detection.

5   Conclusion

The security of mobile computing continues to face threats from attackers who gain access into the communication channel. Such attacks could include Sybil attack, phishing, denial of service attack (DoS), eavesdropping, and spoofing, malware, and message modifications among others. They can be prevented by using respective software such as personal firewall, anti-malware software, and encryption. Although all these solutions have certain weaknesses, extra measures are necessary to overcome such limitations. It is in our opinion that the user should also be knowledgeable of security issues and should not just download any application on his smart phone. Research should be made before downloading apps, and the user should be wary of emails, messages and wireless networks that he is not sure of. Moreover, users should not ignore security warnings that the system may issue. In conclusion, many security measures exist to prevent attacks from occurring however because of the continuous evolvement of the malicious software world, it is necessary for users to be made aware of this issue in order to be protected.

References

1. Adebayo, O.S., AbdulAziz, N.: Android malware classification using static code analysis and apriori algorithm improved with particle swarm optimization. In: Proceedings of 2014 4th World Congress on Information and Communication Technologies (WICT), pp. 123–128 (2014)
2. Bergman, N., Stanfield, M., Rouse, J., Scambray, J.: Hacking Exposed: Mobile Security Secrets and Solutions. McGraw-Hill Education, New York (2013)
3. Chien, E.: Motivations of recent Android malware. Technical report, Symantec Security Response (2011)
4. Deepak, G., Pradeep, B.: Challenging issues and limitations of mobile computing. Int. J. Comput. Technol. Appl. **3**, 177–181 (2012)
5. Desmedt, Y.: Man-in-the-middle attack. In: van Tilborg, H.C.A., Jajodia, S. (eds.) Encyclopedia of Cryptography and Security, p. 759. Springer, Heidelberg (2011)
6. Esposito, F., Matta, I., Ishakian, V.: Slice embedding solutions for distributed service architectures. ACM Comput. Surv. **46**, 6:1–6:29 (2013)
7. Fedler, R., Kulicke, M., Schutte, J.: An antivirus API for Android malware recognition. In: Proceedings of 2013 8th International Conference on Malicious and Unwanted Software: "The Americas" (MALWARE), pp. 77–84 (2013)

8. Felt, A.P., Finifter, M., Chin, E., Hanna, S., Wagner, D.: A survey of mobile malware in the wild. In: Proceedings of 1st ACM Workshop on Security and Privacy in Smartphones and Mobile Devices (SPSM), pp. 3–14 (2011)

9. García-Teodoro, P., Díaz-Verdejo, J., Maciá-Fernández, G., Vázquez, E.: Anomaly-based network intrusion detection: techniques, systems and challenges. Comput. Secur. **28**, 18–28 (2009)

10. He, D., Chan, S., Guizani, M.: Mobile application security: malware threats and defenses. IEEE Wirel. Commun. **22**, 138–144 (2015)

11. Ladan, M.I.: Mobile computing: security issues. In: Proceedings of 2013 International Conference on Wireless Networks (ICWN), pp. 1–6 (2013)

12. Lawton, G.: Is it finally time to worry about mobile malware? Computer **41**, 12–14 (2008)

13. Leavitt, N.: Mobile phones: the next frontier for hackers? Computer **38**, 20–23 (2005)

14. Li, W., Joshi, A.: Security issues in mobile ad hoc networks - a survey. Technical report, University of Maryland, USA (2008)

15. Masoud, N., Karimi, R., Hasanvand, H.A.: Mobile computing: principles, devices and operating systems. World Appl. Program. **2**, 399–408 (2012)

16. mEducation: safeguarding, security and privacy in mobile education. Technical report, GSMA Connected Living Programme: mEducation (2012)

17. Miller, C., Honoroff, J., Mason, J.: Security evaluation of Apple's iPhone. Technical report, Independent Security Evaluators (2007)

18. Nassar, M.: Wireless and mobile computing security challenges and their possible solutions. Am. Sci. Res. J. Eng. Technol. Sci. **3**, 66–74 (2015)

19. Peikari, C.: Protecting embedded devices with integrated permission control (2006). US patent number US20060026687 A1, http://www.google.com/patents/US20060026687

20. Pullela, S.: Security issues in mobile computing. Technical report, University of Texas at Arlington, USA (2002)

21. Quercia, D., Hailes, S.: Sybil attacks against mobile users: friends and foes to the rescue. In: Proceedings of 2010 IEEE International Conference on Computer Communications (INFOCOM), pp. 1–5 (2010)

22. Saha, H.N., Bhattacharyya, D., Banerjee, P.K.: Semi-centralized multi-authenticated RSSI based solution to Sybil attack. Int. J. Netw. Secur. Appl. **1**, 338–341 (2010)

23. Seo, S.H., Gupta, A., Sallam, A.M., Bertino, E., Yim, K.: Detecting mobile malware threats to homeland security through static analysis. J. Netw. Comput. Appl. **38**, 43–53 (2014)

24. Shields, C., Levine, B.N., Margolin, N.B.: A survey of solutions to the Sybil attack. Technical report, University of Massachusetts Amherst, USA (2006)

25. Stamp, M.: Information Security Principles and Practice. Wiley, New York (2011)

26. Vasudeva, A., Sood, M.: Sybil attack on lowest ID clustering algorithm in the mobile ad hoc network. Int. J. Netw. Secur. Appl. **4**, 135–147 (2012)

27. Verton, D.: Critical Threads 2006: IT*Security. Lulu.com, Raleigh (2006)

28. Wu, H., Schwab, S., Peckhams, R.L.: Signature based network intrusion detection system and method (2008). US patent number US7424744 B1, https://www.google.com/patents/US7424744

29. Xiao, Y.: Security in Distributed, Grid, Mobile, and Pervasive Computing. Auerbach Publications, Boston (2007)

30. Yu, H., Kaminsky, M., Gibbons, P.B., Flaxman, A.: SybilGuard: defending against Sybil attacks via social networks. In: Proceedings of 2006 Conference on Applications, Technologies, Architectures, and Protocols for Computer Communications (SIGCOMM), pp. 267–278 (2006)
31. Zhou, Y., Jiang, X.: Dissecting Android malware: characterization and evolution. In: Proceedings of 2012 IEEE Symposium on Security and Privacy (S&P), pp. 95–109 (2012)

Information Security Risk Analysis of Vehicular Ad Hoc Networks

Kanza Bayad[✉], Mohammed Rziza, and Mohammed Oumsis

LRIT Associated Unit with CNRST (URAC No 29), Faculty of Sciences,
Mohammed V University in Rabat, B.P 1014, Rabat, Morocco
bayadkanza17@gmail.com

Abstract. The main purpose of VANETs is to improve road safety and
to provide passengers' comfort. Thus, information security is one of the
most important issue which attracts researchers' attention due to its open
access environment. VANET requires high degree of reliability with an
acceptable risk, that develops the trust between the system and users.
The risk management is an essential method whose main objective is
to advise and determine the appropriate actions as well as priorities to
ensure information security. In this paper, we aim to apply the ISO/IEC
27005 Standard - Information Security Risk Management - on VANETs
in order to classify and mitigate risks in this technology. Our contribution
is an essential process that will help researchers to propose adequate
solutions against the attacks in VANET based on classification results.

Keywords: VANET · Information security risk · ISO/IEC 27005

1 Introduction

In recent years, Vehicular ad hoc networks (VANETs) have become a popular
concept in the Intelligent Transportation System (ITS) due to their application
for improving road safety and providing passengers' comfort. Otherwise, information security has received a lot of executive attention in the new technologies
and products. In this context, the security is a crucial issue in different fields
especially vehicular ad hoc networks which is the scope of our work.

Security is defined as the absence of unacceptable risk, from this point
onwards the analysis of risk is an essential process to determine threats, vulnerabilities and risk estimation of information security. This need is growing to
achieve the final objective of developing trust between the system and users.

The communication of vehicle networks will make them vulnerable to all
sorts of information security related attacks or offensive operations deployed by
individuals or organizations that targets such information systems. Therefore,
there is a lack of application in management tools that facilitate the analysis
of risks and their mitigations in VANETs to obtain the necessary resources for
information security solutions. There are several international methods related
to risk management, such as Cobit and Mehari, but this paper will consider

© ICST Institute for Computer Sciences, Social Informatics and Telecommunications Engineering 2017
R. Agüero et al. (Eds.): MONAMI 2016, LNICST 191, pp. 192–205, 2017.
DOI: 10.1007/978-3-319-52712-3_14

ISO/IEC 27005 (Security Risk Management Information) as being the most recent and recommended standard. So our solution undertakes the application of ISO/IEC 27005 method in VANET in order to mitigate risks in this technology.

The paper is organized as follow, Sect. 2 provides background of VANET security issues. ISO 2700x Family will be presented in Sect. 3. Section 4 will survey ISO 27005 risk management. Section 5 will offer an application of ISO 27005 standard for VANET networks. Finally, a conclusion will be given in Sect. 6.

2   VANET Security Issues

2.1   VANET Concept

The raise of mobile technologies has increased rapidly as well as it becomes more appreciated due to its ease of deployment. It has given rise to establish a new scheme called MANETs (Mobile Ad-hoc Networks), which is established without a centralized infrastructure (ad hoc). Vehicular ad hoc networks (VANET) is a particular case of MANET that provide communications into vehicles and link vehicles with roadside nodes. Its applications have several objectives such as sending safety information to avoid accidents or collisions and comfort applications (traffic jams, parking, collaborative driving, Access Internet, and so forth).

The VANET is a set of communicating entities organized under communication architecture equipped with communication units called OBUs (i.e. On Board Units) and fixed equipment called RSUs (i.e. Roadside Units). Each vehicle must also be equipped with systems to collect its position details, such as GPS (Global Positioning System). Other acronyms used in the VANETs are: V2V (Vehicle-to-Vehicle) for communication between vehicles, V2I (Vehicle-to-Infrastructure) for communication between vehicle and infrastructure - and hybrid architecture which is the combination of two approaches V2V and V2I. Figure 1 illustrates the general architecture in VANET.

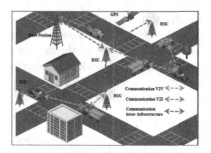

Fig. 1. General architecture in VANET

2.2 VANET Security Issues

Security Requirements

In the concept of vehicular network, several security measures should be taken to prevent cyber attacks and offensive operations. The major security requirements in vehicular network can form an acronym of CIA for Confidentiality, Integrity and Availability [1]. According to ITIL[1] (Information Technology Infrastructure Library), these can be defined as:

– **Confidentiality**: A security principle that requires that data should be accessed by authorized people only;
– **Integrity**: A security principle that ensures data and configuration items are modified by authorized personnel and activities only. Integrity considers all possible causes of modification, including software and hardware failure, environmental events, and human intervention;
– **Availability**: Ability of an IT service or other configuration item to perform its agreed function when required, and its determined by reliability, maintainability, serviceability, performance and security. Availability is usually calculated as a percentage. This calculation is often based on agreed service time and downtime. It is best practice to calculate availability of an IT service using measurements of the business output.

Attacks in VANET

VANET is vulnerable to several threats and attacks which can damage the functionality of a network, decrease its performance or compromise the security requirements [2]. In this section, we will discuss some possible threats and vulnerabilities in VANETs related to the security goals (CIA) through different scenarios.

DoS/DDoS (Denial of Service/Distributed Denial of Service): This attack [3] is one of the most dangerous threat in ITS systems, due to its major impact on the network resources. Indeed, the main goal behind these attacks is to prevent legitimate vehicles from using the network services and accessing its resources. The attacker sends various irrelevant messages to occupy a large amount of bandwidth and to consume more resources of the network. In this end, the communication channel between vehicles is blocked hence those vehicles are unable to communicate with each other on the network. In the case of DDoS Attack, several attacks are launched from different locations for the same purpose.

Message Alteration Attack: The misbehaved vehicles alter the sent messages in order to change their contents to achieve some objectives, such as injecting incorrect messages in the network to affect the behavior of other users. There are a lot of scenarios in this kind of attack that can compromise the integrity of messages in the VANET architecture by modifying, deleting, or intercepting their content [4].

---

[1] ITIL: http://www.itilfrance.com/.

Sybil Attack: This attack uses various false pseudonymous or identities of vehicles [5], and its major objective is to disable the network functionality by creating traffic illusion. Sybil attack makes legitimate vehicles communicate with the attacker who appear as different nodes while hiding the real identity and distribute false traffic congestion. This kind of attacks can inject false information in the network (e.g. traffic jams or accidents) [6].

Jamming Attack: The core purpose of such attack is to disrupt the communication channel between vehicles and RSU stations, by creating jams with high frequency [7]. The attacker can introduce different jamming techniques in a domain to make the network unavailable and to prevent nodes from exchanging messages in that domain.

Eavesdropping/Sniffing: In this type of attack, the adversary tries to listen to the transmission medium in order to extract information about the traffic or to collect data for analysis and perform other types of attacks (e.g. Message Alteration Attack).

3   ISO 2700x Family

The International Organization for Standardization (ISO) and the International Electrotechnical Commission (IEC) created the global standardization system (ISO/IEC). The main purpose of international standards published by ISO/IEC, related to information security, is to maintain trust between the services and treatments of information [8].

ISO/IEC 2700x family is an overview of international standards for Information Security Management System (ISMS), which provides a framework of guidelines necessary for continuous improvement of information security. ISO 2700x family comes in 8 volumes depicted in the Table 1.

4   Methodology: ISO 27005 Risk Management

ISO/IEC 27005:2011 [9] establishes a methodology for information security risk management, which gives more details about the phases of assessment and treatment of information security risks, it is necessary to use the background of ISO/IEC 27001 and ISO/IEC 27002 to implement this standard based on a risk management technique [8].

The main objective of risk management is to advise and determine the appropriate actions as well as priorities for the management of information security risks to protect the organisational information.

ISO 27005 applies the continuous improvement cycle to the management of risks, which is known also as PDCA (Plan, Do, Check and Act) or Deming Cycle. The latter is used in all management system standards. Table 2 shows the existing alignment between the ISMS management system based on the PDCA and the risk management process.

Table 1. Descriptions of ISO/IEC 2700x family [8].

Standard	Description	Publication date
ISO/IEC 27000	This is known as **ISMS standard – Overview and vocabulary**, which provides mostly the definitions, vocabulary and terms used in the family of Information Security Management Systems (ISMS)	2014
ISO/IEC 27001	This is known as **ISMS standard - Requirements**, which is the most popular standard in this family and defines the requirements for designing, planning, implementing, monitoring as well as improving the information security of organization	2013
ISO/IEC 27002	This is known as **Code of practice for information security controls**, which describes the best practices for information security management. This standard provides guidelines for organizations to select, implement and develop their own appropriate controls for information security	2013
ISO/IEC 27003	This is known as **Information security management system implementation guidance**, which describes the steps for design and implementation plans in an ISMS project	2010
ISO/IEC 27004	This is known as **ISMS standard - Measurement**, which concerns the guidance and the assessment of how to measure the effectiveness of such aspects in ISMS of the organization	2009
ISO/IEC 27005	This is known as **Information security risk management** and it provides a methodology for information security risk management. The details of ISO 27005 are explained in the next section	2011
ISO/IEC 27006	This is known as **Requirements for bodies providing audit and certification of ISMS**. This accreditation standard aims to guide the audit and certification bodies on the requirements for being accredited as a certification body of an ISMS	2015
ISO/IEC 27007	This is known as **Guidelines for information security management systems auditing**, which provides guidance for organizations auditing an ISMS, including the compliance auditing and the competence of auditors	2011

Table 2. Alignment of ISMS and information security risk management process [9].

ISMS process	Information security risk management process
Plan	Establishing the context
	Risk assessment
	Developing risk treatment plan
	Risk acceptance
Do	Implementation of risk treatment plan
Check	Continual monitoring and reviewing of risks
Act	Maintain and improve the information security risk
	Management process

According to this standard, the risk management process includes Context Establishment (Clause 7), Risk Assessment (Clause 8), Risk Treatment (Clause 9), Risk Acceptance (Clause 10), Risk Communication (Clause 11) as well as Risk Monitoring and Review (Clause 12). As illustrated in the Fig. 2, the risk assessment process has three main parts: Risk Identification, Risk Analysis and Risk Evaluation. The process can be interactive for both assessment as to the phases of treatment of risks, thus helping increase the breakdown of ratings in every interaction.

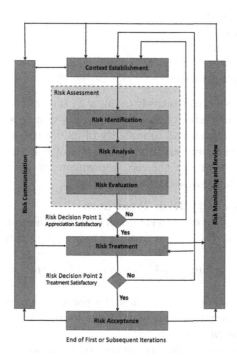

Fig. 2. Information security risk management process [9]

(1) Context Establishment

Establishment of context is the first phase of risk management process and structured in the ISO/IEC 27005 as follows:

General Considerations defines the objective of risk management activities that affects the process in the context establishment. Basic Criteria requires some measures, to warrant the risks, such as: risk evaluation criteria, risk impact criteria and risk acceptance criteria.

The scope and boundaries defines the limitations of risk management process to ensure that all assets are considered, including the definition of the process environment.

Organization for information security risk management defines roles and responsibilities for risk management process approved by the responsible manager in the organization.

(2) Information Security Risk Assessment

The process of risk assessment for information security consists of three phases: Risk Identification, Risk Analysis and Risk Evaluation.

Risk Identification determines those events which can compromise one of security requirements (CIA) following these sub-activities:

- Identification of assets;
- Identification of threats;
- Identify existing controls;
- Identification of vulnerabilities;
- Identification of consequences.

Risk Analysis describes qualitatively or quantify the level of risk in order to sort them depending on their gravity and the criticality of assets. This methodology estimates the impact of risk and probability of its occurrence.

Risk Evaluation is carried out from the results of risk analysis to make decisions about risk, it depends on the risk assessment criteria and risk acceptance criteria determined in the context establishment.

(3) Information Security Risk Treatment

The objective of this step is to establish risk treatment plan as well as define security measures and controls in order to reduce, retain, prevent or transfer risks.

Risk Reduction is accomplished by selecting of controls to make the residual risk as acceptable.

Risk Retention is the decision to allow the risk-existence without any further action based on its evaluation, this may be due to organizational policy or other reasons (e.g. cost, complexity).

Risk Prevention is used in the cases of very high risk where there are no implementing controls feasible for technical or economic reasons, it may be required to avoid them or prevent them.

Risk Transfer, in certain situations, the risk may be transferred to another party capable of treating it more appropriately or better endure the consequences.

(4) Information Security Risk Acceptance

In this phase, a decision is made to accept the risks and validate their treatment, it describes how the risks will be treated to be accepted (risk acceptance criteria). In some cases, the level of residual risk does not conform to the risk acceptance criteria, but it is used because of other reasons for the risks that are accepted.

(5) Information Security Risk Communication

During all stages of risk management, risk information should be communicated to all decision makers and stakeholders, so that all those concerned are well informed to act accordingly to implement the suitable controls and measures for the risks.

(6) Information Security Risk Monitoring and Review

The risks and their factors may vary over time. New threats and vulnerabilities may arise during the steps of risk management.

Monitoring and review of risk factors: The factors of risks must be monitored and reviewed regularly to identify any changes while maintaining a complete view of risk.

Risk management monitoring, reviewing and improving: It is important to monitor the information security incidents, to review and improve the risk factors periodically.

5   Application of ISO 27005 Standard for VANET Networks

This section demonstrates the application of the ISO 27005 standard for vehicular networks, to manage the security risk by identifying and estimating the security risks of existing information in VANETs.

5.1   Risk Identification in VANETs

Assets Identification

According to ISO27005 standard, the assets can be distinguished between primary and secondary.

Concerning the primary assets, it consists the business processes - to achieve the main objective of VANETs and to maintain its functionality as well as the activity information - it consists personal information of vehicle, information shared over the network, storage and gathering information. It can be grouped into three classes (Table 3):

Table 3. Assets identification.

Id assets	Assets	Information type
AS1	Safer roads	Warning
		Collision
		Speed
AS2	Efficient driving	Improve traffic information
		Manage traffic flow
		Parking
AS3	Entertainment information	Internet
		Mp3 download

Secondary assets consists of the support and infrastructure used in VANETs. We can classify the assets in VANETs: Users (Drivers, passengers), physical transmission medium, OBU, RSU, Global Positioning System (GPS) receivers, Control centre, Event Data Recorders (EDR), Omnidirectional antennas, Providers of commercial services, Auto-makers and Maintenance.

Threats, Existing Controls, Vulnerabilities and Consequences Identification

According to ISO 27005 standard, each threat can have one or more origins. It can be due to deliberate, accidental or environmental actions. We presented in Sect. 2.2 some possible attacks that succeed due to the vulnerabilities of VANETs. These threats made the researchers to identify and implement several solutions to address the security issue of VANETs by detecting or preventing the attacks.

The Table 4 presents major vulnerabilities in VANETs that cause such attacks, their impacts on the primary goals of information security and their solutions proposed by researchers.

Table 4. Threats, existing controls, vulnerabilities and consequences identification.

Vulnerabilities	Attacks	Compromised goals	Solutions
High dynamic topology	DOS/DDOS	Availability	Approaches to overcame Denial of Service Attack [3,10,11]
Unprotected wireless communication	Message alteration attack	Integrity	Detection of radio interference in VANET [12,13]
Same secret key used many times	Sybil attack	Availability	Cryptographic countermeasures [4,14]
Difficult to detect the malicious node	Jamming attack	Availability	Anti-jamming attack [15]
Easy to inject fault message	Eavesdropping/ Sniffing	Confidentiality	Sybil attack detection [5]
			Efficient certificate management [16]

5.2   Risk Analysis in VANETs

This phase is very important in risk assessment, it has two methods for measuring risk namely qualitative and quantitative or both. For our risk analysis, we can use a metric to calculate and estimate the level of risk. The degree for impact are 1: negligible; 2: small; 3: Limited: 4: significant and 5: severe. These levels depend on the level of exploitation of the vulnerabilities over the security goals (CIA) and the importance of the assets. However, in general, higher impacts have been assigned to threats involving road safety information, control centres or large areas of VANETs; Average impacts when they involve smaller areas of RSUs; lower impact if they are restricted to only a vehicle of convenience or information and commercial services. We can attribute criteria threat or probability for exploit as 1: rare; 2: unlikely; 3: moderate; 4: susceptible; 5: very likely. These levels depend on the degree of vulnerability of the assets and the existing controls and measures.

For this purpose, we consider scenarios from the previous attacks and estimate the risk according to the criticality of assets, the impact assessment, the frequency of the threat, the degree of vulnerability, the probability of the incident and calculate the level of risk for each identified scenario.

Scenario 1: Overload the resources of one vehicle by sending repeated messages.

Scenario 2: Overload the resources of a set of vehicles, RSUs or wireless devices vehicle by sending repeated messages.

Scenario 3: Configure vehicle sensors to generate false warning messages.

Scenario 4: Modify or delete an important packet that contains critical information.

Scenario 5: Send multiple messages from one node to others with different identifiers.

Scenario 6: Inject a stream of random data on the channel to disrupt communication.

Scenario 7: Send a malicious code to the neighbours of the target vehicle to listen to the data traffic and obtain the target vehicles ID and its location.

The final determination of the risk which is used for the estimation value of attacks is obtained by multiplying the probability of threats and their impact.

$$Risk = Impact \times Probability\,(Threat) \tag{1}$$

We can notice from the table that the value of impact and probability of threat can be inconstant depending on the scenario, for example, the first scenario (DOS Attack) has a small impact 2 on efficient driving assets because it can affect only one vehicle, the probability of threat is estimated as very likely 5 because of the ease of this attack simulation. The fifth scenario (Sybil Attack) has a severe impact 5 on safer roads and efficient driving assets, because this kind of attacks can inject false information in the network to cause incidents, the probability of threat is estimated as susceptible 4 (Table 5).

This phase can give a risk classification previously calculated, we'll derive ranking matrix from that used by ISO-27005 (Fig. 3):

We can attribute our proposed scenarios in the matrix to classify the risk of each scenario. We are limited to these scenarios because we want to provide different examples to calculate risk.

5.3   Risk Evaluation in VANETs

This matrix shows the risk assessment of our scenarios that may result in impacts on primary assets. Incident scenarios positioned in the green area are considered

Table 5. Risk values of our scenarios.

Scenario	Assets	Impact	Probability of threat	Risk
1	2	2	5	10
2	2	4	4	16
3	1	4	3	12
4	1, 2, 3	4	3	12
5	1, 2	5	4	20
6	1, 2, 3	4	4	16
7	2	5	3	15

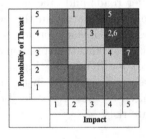

Interval	Risk Classification
1-5	Low
6-12	Medium
15-25	High

Fig. 3. Ranking matrix used by ISO-27005

as low risk; those positioned in the yellow area are considered as medium risk; and those placed in the red area are considered as high risk for the information security of VANETs. As we observe in our scenarios that is no low-risk scenario that is obvious in risk assessment, hence zero risk does not exist and we cannot guarantee a total security.

We tried to give examples from the attacks presented in the first section to give an idea about the risk value of each scenario, researchers may use this method to think about the risk that reached a high risk level for developing their own solutions against that attack (Fig. 4).

Fig. 4. Risk assessment of our scenarios (Color figure online)

5.4   Risk Treatment in VANETs

According to ISO 27005 Standard, each scenario carries out an analysis of risk treatment in order to reduce, retain, prevent or transfer risks, based on the establishment of controls and solutions suggested in the literature. In this vein, those solutions are used to reduce the risk, the other options are used according to the level and the type of risks.

The solutions, measures and controls against those attacks [17] will be applied to reduce the risks of our scenarios. As depicted in the following table, the risks of the scenarios are lowered - from high level to medium, and from medium to low level - due to the solutions proposed (Table 6).

The objective of this phase is to eliminate high-risk scenario by removing the possible scenarios from the red zone as shown in the Fig. 6.

Table 6. Risk values after risk treatment.

Scenario	Assets	Impact	Probability of threat	Risk
1	2	1	3	3
2	2	4	3	12
3	1	3	2	6
4	1, 2, 3	2	1	2
5	1, 2	4	1	4
6	1, 2, 3	4	2	8
7	2	3	3	9

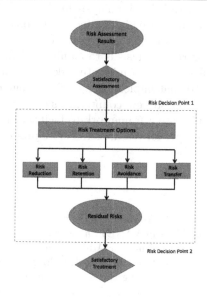

Fig. 5. Risk treatment activity [9]

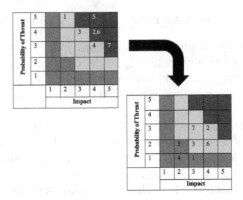

Fig. 6. Risk treatment of our scenarios (Color figure online)

According to Fig. 5, the last step after the treatment of risks is to check whether the measures are satisfactory, that is, if those steps meet the risk acceptance criteria set out above.

In this study it was assumed that all the solutions presented are efficient to achieve the risk reduction estimated, and that the residual risk meet the acceptance criteria established for VANETs. Otherwise, it would take new interactions of the risk management process as illustrated in Fig. 2.

6 Conclusion

This paper performed a detailed risk analysis for VANET based on ISO 27005 standard. Through this analysis we highlighted all the phases of this standard to determine its application feasibility based on the different contexts of VANET. The main purpose of this risk analysis is to monitor incidents and process continuous improvement of security to mitigate risk as much as possible. In this paper, We have illustrated that implementing risk management on VANET will help the researchers to propose new countermeasures for any kind of attacks. Our future target is to propose a framework to facilitate risk management over VANET, it will be a pre-study for researchers before proposing solutions against attacks.

References

1. Sumra, I.A., Hasbullah, H.B., AbManan, J.B.: Attacks on security goals (confidentiality, integrity, availability) in VANET: a survey. In: Laouiti, A., Qayyum, A., Mohamad Saad, M.N. (eds.) Vehicular Ad-hoc Networks for Smart Cities. AISC, vol. 306, pp. 51–61. Springer, Heidelberg (2015). doi:10.1007/978-981-287-158-9_5
2. Tyagi, P., Dembla, D.: Investigating the security threats in vehicular ad hoc networks (VANETs): towards security engineering for safer on-road transportation. In: 2014 International Conference on Advances in Computing, Communications and Informatics (ICACCI), pp. 2084–2090. IEEE (2014)

3. Malla, A.M., Sahu, R.K.: Security attacks with an effective solution for dos attacks in VANET. Int. J. Comput. Appl. **66**(22), 45–49 (2013)
4. Hamida, E.B., Noura, H., Znaidi, W.: Security of cooperative intelligent transport systems: standards, threats analysis and cryptographic countermeasures. Electronics **4**(3), 380–423 (2015)
5. Hussain, R., Oh, H.: On secure and privacy-aware sybil attack detection in vehicular communications. Wirel. Pers. Commun. **77**(4), 2649–2673 (2014)
6. Ali Mohammad, M., Pouyan, A.A.: Defense mechanisms against sybil attack in vehicular ad hoc network. Secur. Commun. Netw. **8**(6), 917–936 (2015)
7. Malebary, S., Xu, W.: A survey on jamming in VANET. Int. J. Sci. Res. Innovative Technol. **2**, 142–156 (2015)
8. ISO/IEC 2700x Family (2016). http://www.iso.org/
9. ISO/IEC, ISO/IEC 27005, Information technology - Security techniques - Information security risk management. ISO/IEC (2011)
10. Hasbullah, H., Soomro, I.A., et al.: Denial of service (dos) attack and its possible solutions in VANET. World Acad. Sci. Eng. Technol. Int. J. Electr. Comput. Energ. Electron. Commun. Eng. **4**(5), 813–817 (2010)
11. Pathre, A.: Identification of malicious vehicle in VANET environment from ddos attack. J. Glob. Res. Comput. Sci. **4**(6), 30–34 (2013)
12. Hamieh, A., Ben-Othman, J., Mokdad, L.: Detection of radio interference attacks in VANET. In: IEEE Global Telecommunications Conference, GLOBECOM 2009, pp. 1–5. IEEE (2009)
13. Vijayalakshmi, V., Sathya, M., Saranya, S., Selvaroopini, C.: Survey on various mechanisms for secure and efficient VANET communication. In: 2014 International Conference on Information Communication and Embedded Systems (ICICES), pp. 1–5. IEEE (2014)
14. Mejri, M.N., Ben-Othman, J., Hamdi, M.: Survey on vanet security challenges and possible cryptographic solutions. Veh. Commun. **1**(2), 53–66 (2014)
15. Azogu, I.K., Ferreira, M.T., Larcom, J.A., Liu, H.: A new anti-jamming strategy for VANET metrics-directed security defense. In: 2013 IEEE Globecom Workshops (GC Wkshps), pp. 1344–1349, IEEE (2013)
16. Horng, S.-J., Tzeng, S.-F., Huang, P.-H., Wang, X., Li, T., Khan, M.K.: An efficient certificateless aggregate signature with conditional privacy-preserving for vehicular sensor networks. Inf. Sci. **317**, 48–66 (2015)
17. Mokhtar, B., Azab, M.: Survey on security issues in vehicular ad hoc networks. Alexandria Eng. J. **54**(4), 1115–1126 (2015)

Automatic Definition and Application of Similarity Measures for Self-operation of Network

Haitao Tang[1(✉)], Kaj Stenberg[2], Kasper Apajalahti[3], Juha Niiranen[4], and Vilho Räisänen[1]

[1] Bell Labs, Nokia, Espoo, Finland
haitao.tang@nokia.com
[2] Mobile Network Products, Nokia, Espoo, Finland
[3] Semantic Computing Research Group, Aalto University, Espoo, Finland
[4] Department of Mathematics and Statistics, University of Helsinki, Helsinki, Finland

Abstract. Self-operation concept is proposed to learn the past experiences of network operations and apply the learned operation experiences to solve new but similar problems. It works based upon the observation that actions appropriate for achieving an objective resemble each other in similar network contexts. Plenty of such similarities exist at the level of network elements, functions, and their relations. Similarity measure definition and application are essential components for the self-operation to apply the learned operation experiences. This paper provides a solution for self-operation to define and apply two types of similarity measures for two self-operation use cases. The first use case answers how to select a best suitable function to achieve any given objective. The second use case tells how the selected function should be configured with the most optimal parameter values so that the given objective could be achieved. This solution is realized on a demonstrator implementing the self-operation concept. Corresponding experiments are made with the demonstrator. The experimental results show that the self-operation solution works well.

Keywords: Similarity measure · Context aware · Network operations · Self-operation · Operation experience · OSS · Cellular network · Case based reasoning

1 Introduction

The network environments of multi-RAT, multi-access, and multi-vendor have added significant complexity to the network operations. Self-x functions (e.g., SON and traffic steering functions [1–3]) have become an essential part of the 3–4G networks and their management. These self-x functions have reduced a clear part of manual work related to operations that would be needed otherwise for the 3–4G networks. This effectively reduces the operational complexity perceived by human operators as well. The coming 5G systems (i.e., their networks and management systems [4]) are expected to have a much wider scope and, a larger number and variety, of self-x functions and multi-x

© ICST Institute for Computer Sciences, Social Informatics and Telecommunications Engineering 2017
R. Agüero et al. (Eds.): MONAMI 2016, LNICST 191, pp. 206–219, 2017.
DOI: 10.1007/978-3-319-52712-3_15

network environments. In addition, one of the 5G goals is to minimize the need of human involvement in their operations.

These fundamental developments have created the industry-wide determination to gradually evolve towards cognitive network management systems. In such systems, relevant past experiences could be used to predict the future status of a network. The corresponding decisions could thus be made to improve either network performance or subscriber perceived experience. In such systems, the minimal but still critically needed role of human operator can be seamlessly integrated to observe the systems and instruct them when the non-human parts of systems have no knowledge to deal with certain situations or are otherwise incapable of drawing conclusions or making decisions by their own based on their predefined logics. Such systems can prevent the functions (self-x or not) of the systems from executing the operations that may cause (and are known to have caused already earlier) degradation in network performance metrics or unfavorable user experience. Such systems can also make an operation of a function favorable if its execution is expected to induce improvement in network performance or customer experience.

Self-operation [5] proposes a solution to realize such an aforementioned cognitive network management system. It creates a self-operation case for each relevant event, learns every corresponding operation and outcome of the system, and stores the learned experience to the self-operation case. The outcome consists of the performance metrics and customer experience, etc. The self-operation case also stores the learned context data such as system conditions and other relevant circumstances (e.g. cell configuration, location, and traffic profile) that may have impacted the triggering of the event. All the data relevant to a corresponding operation execution are learned and collected in the data elements of the self-operation case, and thus inherently linked into a piece of useful corresponding experience, which can thus be applied on the fly. The availability of such experience is very important. As of today, these data (if any) are quite scattered and distributed in a system. Some data elements are stored in different locations. Other necessary data elements may not yet be stored at all. In such a situation, data mining cannot help to find the experience. In addition, data mining is usually time/resource consuming, and cannot therefore meet a request for such experience in timely fashion.

The self-operation solution in [5] does not answer how to define a similarity measure to find the corresponding operation experiences from the potentially large number of learned but different self-operation cases. The similarity measure definition is an essential and critical component of the self-operability and, it is specific to the given use case of self-operation. It determines if the operation experience cases (i.e., knowledge) learned from the earlier executed operations can be applied to future operations of a given use case.

As a major use case of self-operation, an operator may want to request the self-operation for guidance on how to achieve given objective(s) for network performance or service in a certain area (i.e. scope of the network). The objectives are usually related to improvement of certain Key Performance Indicators (KPI) regarding for example coverage, traffic, mobility, or quality. Different functions may however cause impacts on many of those KPIs at the same time. It is thus difficult for the operator to select the best function (out of several candidate functions) to achieve the objective.

This is where the definition and application of the corresponding similarity measure can help. The relevant self-operation cases can be matched from the knowledge database, with the corresponding objective-specific similarity measure. The information about the best suitable function can then be extracted from the relevant self-operation cases.

As another major use case of self-operation, the operator can have difficulty to determine the (best) suitable configuration (e.g., SCV - SON function Configuration parameter Value) for the selected function to achieve the result expected by the objective. The suitable configuration of the function depends on the corresponding conditions (network configurations, status, traffic, etc.) of the managed objects (MOs) where the function is planned to be executed. This is again where the definition and application of the corresponding similarity measure can help. The relevant self-operation cases could be matched from the knowledge database, with the corresponding function-specific similarity measure. The information of the (best) suitable function configuration can then be extracted from the relevant self-operation cases.

The function-specific similarity measure could also be used to find the corresponding operation experience case(s) and extract the knowledge concerning another related major use case of self-operation that answers the question: "Can an action request for the function be executed or not?" Thus, the function-specific similarity measure enables both the operation to select the corresponding configuration for the chosen function, and the decision on an action of the function.

The motivation of this paper is therefore to design a complete solution by solving the following problems: (1) how to define an objective-specific similarity measure to match an objective to its corresponding function; (2) how to automatically match the objective and corresponding rule given by an operator to the best suitable function for achieving the given objective; (3) how to automatically define the corresponding function-specific similarity measure; (4) how to automatically apply the function-specific similarity measure for a function-specific operation. For example, the corresponding operation information and the configuration(s) can be found from the matching operation experience cases.

The sections of this paper are organized as the follows. In Sect. 2, the self-operation architecture to define and apply a similarity measure is described. In Sect. 3, the approach to define an objective-specific similarity measure is introduced. In Sect. 4, it is explained how an objective-specific similarity measure is used to find the relevant function. In Sect. 5, the approach to define a function-specific similarity measure is presented. Section 6 depicts how a function-specific similarity measure is used to find the proper configuration value for the selected function. Section 7 introduces the example implementation of a self-operation system and its experiment results. Section 8 summarizes and discusses the major finding of the current work.

2   Self-operation Architecture for Similarity Definition and Application

Figure 1 shows the architecture of defining and applying similarity measures based on stored operation experience cases. The arrows are logical and can be implemented by direct or indirect connections between the entities in the real implementations.

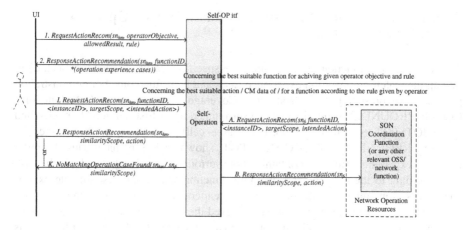

Fig. 1. The architecture of defining and applying similarity measures based on stored operation experience cases.

The definition of a similarity measure is started when a request message for action recommendation (i.e., Message 1, A, or I) is received. These messages serve as the triggers to define relevant similarity measures and use them to find the matching self-operation cases with the principle of case based reasoning [6]. The corresponding experiences in the matching self-operation cases are replied back to the requesting entities.

There are different types of similarity measures, which are usually specific to their actual applications (i.e., use cases) [7–9]. The similarity measures of this paper belongs to the family of semantic similarity measures. The similarity measures of this paper are used to find the exactly matching self-operation cases (if any) stored in the database of the self-operation entity. Their specific definitions and applications of the similarity measures are given in the following sections.

3 Definition of Similarity Measure for a Given Operator Objective and Rule

The operational objectives and rules of a network (e.g., [10]) are usually defined with a set of high level KPIs (e.g., [11, 12]) for the network operations. When an operator needs to achieve a specific objective for network performance under certain rules (i.e., constrains and options), the operator sends a request (Message 1 in the Fig. 1) to self-operation function. This message carries the information of the operation objective including the target scope (i.e., the targeted MOs), allowed result, and rules. The rules can be created either by the system vendor or by the operator via means of Rule Editor, which is a specialized tool for the creation and maintenance of the rules.

The self-operation function uses the received information to define the corresponding objective-specific similarity measure, which can be simply in the form of a text string carrying the provided information elements.

4   Selection of a Suitable Function for the Given Operator Objective and Rule

The self-operation function uses the objective-specific measure (defined in Sect. 3) to find all the matching operation experience cases and their functions. For demonstration purposes, we present two Capacity and Coverage Optimization (CCO) functions, CCO-SURROUNDED (optimizing a cell surrounded by its first-tier neighbor cells) and CCO-HOTSPOT (optimizing a hotspot source cell). For example, these functions (CCO-SURROUNDED and CCO-HOTSPOT, shown in Fig. 6) have caused similar operation experiences (in areas containing both surrounded and hotspot cells) in the past.

According to the rule, the self-operation function selects the best suitable experience cases from all the matching operation experience cases. For example, *CCO-SURROUNDED* is the function that has achieved the optimization objective in most of the matching cases (96% of all the matching cases). *CCO-SURROUNDED* function is thus selected automatically as the best suitable function to achieve the intended operation. The decision for the selection can be made based on several different criteria such as the highest probability to achieve successful results, operations' priorities or operator's preferences and policies. The criteria is actually defined by the rules

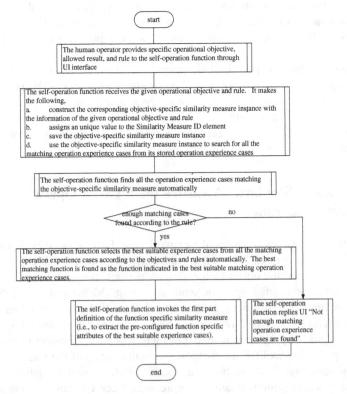

Fig. 2. Procedure to find the best matching function and its corresponding operation experience cases that can achieve a given operator objective.

provided by the operator. The general procedure of objective specific similarity definition and function selection is described with the diagram shown in Fig. 2.

5 Definition of Similarity Measure for the Selected Function

The common information elements needed by a function-specific similarity measure instance are defined as a set of general similarity attributes and function-specific attributes, as shown in Table 1. The function-specific attributes are always explicitly

Table 1. The common information elements of a function-specific similarity measure instance.

	Element name	Definition
General attributes	Function-specific Similarity Measure ID (F_SM_ID)	A character string that uniquely identifies this similarity measure instance. It helps the further process and application of this similarity measure instance
	Similarity scope	The type of the managed objects (MOs) relate to this similarity measure instance. For example, A similarity scope can be one type of {*individual cell, cell pair, first-tier neighbor cells, second-tier neighbor cells, subnetwork, network, etc.*}. A similarity scope is usually specific to a function. For example, a *CCO-SURROUNDED* function is optimizing the coverage performance of the given cells. Thus, the similarity scope for this function is the given cell and its 1st-tier neighbors of the same type
Function-specific attributes	Function ID	The unique ID of a function (e.g., *CCO-SURROUNDED*) that is selected as the most relevant function to pursue the requested operation
	Function specific attribute1	The first feature specific attribute and value that is automatically extracted from the selected experience cases. Note: an attribute and its value are extracted only when this attribute is impacting the function or is impacted by the output of the function. The attribute is identified according to the impacting scopes [14] of the function
	...	
	Function specific attribute$_n$	The nth feature specific attribute and value that is automatically extracted from the selected experience cases, where $n \geq 0$ and, $n = 0$ means there is no feature specific attribute for the specific similarity measure instance

defined for the specific function selected. A function-specific similarity measure instance is always operation specific.

After the best suitable function is found by self-operation, the self-operation is invoked to define its function specific similarity measure, which consists of two parts. With the information of the function (e.g., *CCO-SURROUNDED*) and the objective-specific similarity measure (e.g., coverage-related optimization of the cells with ID 1–5), the self-operation function defines the first part of the corresponding function specific similarity measure. Here, the information of any function in the network is pre-defined and made available in the form of function metadata [13] by the operator or its vendor. The function information also defines the impacting scopes [14] of the function.

The first part of the function-specific similarity measure is the static information of the function and the MOs that are either pre-defined or available beforehand. This "static" part is defined by extracting the information of the function, the corresponding cells, and the relevant rule. For example, the first part of *CCO-SURROUNDED* - specific similarity measure can consist of the information elements (and their values) of such as CCO ID, cell technology, cell type, and antenna mode. For simplicity, we assume the target scope consists of only one similarity scope in this example. In reality, if multiple similarity scopes exist in a given target scope (as often the case), their corresponding function-specific similarity measures are defined one by one with the same approach shown in this example.

The self-operation function then uses the defined first part of the function-specific similarity measure to further select the matching operation experience cases from all the cases still fulfilling the search criteria. For example, there are 51 self-operation cases found under the selected *CCO-SURROUNDED* function. 25 self-operation cases match the defined first part of the CCO-specific similarity measure.

The self-operation function extracts the information of the 25 cases. What to extract depends on the given rule or otherwise a default configuration. For example, an extraction can be done from all those performance metrics information elements and their value ranges shared by some or all of the 25 cases. These performance metrics are, for example, the impacting and impacted metrics of *RLF INPUT* and *RLF OUTPUT*. The extracted result serves and becomes the remaining part of the similarity measure definition. Now, the complete function-specific similarity measure has been defined.

6   Selection of Suitable Configuration for the Selected Function

With the defined function-specific similarity measure, self-operation function finds, e.g., 9 self-operation cases (out of the 25 cases) matching the similarity measure exactly. The configuration values (SCVs) of the 9 self-operation cases are collected into a configuration set called "*CCO-SURROUNDED Config Set$_1$*". The self-operation function then uses the extracted configuration value to configure the *CCO-SUR-ROUNDED* function and activate it to achieve the given objective.

The general procedure of the definition and application of function specific similarity measure is described with the diagram shown in Fig. 3. In this procedure, the

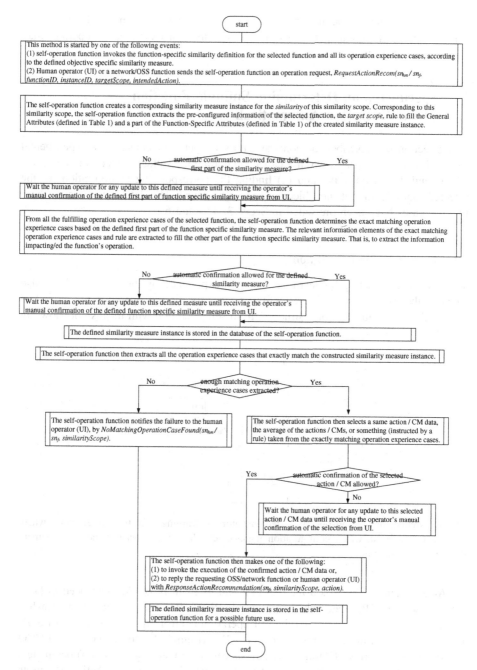

Fig. 3. Procedure for the automatic function-specific similarity measure construction and application.

intervention of human operator is supported in the otherwise automatic definition and application of a function-specific similarity measure. For example, the operator may need to update or confirm a selection.

7 Experiments on Determining Suitable Function and Configuration Automatically

In this section, we describe a demonstrator for self-operation and show its experimental results. It currently realizes two use cases: (1) finding the suitable function to achieve a given (high level) objective and (2) finding the corresponding configuration for the selected function so that the objective can be achieved. The details concerning these two use cases have been presented in Sects. 3, 4, 5 and 6.

7.1 Demonstrator Description

The demonstrator set-up for learning operation experiences is shown in Fig. 4. It also supports the applications of operation experiences for the self-operation use cases that receive their configuration or instruction from self-operation with means not shown in Fig. 4.

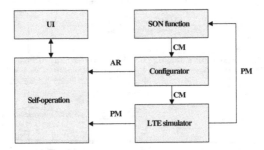

Fig. 4. Architecture of self-operation demonstrator for learning operation experiences, where AR = action request, CM = configuration management data, PM = performance management data, and UI = user interface.

An LTE simulator (Nokia internal tool and its main principle introduced in [15]) acts as a source of PM data, which are sent via REST (Representational State Transfer) interfaces to a SON function and the self-operation control logic. Two groups of SON functions are used in the demonstrator, i.e., RET (Remote Electrical Tilt)-based CCO and energy saving (ES). Configurator adjusts cell and other (e.g., function) parameters on the one hand, and amends CM data with metadata to create Action Requests (ARs) for self-operation on the other. The UI can be used for similarity definitions and related operation case searches. Direct configuration from the UI is not implemented at the moment.

PM data are stored into self-operation internal database as they arrive. ARs are received by the self-operation system in such a way that each received AR triggers the creation of a corresponding operation case. A MongoDB NoSQL database is used for storing PM data, operation cases, and function profiles. The REST interface is implemented with Java, the self-operation control logic with Clojure, and the user interface with HTML 5/JavaScript. SON functions, self-operation, and UI JavaScript back-end are run on Ubuntu desktop machine (Intel Core2 2.5 GHz, 2 GB memory, 64-bit Ubuntu). UI front-end is run on browser (Chrome) over a Windows 7 laptop (8 GB).

7.2 Experiment and Result

This section shows an example experiment and results in which a human operator provides high-level operation objective and then finds a best matching function and its configuration set in a desired context. The experiment is done in three phases, i.e., defining goal and preconditions, retrieving relevant search results based on the automatically defined similarity measure, and, if needed, sharpening the results by adjusting similarity measure.

7.2.1 Defining Goal and Precondition for the Objective-Specific Similarity Measure

Figure 5 depicts the first phase in the view. Through UI, the user can define a goal and its context by Wizard 1 of Fig. 5 and set numerical boundaries (or other rules) for the search results by Wizard 2 of Fig. 5.

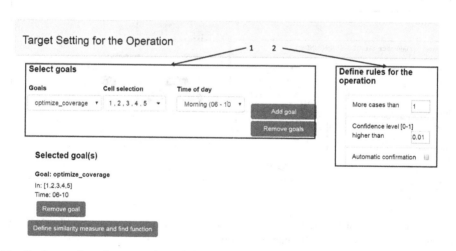

Fig. 5. A snapshot of an example to define objective specific similarity measure via specifying corresponding goal, network context, and numerical boundaries.

In this use case, the user wants to find suitable operations for optimizing coverage for an area including, e.g., five cells (1, 2, 3, 4, and 5), and with a time range from, e.g.,

6AM to 10AM. In the rule definition form (Wizard 2), numerical boundaries can be selected to further exclude irrelevant search results. For example, the minimum amount of cases per retrieved SON function is set to 1. The minimum confidence level (success ratio to achieve a goal) is set to 0.01. Here, the boundaries have low values in order to maximize the amount of operation cases in the search results.

The above information is used to define the objective-specific similarity measure. With this similarity measure, Wizard 3 of Fig. 6 searches and shows the result of the self-operation cases matching the objective-specific similarity measure. The self-operation analysed approximately 500 cases in several seconds. Two SON functions are then identified in these self-operation cases. *CCO-SURROUNDED* is a CCO function instance that optimizes a source cell surrounded completely by its 1st-tier neighbor cells. *CCO-HOTSPOT* is a CCO function instance that optimizes a hotspot source cell. The columns in Wizard 3 describe the name of the function (*function_-name*), the total amount of self-operation cases matching the target that the SON function has been involved with (*matching_cases*), the amount of successful cases achieved the target (*successful_cases*), the success ratio of the matching cases (*confidence*), and the proportion of the number of matching cases of the function to the total number of the matching cases of all functions (*proportion*). The function (*CCO-SURROUNDED*) and its 51 self-operation cases in the first row are selected as this function has the highest proportion value.

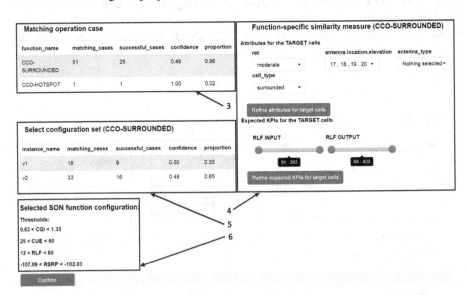

Fig. 6. A snapshot of the objective-based function selection, the function-specific similarity definition, and the function configuration selections.

7.2.2   Function-Specific Similarity Definition and Search
for Configuration

For the selected function *CCO-SURROUNDED*, the available function-specific similarity attributes are antenna elevation, antenna type, and cell type of the source cells, as well as their value ranges for RLF. The value ranges indicate the values before (*RLF INPUT*) and after (*RLF OUTPUT*) the operation case has been executed.

Wizard 4 of Fig. 6 collects the relevant attributes of the source cells to define the first part of the function-specific similarity measure for the selected function. With this first part of the similarity measure, the 25 matching self-operation cases (found by Wizards 3) are further filtered. The remaining part of the function-specific similarity measure is then defined by extracting the relevant KPI information of the further matched self-operation cases. With this fully defined function-specific similarity measure, the first configuration set (*v1*) of the 9 self-operation cases is selected, as shown in Wizard 5. The actual configuration values of the selected configuration set are presented in the configuration list shown in Wizard 6.

The selected configuration can now be confirmed (automatically or manually) and configured to the selected function so that the selected function can make its decision (e.g., CM output) accordingly. If not, the function-specific similarity measure can be updated to find another configuration set, or another function can be re-selected and the process is repeated from Wizard 3.

7.2.3 Refining Function Specific Similarity Definition and Its Match Results

In addition to the automatic confirmation of a matching result, a user can also take the manual control of the confirmation when needed. In this mode, the user can explore the current search results to see if more accurate results for the context are needed. Figure 7 demonstrates such a situation, in which the user has decided to refine the results by reducing the value range of the *RLF OUTPUT* shown in Entry A and the elevation value shown in Entry B.

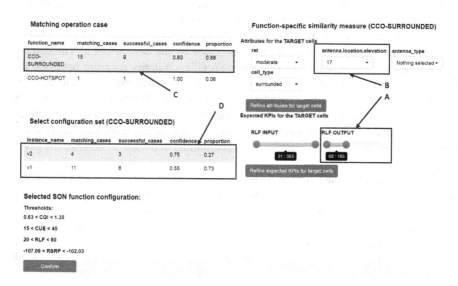

Fig. 7. A snapshot of the match result and configuration via refining the values of the function specific similarity measure.

Figure 7 shows how the amount of cases has reduced (with respect to Fig. 6.) for the *CCO-SURROUNDED* and for its configurations *v1* and *v2*, shown in Entry C and Entry D. The confidence levels of these elements have increased. Configuration set *v2* is now automatically selected as the preferred configuration for the user to confirm. The user could even pick and confirm the configuration set *v1*, if the user would prefer so instead.

8   Conclusion and Discussion

This work provides a solution to define and apply two types of similarity measures for two self-operation use cases. The use cases are as follows: Self-operation uses its learned operation experiences to answer the question "Given any objective and its corresponding network context, what function should be used to achieve it?" Self-operation uses its learned operation experiences to answer the question "Given any objective and network context, what should be the suitable configuration for that function so that it could achieve the objective?"

The solution consists of the self-operation architecture for similarity measure definition and application, the data elements needed by the two types of similarity measures, and their definition and application procedures.

This work also describes a demonstrator implementation of self-operation, which learns operation experiences into self-operation cases and applies operation experiences for certain self-operation use cases. These use cases receive their configuration or instruction from self-operation with the means not shown in the demo architecture. The demonstrator uses an LTE simulator and SON function instances as a source of data, where the LTE simulator simulates a whole LTE network. In the experiments, the demonstrator defines an objective-specific similarity measure based on the given network context, objective, and rule. It then matches the corresponding self-operation cases with the defined objective-specific similarity measure. The best suitable function is extracted from the matching self-operation cases by the demonstrator. The demonstrator then automatically defines a function-specific similarity measure based on the selected function and the given network context, objective, and rule. The more relevant self-operation cases are further matched with the defined function-specific similarity measure by the demonstrator. The (best) suitable function configuration is extracted from the further matched self-operation cases by the demonstrator. The function can then be configured with the suitable configuration and activated to achieve the given objective.

The experimental results of the demonstrator (including the implemented solution, proposed by this paper) show the concept of self-operation (including the solution) work well as expected. This self-operation scales well (with respect to use of a distributed database, MongoDB) and works automatically while being able to interact with human operator through UI during the network operations.

The network operations of 5G networks are expected to have much more automation capabilities when compared with the current network operations. The proposed solution for self-operation by this paper serves naturally as an important part of the 5G network operations.

As the future work, the current demonstrator is expected to be enhanced to support the direct configuration of the functions and the network from UI. In addition, a machine to machine interface is expected to be added to the demonstrator so that self-operation can directly control and configure the functions and the network.

References

1. 3GPP: Evolved Universal Terrestrial Radio Access Network (E-UTRAN); Self-configuration and self-optimizing network use cases and solutions (Release 8). 3GPP TR 36.902 V1.0.1, September 2008
2. NGMN: NGMN Use Cases related to Self Organising Network, Overall Description. Deliverable, NGMN Alliance, December 2008. https://www.ngmn.org/uploads/media/
3. Nokia: Business aware traffic steering. White Paper of Nokia Networks (2013). http:// networks.nokia.com/sites/default/files/document/nokia_traffic_steering_white_paper.pdf
4. 5G-PPP: 5G Empowering Vertical Industries. Brochure, February 2016. https://5g-ppp.eu/ wp-content/uploads/2016/02/BROCHURE_5PPP_BAT2_PL.pdf
5. Tang, H., Stenberg, K.: Self-operation of a network. In: Proceedings of IEEE DataCom 2016, pp. 647–653, August 2016
6. Aamodt, A., Plaza, E.: Case-based reasoning: foundational issues, methodological variations, and system approaches. Artif. Intell. Commun. **7**(1), 39–52 (1994)
7. Rawashdeh, A., Ralescu, A.L.: Similarity measure for social networks – a brief survey. In: Proceedings of Modern AI and Cognitive Science Conference (MAICS), pp. 153–159, April 2015
8. Guessoum, D., Miraoui, M., Tadj, C.: Survey of semantic similarity measures in pervasive computing. Int. J. Smart Sens. Intell. Syst. **8**(1), 125–158 (2015)
9. Gomaa, W.H., Fahmy, A.A.: A survey of text similarity approaches. Int. J. Comput. Appl. **68**(13), 13–18 (2013)
10. TRAI: The Standards of Quality of Service for Wireless Data Services (Amendment) Regulations. Regulation, Telecom Regulatory Authority of India, New Delhi, India, July 2014. http://www.trai.gov.in/Content/Regulation/1_0_RegulationUser.aspx
11. 3GPP: Key Performance Indicators (KPI) for Evolved Universal Terrestrial Radio Access Network (E-UTRAN): Definitions, v13.0.0. 3GPP TS32.450, January 2016
12. TRAI: The Indian Telecom Services Performance Indicators, July - September, 2015. Indicator Report, Telecom Regulatory Authority of India, New Delhi, India, pp. 61–84, February 2016. http://www.trai.gov.in/WriteReadData/PIRReport/Documents/Indicator_Reports.pdf
13. NGMN: NGMN Informative List of SON Use Cases. An Annex Deliverable, NGMN Alliance, pp. 6–47, April 2007. https://www.ngmn.org/uploads/media/NGMN_Informative_List_of_SON_Use_Cases.pdf
14. Bandh, T., Tang, H., Sanneck, H., Schmelz, C.: SON operation. In: LTE Self-Organizing Networks (SON), Chap. 9, pp. 322–356. Wiley (2012). ISBN 978-1-119-97067-5
15. Viering, I., Döttling, M., Lobinger, A.: A mathematical perspective of self-optimizing wireless networks. In: Proceedings of ICC 2009, p. 1 ff., Dresden, Germany, June 2009

Processing Time Comparison of a Hardware-Based Firewall and Its Virtualized Counterpart

Steffen Gebert, Alexander Müssig, Stanislav Lange, Thomas Zinner,
Nicholas Gray$^{(\boxtimes)}$, and Phuoc Tran-Gia

Institute of Computer Science, University of Würzburg, Am Hubland,
97074 Würzburg, Germany
{steffen.gebert,alexander.muessig,stanislav.lange,zinner,
nicholas.gray,trangia}@informatik.uni-wuerzburg.de

Abstract. The network functions virtualization (NFV) paradigm promises higher flexibility, vendor-independence, and higher cost-efficiency for network operators. Its key concept consists of virtualizing the functions of specialized hardware-based middleboxes like load balancers or firewalls and running them on commercial off-the-shelf (COTS) hardware.

This work aims at investigating the performance implications that result from migrating from a middlebox-based hardware deployment to a NFV-based software solution. Such analyses pave the way towards deriving guidelines that help determining in which network environments NFV poses a viable alternative to today's middlebox-heavy architectures. To this end, a firewall is chosen as an exemplary network function and a performance comparison between a dedicated hardware device and a commercially distributed virtualized solution by the same vendor is drawn. This comparison focuses on the packet delay, while varying the load level that is applied to the network function under test. Based on traffic measurements of a university campus network, conclusions regarding possible fields of application are drawn.

1 Introduction

Today's networks rely heavily on specialized, hardware-based middleboxes for a multitude of networking tasks such as firewalling or load balancing. Despite their advantages with respect to performance, these specialized middleboxes exhibit drawbacks in terms of acquisition costs, flexibility, and vendor-dependence, favoring a paradigm shift towards NFV. By leveraging virtualization techniques, the NFV concept allows migrating the functionality of the specialized middleboxes to software running on COTS hardware. On the one hand, this reduces the high acquisition costs associated with the former. On the other hand, network operators can benefit from vendor independence and an increase in flexibility.

Before deploying virtualized network functions (VNFs) in an existing network, its operator needs to determine whether the resulting system can still

© ICST Institute for Computer Sciences, Social Informatics and Telecommunications Engineering 2017
R. Agüero et al. (Eds.): MONAMI 2016, LNICST 191, pp. 220–228, 2017.
DOI: 10.1007/978-3-319-52712-3_16

cope with the load offered by the network. Due to the fact that different network functions behave differently and have specific requirements, such a question can not be addressed in a general way. Hence, this work focuses on the performance evaluation of a firewall which is commercially available both as a hardware entity as well as a VNF. In particular, Cisco's *Adaptive Security Appliance Service Module* (ASASM)[1] and its virtualized counterpart *Adaptive Security Virtual Appliance* (ASAv)[2] are utilized in our experiments. Based on traffic statistics of a university campus network, the feasibility of the two deployment types in this environment is investigated.

Measurements focus on the packet processing time while varying the system load in terms of number of concurrent sessions. By using a dedicated hardware-based traffic generator which applies realistic load profiles to the device under test (DuT), such an analysis sheds light on the feasibility of NFV-based solutions in realistic environments and thus, can contribute towards identifying scenarios in which adopting the NFV paradigm makes the most sense.

This work is structured as follows. Section 2 provides an overview of related work regarding the general topic of VNF benchmarking as well as performance evaluation of virtualized firewalls in particular. In Sect. 3, the testbed setup is presented alongside the different scenarios and parameters that are used in this work. After discussing the results of the measurements in Sects. 4 and 5 concludes the paper.

2 Related Work

While different network functions have different characteristics in terms of their behavior and requirements, there is a common ground when it comes to evaluating their performance. RFC 2544 [3] provides benchmarking guidelines for networking devices such as routers, switches, or firewalls. These guidelines include key performance indicators for various DuTs as well as the methodology for measuring latency and throughput of these devices. Several additional documents were released in order to take into account the increased set of features and capabilities of network elements [1,2].

When attempting to evaluate the performance of virtualized network functions that run on COTS hardware, additional challenges need to be addressed. Due to the additional abstraction layer introduced by the softwarization of network functions, system performance does not only depend on the underlying hardware but also on the particular VNF implementation [5]. In contrast to ASIC-based packet processing, effects like scheduling and caching also impact the predictability and reliability of software solutions. Furthermore, interdependencies between VNF instances running on the same physical substrate can affect the system's behavior [6,7].

---

[1] http://www.cisco.com/c/en/us/products/interfaces-modules/
catalyst-6500-series-7600-series-asa-services-module/index.html.

[2] http://www.cisco.com/c/en/us/products/collateral/security/
adaptive-security-virtual-appliance-asav/datasheet-c78-733399.html.

For the specific case of firewall benchmarking, a methodology is presented in RFC 3511 [4] that characterizes the performance of a firewall and describes formats for presenting benchmarking results. The measurements conducted in the remainder of this paper follow this RFC as a guideline.

A performance comparison between a Cisco ASA 5505 hardware and the software-based Linux *iptables* is presented in [9]. The work focuses on three main performance metrics: throughput, latency, and concurrent connections. While the Cisco ASA outperforms Linux iptables in terms of throughput and latency, the latter is capable of handling bursts of packets better and achieves a higher number of concurrent sessions.

3   Methodology

In order to investigate whether a virtualized firewall can replace its more expensive and inflexible hardware-based counterpart in a particular scenario, we evaluate and compare their performance in a dedicated testbed. First, the testbed setup is presented alongside the specifications of its hardware and software components. Second, the course of experiments for the aforementioned performance evaluation as well as parameters and performance indicators are described.

3.1   Measurement Setup

Figure 1 shows the main components of the testbed utilized in this work. It is comprised of two networks, an external and an internal network, which are separated by the firewall. The networks are represented by two switches that are connected to the firewall and different types of traffic are generated using two Spirent C1[3][4] traffic generators. The Spirent C1 is a dedicated FPGA-based traffic generator equipped with four 1 GbE interfaces and allows highly accurate and reliable measurements of various performance indicators like packet delay.

The first traffic generator produces stateful TCP traffic using the Avalanche software. In this context, "stateful" refers to the fact that the firewall needs to keep track of the state of each connection according to the TCP state machine. This traffic is used to set the DuT under different load levels in terms of varying numbers of active connections. The second C1 device is controlled by the TestCenter software in order to benefit from the highly precise hardware-based delay measurement that, however, only supports stateless traffic. Probe packets are sent once per second through a TCP connection that was previously opened by emulating the TCP handshake.

As mentioned earlier, two different firewall deployments are analyzed in this work and detailed in Table 1. The first component is the Cisco *Adaptive Security Appliance Service Module* (ASASM), a hardware solution. While layer 3 and 4 processing is performed in ASIC/TCAM, the general purpose Xeon CPUs of

---

[3] http://www.spirent.com/ethernet_testing/platforms/c1_chassis.

[4] http://www.spirent.com/~/media/Datasheets/Broadband/PAB/
SpirentTestCenter/STC_C1-Appliance_Datasheet.pdf.

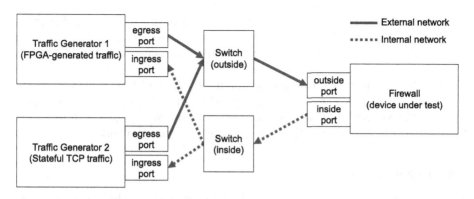

Fig. 1. Hardware setup used in this work.

Table 1. Devices under test.

Product		
Vendor	Cisco	Cisco
Series	ASASM	ASAv
Model	WS-SVC-ASA-SM1	ASAv30 v9.4(1)3
Deployment type	Physical, switch blade	virtual
CPU	2x Xeon 5600 2.00 GHz, 6 cores	4 vCPUs
Memory	24 GB	8 GB
Pricing		
Perpetual[a]	$97,750	$15,980
On-demand[b]	–	$1.39 per hour
Hardware base platform		
Platform	Catalyst 6509 Switch	Cisco UCS C220 M3
CPU	VS-S720-10G, 600 MHz	Xeon E5-2680, 8 cores
Memory	–	64 GB DDR3
Hypervisor	–	VMware ESXi 5.5
Specifications		
Max. throughput	20 Gbps	2 Gbps
Connections/sec	300,000	60,000
Concurrent conn	10,000,000	500,000

[a]according to http://ciscoprice.com/
[b]on Amazon AWS

the ASASM are used for tasks like VPN, content inspections, and management. The Cisco *Adaptive Security Virtual Appliance* (ASAv) ASAv30 runs virtualized using VMware ESXi on a Cisco *UCS* server and is configured as per vendor recommendations. While the data sheet of the ASASM provides basic information on the processing delay of the appliance, no information is available in case of the ASAv. This work sheds some light on the performance differences between these commercially available solutions.

In order to achieve realistic testing conditions, around 1300 rules are configured on the firewalls. These rules correspond to those installed on our campus firewall. Hence, the resulting measurements can provide insights regarding the feasibility of the two firewall deployment types in such a network.

3.2 Experiments

Using the testbed setup described in the previous section, the performance of the two firewall types is evaluated with respect to the achieved processing time. This section presents the methodology for investigations regarding the effects of different load levels on the processing time of TCP packets. The test scenarios were developed together with firewall administrators and campus network administrators at the computing center of our university.

The main test case investigates the processing times of TCP packets while the firewall is exposed to various amounts of load in terms of open TCP connections. Before the measurement is started, the TCP connections are opened by utilizing Avalanche in order to simulate users in the internal network that request file downloads from servers in the external network (cf. Fig. 1). After downloading a small 1 kilobyte file, the TCP connection is left open and users keep on requesting other files from different servers until the desired number of TCP connections is established. In order to avoid completely idle connections, a 1 kilobyte file is requested via HTTP for each connection every 10 s. The total number of active connections is varied between 1,000 and more than 500,000 in order to cover a diverse set of scenarios. Finally, the TestCenter software is used to instruct the FPGA to generate one TCP packet per second and capture the resulting packet delays.

4 Results

As the firewall is the access gate to a network where all traffic from or to this network passes, it can become a bottleneck between the internal and external network. Especially the software implementation of the firewall raises the question whether it can keep pace with its hardware counterpart. Therefore, the performance of the two firewall deployment types according to the methodology described in Sect. 3 is evaluated in this chapter. Each experiment lasts 5 min and is repeated 5 times.

4.1 Processing Time

In Fig. 2, an overview of the distribution of processing times of the ASASM is provided. While the x-axis displays the processing times, the y-axis represents

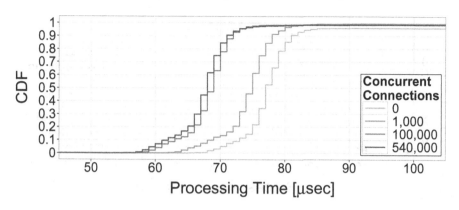

Fig. 2. Processing times achieved by the ASASM.

the fraction of observations in which the corresponding value was not exceeded. Furthermore, differently colored curves mark different load levels in terms of concurrent connections. For the sake of readability, only the most relevant range of x-values is depicted.

There are three main observations. First, the processing time has a low variability for all scenarios, i.e., an interquartile range of roughly $4\,\mu$ s with values between 60 and $85\,\mu$ s. Second, processing times show a strictly decreasing behavior with increasing numbers of concurrent connections. This phenomenon could stem from interrupt mitigation mechanisms similar to those of the *New API* [8], the network I/O API that is utilized by Linux operating systems. In order to decrease the overhead that results from each individual packet causing an interrupt, this mechanism accumulates packets until either a certain amount of packets is collected or processing is initiated by a timeout. Hence, lower load levels cause higher delays as packets need to wait for the timeout to trigger processing, while packets exceed the threshold at an increasing rate in case of high load levels, resulting in lower delays. Finally, the small gap between the two highest load levels indicates a converging behavior with respect to processing times.

Similar to the previous figure, Fig. 3 displays the distribution of processing times achieved by the virtualized firewall ASAv. Again, the x-axis is limited to the most relevant interval. In contrast to the maximum number of connections of 540,000 that was used in the context of the ASASM-related measurements, the maximum for the ASAv-related measurements is at 500,000. The reason for this parameter choice is a hard-coded capacity limit implemented in the ASAv software (cf. Table 1).

The ASAv exhibits two modes regarding the processing times. For low numbers of TCP sessions, higher delays and a significantly higher variance are observed. In these cases, the ASAv introduces packet delays between 100 and 800 *upmu* s, roughly ten times higher than when using an ASASM. When increasing the load, however, the variance and the absolute values decrease and stabilize in an interval between 100 and 350 *upmu* s. As in case of the hardware-based

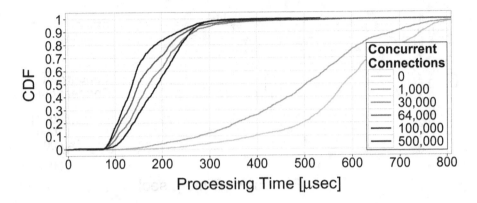

Fig. 3. Processing times achieved by the ASAv.

ASASM, there seems to be a mechanism that positively affects packet processing delays of the firewall at higher load levels.

4.2 Suitability for a Campus Network

In order to put the measurement results into the context of a real network, traffic measurements have been conducted in the university's campus network using NetFlow. During two working days of observation, the highest number of parallel connections at the Internet uplink with a capacity of 2×3.5 Gbps was found to be around 420,000 connections. Further, the highest number of new connections per second was found to be around 6,500–6,800, with two exceptions, during which 14,700 and 20,300 new connections were opened within one second, respectively. At the 10 G connection of a single building (computer science faculty), a maximum of around 177,000 concurrent connections with peaks of up to 4,400 new connections per second were observed.

Given the ability of ASAv to handle up to 500,000 concurrent connections, it seems to be a feasible approach for both scenarios. However, the total throughput of only up to 2 Gbps is the limiting factor, which would restrict the use of ASAv in the investigated network, e.g., to the protection of clusters of servers or buildings connecting only few users through smaller links. An investigation of the maximum number of connections per second that the ASAv can handle remains for future work.

5   Conclusion

This work presents a comparison of processing delays introduced by two types of firewall deployments, namely a hardware-based approach and an NFV-based virtualized approach. In particular, Cisco's Adaptive Security Appliance Service Module (ASASM) and its virtualized counterpart, the Adaptive Security Virtual Appliance (ASAv), are tested. Both of these are commercially available products.

By comparing these two firewall deployment types, this work provides guidance for dimensioning of NFV systems.

All measurements are performed in a testbed featuring two Spirent C1 traffic generators, an industrial-grade packet generator and test platform. The evaluations presented in this paper allow characterizing scenarios in which the more flexible and cost-efficient virtualized approach can provide a sufficient level of performance and thus poses a viable alternative to purchasing specialized hardware.

In all investigated scenarios, using the virtualized ASAv results in an increase of packet delays by a factor of up to ten. Furthermore, a higher variance of the processing times is observed. However, even in the virtualized case, the majority of measured processing times is below 1 ms. Depending on the usage scenario, delays in this order of magnitude might be acceptable, e.g., for perimeter firewalls connecting networks to the Internet.

Future investigations with a better-equipped 10 GbE traffic generator could extend this work by providing additional insights into the performance limits of the DuTs. More directions for future work include a comparison between different hypervisors like the KVM-based ASAv, as well as different virtualization strategies such as paravirtualization. Additionally, investigations regarding the load in terms of the number of new connections per second would help identifying performance bottlenecks. Consequently, such analyses can provide guidelines for network operators to decide between a hardware-based solution and a virtualized one.

To further benefit from running virtual instances, e.g., by dynamically scaling up and down, the current version of the ASAv lacks the feature of operating in a cluster. Once available or when investigating alternative implementations, this important aspect of a VNF deployment offers even more room for further measurements.

Acknowledgment. This work has been performed in the framework of the SARDINE project and is partly funded by the BMBF (Project ID 16KIS0261). The authors alone are responsible for the content of the paper.

References

1. Asati, R., Pignataro, C., Calabria, F., Olvera, C.: RFC26201: Device Reset Characterization. IETF (2011)
2. Bradner, S., Dubray, K., McQuaid, J., Morton, A.: RFC6815: Applicability Statement for RFC 2544: Use on Production Networks Considered Harmful. IETF (2012)
3. Bradner, S., McQuaid, J.: RFC2544: Benchmarking Methodology for Network Interconnect Devices. IETF (1999)
4. Hickman, B., Newman, D., Tadjudin, S., Martin, T.: RFC3511: Benchmarking Methodology for Firewall Performance. IETF (2003)
5. Lange, S., Nguyen-Ngoc, A., Gebert, S., et al.: Performance benchmarking of a software-based LTE SGW. In: 2nd International Workshop on Management of SDN and NFV Systems (2015)
6. Morton, A.: Considerations for Benchmarking Virtual Network Functions and Their Infrastructure. Internet-Draft draft-morton-bmwg-virtual-net-03 (2015)

7. Overture, Brocade: Intel, Spirent, and Integra. NFV Performance Benchmarking for vCPE, Executive Summary (2015)
8. Salim, J.H., Olsson, R., Kuznetsov, A.: Beyond softnet. In: Proceedings of the 5th Annual Linux Showcase & Conference (2001)
9. Xu, J., Su, W.: Performance evaluations of Cisco ASA and linux IPTables firewall solutions. Master's thesis, Halmstad University (2013)

Author Index